D0742838

MDDL and the Quest for a Market Data Standard

ELSEVIER WORLD CAPITAL MARKETS SERIES

Series Editor: Herbie Skeete

The Elsevier World Capital Markets Series consists of books that cover the developments in the capital markets, as well as basic texts introducing the markets to those working directly or indirectly in the capital markets. Investors are more knowledgeable and demanding than ever before and there is a thirst for information by professional investors and those who sell and provide services to them. Regulators are demanding more transparency and new rules and regulations are being introduced constantly. The impact of competition means that markets are constantly changing and merging, and new instruments are being devised. The Series provides cutting-edge information and discussion about these and other developments affecting the capital markets. Technology underpins and is driving innovation in the markets. Inappropriate technology or no technology can bring down even the soundest financial institution. This series therefore also includes books that enable market experts to understand aspects of technology that are driving the markets.

Series Editor Herbie Skeete is a well known figure in the financial information industry having spent twenty-six years at Reuters. During his many senior positions with Reuters—most recently as Head of Equities Content and Head of Exchange Strategy—Mr Skeete has become recognized globally as an expert on exchanges and content issues. He is frequently asked to address conferences and to contribute to roundtable discussions. Mr Skeete runs the exchange information publisher Mondo Visione Ltd, edits the industry-standard *Handbook of World Stock, Commodity, and Derivatives Exchanges*, which celebrates its seventeenth edition in 2007, and operates the exchange information website www.exchange-handbook.com

MDDL and the Quest for a Market Data Standard

Explanation, Rationale and Implementation

Martin Christopher Sexton

AMSTERDAM • BOSTON • HEIDELBERG • LONDON
NEW YORK • OXFORD • PARIS • SAN DIEGO
SAN FRANCISCO • SINGAPORE • SYDNEY • TOKYO

Butterworth-Heinemann is an imprint of Elsevier

Butterworth-Heinemann is an imprint of Elsevier
Linacre House, Jordan Hill, Oxford OX2 8DP, UK
30 Corporate Drive, Suite 400, Burlington, MA 01803, USA

First edition 2008

British Library Cataloguing in Publication Data
A catalogue record for this book is available from the British Library

Library of Congress Control Number: 2007922083

ISBN: 978-0-7506-6839-2

For information on all Butterworth-Heinemann publications
visit our website at http://books.elsevier.com

Printed and bound in Great Britain
08 09 10 11 10 9 8 7 6 5 4 3 2 1

This publication is dedicated to my son, George Christopher, who stole the limelight by leapfrogging the due date of completion of this book by being born a week early, resulting in it being completed on the back seat of my car, which became my makeshift office.

Contents

Series Editor's preface

Someone once said that the trouble with standards is that there are too many of them. Fortunately for those of us who work in the world of market data, a single dominant standard is now emerging governing the way in which market data is exchanged, and that is MDDL.

This book by Martin Sexton sets MDDL within a business context and takes the user – whether from the world of business or technology – through the intricacies of the language. Because this is such a dynamic area at present, Martin also discusses the Quest for a Market Data Standard, and all the considerations this involves for any business or undertaking that has market data as a component.

For a technical book, it is surprisingly jargon free and has something in it for everyone. Whether you are a business analyst wanting to know more about the black art of market data, a developer needing a crash course in the practicalities of deploying MDDL within a financial organization, or a decision maker who wants to understand how and where MDDL could improve the performance of your business, this book identifies and explains the key issues.

Martin is in my opinion the perfect author for this book. He is steeped in the world of market data and the sometimes arcane business of data structures and shipping market data throughout organizations, and has many years experience of helping others to understand the issues involved.

Readers of this book may be left with the impression that Martin lives, breathes and dreams market data. Let me assure you that there is another side to Martin. I first met Martin about six years ago when we were both guests of FTSE (the index group) at a football match, Spurs versus Chelsea at White Hart Lane. The game itself was a boring 0-0 draw, but before the game was over I had persuaded Martin to contribute an article on data standards to my annual publication, the *Handbook of World Stock, Derivative and Commodities Exchanges*. He has been a regular contributor since then.

So I am pleased to include this book in the **Elsevier World Capital Markets Series**. This series of books is designed to cover developments in the capital markets, as well as basic texts introducing the markets to those working directly or indirectly in the capital markets. The first book in the series, *Market Data Explained* by Marc Alvarez, was published in October 2006.

Herbie Skeete
London

Chapter 1

Introduction

The aim of this publication is to provide an objective, vendor-independent assessment of the Market Data Definition Language (MDDL). The book assumes no previous knowledge of the standard, of computers or systems networking; however, a rudimentary understanding of the financial markets would be an advantage although it is not essential.

So why give the book the title *MDDL and the Quest for a Market Data Standard*, and not just *MDDL*? I felt it's important to make the reader aware of other industry standards that support elements of market data and the business context in which they do. FIX, FIXml, ISO 20022 and FpML are all explored, as well as mechanisms for delivering the market data payload.

MDDL has been designed to support the data interchange of financial market information, known as market data, and, more specifically, the investment decision-making, reference data management and market reporting processes. The MDDL mission statement defines the intended usage context as being 'The XML specification to enable the interchange of information necessary to account, to analyse, and to trade financial instruments of the world's markets' (www.mddl.org).

MDDL has a universal perspective, as the owner of the standard – the Financial Information Services Division (FISD) of the Software and Information Industry Association (SIIA) – has managed to attract membership from all four corners of the globe. In 2005, the FISD set up the Securities Model Working Group (SMWG) to ensure the continued development and take-up of the standard.

The 'Big Three' data vendors (Bloomberg, Reuters, and Thomson Financial) have all contributed to the development of the standard, as have other data and system vendors. Stock exchanges, buy-side (fund and asset managers) and sell-side (investment banks) institutions have also played their part in its design.

The book provides the business context in which the MDDL resides and helps to identify the possible scenarios in which it can be used, supported by a comprehensive set of examples.

A study is made into the use of MDDL across the enterprise, linking its deployment to corporate goals and business benefit realization.

The financial standards landscape is also examined, and a briefing is provided as to where MDDL fits within. An investigation into the future of the standard is made, and into how the advent of the ISO standards 19312 and 20022 may impact the design of the standard.

Audience of this book

There are no prerequisites for this book, other than a desire to learn about the capabilities of the only industry standard in the market data arena.

One key aspect to this publication is that I have attempted to convey not only my experience of working with trading floor environments for nearly 20 years, but also my knowledge of management techniques acquired throughout that period.

The book identifies the challenges and significance of the standard. It examines the business and market drivers, and presents decision-makers with a clear, concise and jargon-free read.

It confers the knowledge to enable business and technology professionals to converse comfortably regarding financial systems integration.

The publication has been written for business decision-makers, hybrid professionals (i.e. individuals, sometimes known as 'business systems analysts', who are able to converse/liaise with senior management, business users and IT technicians) who require pointers as how an organization's reference and market data processes might be decoupled from its transactional systems, allowing it to reduce costs as well as move towards a grid-based infrastructure. Grid computing can be seen as the Nirvana of IT operation managers, and is where business functions are decoupled from the data dissemination and acquisition processes, providing a closer relationship between business and IT functions and thus enabling the organization to make the most effective use of the resources available on the network.

Developers are provided with a comprehensive selection of examples and with the training needed to extend the standard to meet the specific requirements of their organization.

Business systems analysts are given an explanation of the standard's business terms, context and hierarchical structure, thus enabling them to design MDDL-compliant interfaces.

This is an essential reference book, assisting managers at all stages of a project's lifecycle, including defining the business case, writing the feasibility study and planning the deployment of new interfaces across the enterprise.

The subject of creating schemas to support specific business functions and taxonomies is discussed; however, technical considerations surrounding designing XML schemas and, in particular, modifying the MDDL schema itself, is not. Naturally, anyone contemplating this should consider taking some advice before doing so.

This book is not intended for advanced-level technicians seeking advice on how to compile the schema into objects using JAXB/JAXB2, Apache XMLBeans, Castor or any proprietary product.

If you are a non-technician, please don't be put off by the use of angle brackets used in XML; this is merely the mechanism deployed to define the terms (or metadata) and the data itself, thus allowing meaning and context to be conveyed in its hierarchical structure. To allay any fears, reading the section titled 'How MDDL works' may be particularly useful.

One aspect that the reader may have noticed when examining the material available in the public domain is that MDDL lacks a business layer, providing meaning to the diverse collection of terms in the standard itself. It is not my intention to define this missing component within this publication; however, by providing real-life examples that show how MDDL and other standards (FIX, FpML and ISO 20022) can be deployed, it is hoped that the reader may be able to appreciate the opportunities available.

After completing this book, the reader will understand how their business can benefit from the deployment of industry standards.

Structure of the book

The material in this book has been arranged so that it can be read from start to finish, or used as a reference guide. The structure of the book and its comprehensive index allows the user to select a specific topic of interest.

Examples

All the examples shown in this publication, compliant to the latest version of the standard, can be downloaded from www.questfor.tv.

Conventions

To help the reader get the most out of this publication, a number of conventions have been used.

Technical material, such as XML samples, is enclosed within a shaded box (see Figure 1.1).

```
<trade>
    <close>500</ close>
    <size>550</size>
</trade>
```

Figure 1.1 A closing price report

Where appropriate, some of the examples are presented in different visual form; Figure 1.2 shows an alternate representation of the raw XML sample in Figure 1.1.

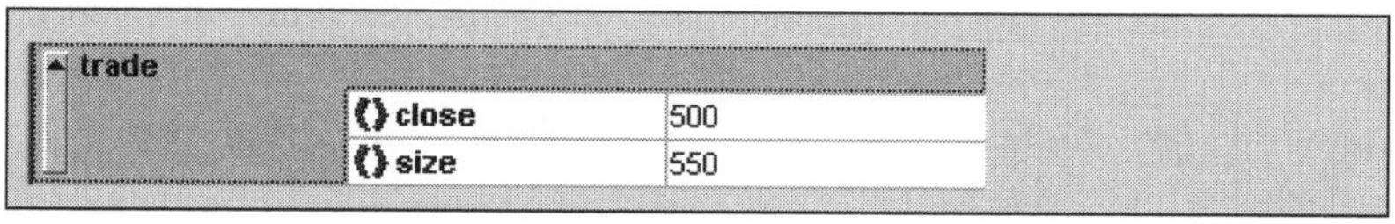

trade		
	() close	500
	() size	550

Figure 1.2 Visual representation of a raw XML document

Other conventions include the following:

- Words or items of importance are highlighted
- Code and filenames are shown in the Verdana shrift (or font); likewise with web page addresses and URLs (www.questfor.tv)
- Text equivalent to menu options on user interfaces is in Arial Black (File|Open).

Chapter 2

What is market data?

It's quite interesting that I have never seen a definitive statement that succinctly defines what market data is. Put simply, it is information (a collective term for instrument prices, trading statistics and news) that supports the investment decision-making process.

Over 300 years ago, market data took the form of price lists. The first of these issued in London was by Jonathan Castaing, a broker whose office was a Jonathan's Coffee House situated just off Cornhill, in Change Alley – a plaque commemorates its location, just a short walk from the Bank Tube station (see Figure 2.1).

I really like the idea of deals being conducted over a cup of coffee – a far open-outcry from today's world of electronic trading. (I couldn't go without a reference to traders crying out their bids on the trading floor, one of which I had the privilege

Figure 2.1 Jonathan's Coffee House plaque

of working on – the London International Financial Futures and Options Exchange, from 1998 to 2000.)

Even when Castaing's price list first went to press (Figure 2.2), the fundamental elements of market data were identified. The 'Course of the Exchange, and other things', appearing twice weekly (on Tuesdays and Fridays) from 1698, continued throughout the following century. Without such publications, would we be in the position where there are over 300 stock exchanges world-wide in existence today?

To this day, stock exchanges world-wide disseminate electronically daily official price lists. It's amazing to think in this modern world of the world-wide web and instant access to stock prices that market data originates from a sheet of paper measuring 10 × 4 inches! Jonathan Castaing's place in history is assured.

The financial markets are a lot more complex today compared to 300 years ago, when there were only 15 joint-stock companies with a capitalization of over 900 000 pounds sterling each. At that time, there was a one-to-one relationship between an issuer and the stock itself. Nowadays, market data plays a key role in the identification of the issuer, and the various financial products the issuer uses to finance its activities. An example of this can be seen by examining the shares of DaimlerChrysler. Its ordinary shares are officially listed in 7 countries, traded on 22 exchanges and priced in 5 currencies!

Unlike Jonathan Castaing's day, market data is no longer just a joint-stock name and its end of day closing price; it encompasses:

- reference data – a term that refers to information needed to identify correctly a financial instrument, an issuer, a trading counterparty (used for transaction routing) or a business entity
- the current pricing and trading activity of an instrument
- the historical pricing and trading activity of an instrument
- corporate actions that result from corporate or regulatory announcements
- financial indices, rates (instrument and issuer), ratings and other indictors.

(1)

The Courſe of the *Ex-change*, and other things.

London, Tueſday *4th January*, 1698.

Amſterdam	35	9a10
Rotterdam	35	11a36
Antwerp	35	9a10
Hamburgh	35	2a3
Paris	47	$\frac{1}{4}$
Lyons	47	$\frac{1}{4}$
Cadiz	51	$\frac{1}{4}$a51
Madrid	51	$\frac{1}{4}$
Leghorn	52	$\frac{1}{4}$
Genoua	51	$\frac{1}{4}$
Venice	49	$\frac{1}{2}$
Lisbon	5	$7\frac{3}{4}$
Porto	5	$6\frac{3}{4}$
Dublin	16	$\frac{1}{2}$
Gold	4 *l.* 00 *s.* 6 *d.*	
Ditto Ducats	4 · 5 6	
Silver Sta.	5 *s.* 1 *d.* $\frac{1}{2}$ a 2 *d.*	
Foreign Bars	5 3 $\frac{1}{8}$	
Pieces of Eight	5 3 $\frac{1}{8}$	

	Saturd	*Monday*	*Tueſd.*
Bank *Stock*	$86\frac{1}{2}$ a $\frac{3}{4}$	$86\frac{1}{2}$ a $\frac{3}{4}$	86 $\frac{3}{4}$
India	53 $\frac{3}{4}$	53 $\frac{3}{4}$	53 $\frac{3}{4}$
African	11 $\frac{3}{4}$	11 $\frac{3}{4}$	11 $\frac{3}{4}$
Hudſon Bay	110	110	110
Orphans Chamb.	53	53	53
Blank Tick.M.L.	6 15	6 15	6 15

No Transfer of the Bank *till* January 7.

In the Exchequer	*Advanced.*	*Paid off.*
1ſt 4 Shill.Aid	1896874	1814575
3d 4 Shill. Aid	1800000	1392377
4th 4 Shill.Aid	1800000	886492
$\frac{3}{4}$ Cuſtom	967985	764328
New Cuſtom	1250000	655200
Tobacco, *&c.*	1500000	119400
$\frac{2}{3}$ Exciſe	999815	864260
Poll-Tax	569293	479328
Paper, *&c.*	324114	65512
Salt Act	1904519	73772
Low Wines, *&c.*	69959	11100
Coal Act&Leath.	564700	17162
Births and Marr.	650000	2000
3 Shill. Aid	1500000	601555
Malt Act	200000	163746
Exchequer Notes, ſunk		585000*l.*

Coyn'd in the *Tower*, laſt Week, 0000*l.*

By John Caſtaing, *Broker, at his Office at* Jonathans *Coffee-houſe.*

Figure 2.2 Jonathan Castaing Price List published in 1698 (reproduced by kind permission of The Guildhall Library, City of London)

All this information is required to be able to make effective investment decisions, and with the advent of the 'Big Bang' (a term referring to the automation of the London Stock Exchange, which closed its trading floor in 1978) and the automation of the financial markets, accurate and timely delivery of information has become an integral part of every organization. Without the market data disseminated by exchanges (regulated markets) or Multilateral Trading Facilities (unregulated markets), the financial markets grind to a halt. For example, when on 5 April 2000 the start of trading at the London Stock Exchange (LSE) was delayed for approximately 8 hours and the LSE was out of action for nearly a whole business day, trading in London stocks virtually dried up. Although trading was extended into the evening to compensate for some of the lost time, the trading volume was only half the normal amount on a day that generally had a large volume. This emphasizes the importance of the timely delivery of accurate market data.

So where does market data fit within the world of finance?

A way of visualizing the multi-dimensional world of financial data is to describe it in terms of 'View' or 'Do', as shown in Figure 2.3.

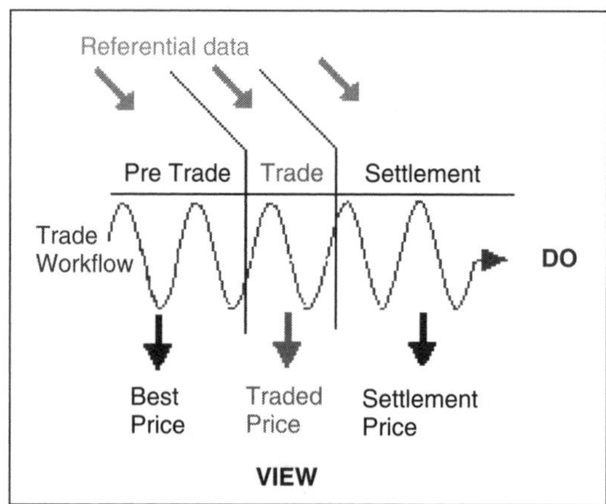

Figure 2.3 Multi-dimensional world of financial data

A snapshot of the market or an instrument at given point within the trade lifecycle is classified as a 'View'. This can be the best price listed on an Order Book, the last traded price and quantity, or the collective prices of instruments that are used to calculate an index such as the Dow Jones Industrial Average. View data is primarily published by exchanges, Multilateral Trading Facilities (MTFs) and vendors, and is market data. 'Do', on the other hand, is workflow information needed to take a deal from its inception through to settlement.

These two distinct dimensions can be observed in actual services offered by the London Stock Exchange. The London Market Information Link (LMIL) feed (or Infolect its enhanced successor) disseminates View information, whilst the SETS trading platform offers an Order Book facility handling workflow (Do) data.

Semantically, it can be argued that a third dimension exists – that being the acquisition and dissemination of referential data (instrument identifiers, business entities and corporate action events). This also comes under the heading of market data. MDDL supports both View and referential data.

Financial data also has properties akin to those of light, and some firms are considering the quantum world to obtain a market advantage. The subject of improving data delivery times is examined in detail later within this book.

Light cannot just be thought of as a simple wave-like phenomenon or as merely being composed of hard particles (or corpuscles, as Isaac Newton called them). Whether the properties are those of localized particles or those of waves depends on how they are observed. The dual nature of light and matter, known as 'wave particle duality', can also be observed within the world of finance. In particular, when observing the trade workflow, information flows through the organization from Front Office to Back Office, Back Office to Settlements, and Settlements to the General Ledger. Transactional information also flows outwards to regulatory authorities, trading partners and individuals that are involved in a deal. Data flows back into the organization from exchanges and vendors, and the cycle repeats itself ... This ripple of information starts at initial Indication of Interest (IOI) or placement of a quote, and continues through to settlement. A snapshot of information can be taken at any point within the trade lifecycle; at this point the observed data becomes 'market data'. It can be said that the data converts from a wave-like phenomenon back to a physical localized particle – which is exactly how light behaves.

It is worth considering whether the financial markets, share price movements, can be modelled using quantum physics wave function calculations. Maybe one of the major financial institutions is already using such equations to automate its trading processes or within its systematic internalizers (internal order book systems). Imagine the competitive advantage this would give the organization! I digress.

Chapter 3

Executive summary

Any firm within the financial sector, providing banking, investment, or intermediation or advisory services, is dependent on accurate, reliable and timely delivery of market data. It is used across the enterprise, from the investment decision-making on the trading desks through to calculating 'gain and loss' entries in the General Ledger, as well as in the more obvious external data feed scenario from the vendor to the customer. MDDL is a standard that fills these requirements by defining a common set of terms for use by exchanges, vendors and end-user clients alike. Messages are constructed by using the hierarchal relationship of terms. These messages may contain reference data (security definitions, business entity information) and quote, reporting and analytical information – in some cases all this information within a single document.

One of MDDL's main strengths is its extensible design, with user extensions being kept separately from the core schema. The extension mechanism has been developed such that extensions can easily be migrated into later releases of the standard. Instrument, business entity and other identification codings are also not part of the schema, therefore as and when new ones appear these can immediately be supported without the need to modify the standard itself. An example of this is the creation of the new ISO 16372 IBEI (International Business Entity Identifier).

The future evolution looks good. MDDL is a major contributor to and is committed to the ISO 19312 effort – the Securities Data model initiative. This means that MDDL should evolve towards ISO 19312, and *vice versa*. However, there is a risk that MDDL is driven by its users, many of whom are impatient with the relatively slow ISO standards approval process, and as a result it may get ahead and ultimately out of step with ISO 19312. It is hoped that this ISO model will eventually reflect the contents of MDDL in full. Similarly, MDDL will start to pick up terms from the ISO standard as this becomes more mature.

How important is market data to the business? The term 'market data' encompasses various types of financial information, including reference data (i.e. instrument issue data, business entity information – issuers, trading parties, etc.), pricing data and corporate action events. On examining a typical end-user of market data (Figure 3.1), it can be seen that it plays an important role in the operations of the business. Therefore, clean, consistent and up-to-date data helps the organization to operate efficiently. Similarly, given the importance of market data, savings can always be made by deploying industry standards that reside within its scope.

Upgrading of an organization's infrastructure, systems and business processes must be linked to the realization of business benefits. A financially conscious governing board is unlikely to accept change without it being shown to meet at least one corporate goal. Gone are the days of upgrading systems on the recommendation of the IT department or at the whim of a pushy, self-confident IT manager wanting the latest technology on his résumé! Similarly, the technology department should not be able to put a block on a deployment when the business case indicates otherwise. Business change may be driven by at least one tangible benefit (such as the reduction of staff, migration to a less expensive vendor, etc.) or by intangible benefits (like the need to meet new regulatory frameworks).

Before defining a strategic change based around the delivery of market data, the first task that needs to be undertaken is a review of data usage across the enterprise. Having undertaken this exercise a number of times, I can say with near certainty that there will be a number of services that are no longer required. People move on and others join, but the services are rarely discontinued. The exception to this rule is where a firm has implemented a market data usage management software that provides the link between a human resource and his or her data usage. This is an extremely useful tool, as it provides the organization not only with a verifiable

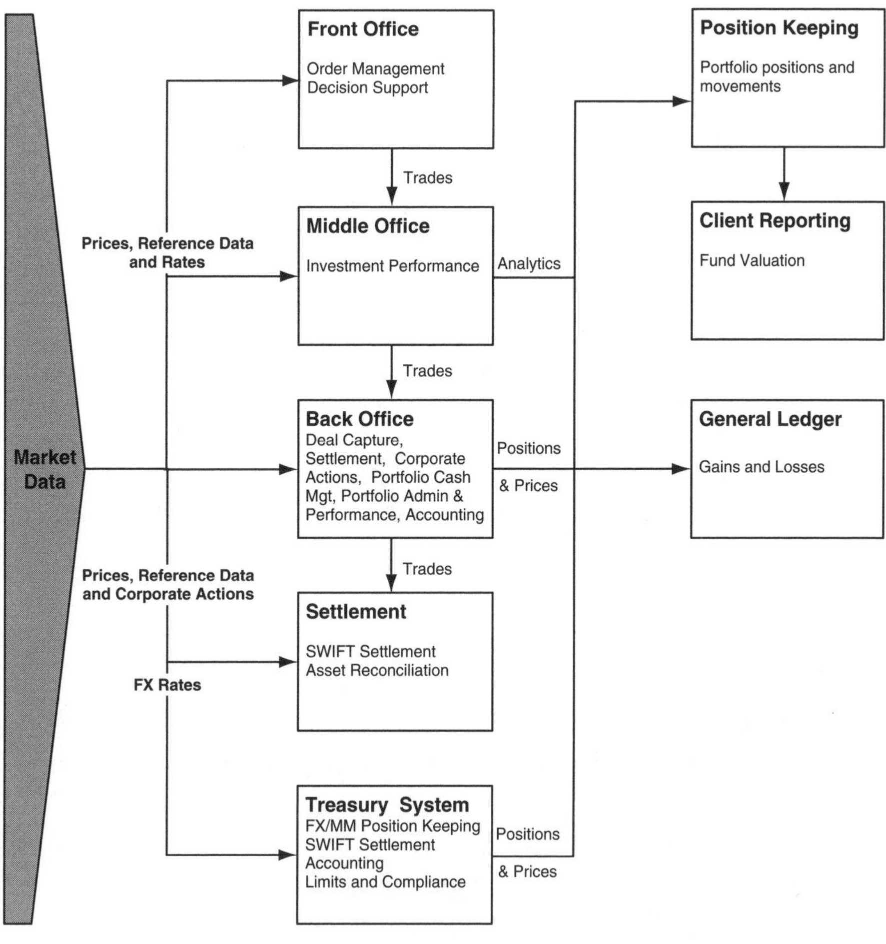

Figure 3.1 Market data use within a typical financial organization

mechanism to report data usage when external auditors come a-knocking, but also with the 'real' cost of each individual and thus their value to the business. When market data management software is in place, the chance of finding overspend is greatly reduced. However, a regular audit can still bring up the occasional saving.

The market data review will identify opportunities for savings, by eliminating duplicate services and unnecessary contract renewals. This review exercise can be seen as self-funding, as it results in the elimination of waste. Once the review is complete it will then be possible to analyse the organization's current situation and objectives, and to identify change initiatives.

The Vision

Any business change will need to be driven by the vision of the governing board. Armed with the results of the market data review, senior management can start to examine a new vision for the business and define the blueprint for the future. Most programs are specification-led and output-driven; in the case of the deployment of industry standards, these programs tend to be vision-led and benefits-driven. The implementation of a policy based around new regulations, such as REG NMS (Regulation National Market System) or MiFID (Markets in Financial Instruments Directive), is a program founded on a vision. The capacity to deliver the requirements of such legislation can only realistically be met through the use of industry standards. The creation of a centrally managed repository of reference data is one way of ensuring that it can be shown that an organization has control over its data, and a messaging standard that can support the dissemination of such information is an integral part.

From a corporate perspective, some of the drivers behind this vision are:

- better data accuracy
- faster trade throughput
- reduced staffing and office facilities
- outsourcing of business functions
- reduced dependency of the business on specific suppliers and sources of data
- improved quality of data
- reducing the need for specialist staff
- better financial controls and compliance adherence
- integration of new systems
- the amalgamation of businesses (the merges/acquisition of funds and/or institutions).

It's unlikely at this stage that the use of a specific industry standard or standards will have been identified or agreed upon. However, an awareness of the standards within the marketplace will help in identifying business opportunities and benefits.

Managers, management consultants and analysts may find Chapters 4 and 9, that examines the financial standards landscape and regulatory adherence, respectively, of particular interest.

The governing board must ensure that the vision is clearly described within the outward-facing vision statement, and then work can be started on the model of the future business; its working practices, structures and processes. The governing board can start formulating the information it requires and the technology that will be needed to deliver the capability outlined by the vision.

The aim of the blueprint is to define the structure and composition of the organization after the delivery of the program, and to identify quantifiable business benefits specific to the operations of the firm. These may include the replacement of all legacy systems within 21 months, a 10 per cent reduction in IT and operation staff, and reduced 'time to settle' from T + 5 to T + 1 by Q3, 2007 through trade automation. Other benefits may include greater fiscal control resulting from the creation of a central repository of market and trading data, as well as the opportunity to reduce costs by the simplification of the data dissemination processes, which in turn provides the increased possibility to outsource business functions.

Linking MDDL to corporate goals

The governing board is ultimately responsible for defining business strategy, and is unlikely to have time to consider the whys and wherefores of what messaging standards should be used and how they might assist in the achievement of the corporate goals. Given this, it is recommended that the board should consider identifying a resource capable of examining the business case for using an XML market data standard. This person will need to be experienced in the operations of the business as well as technology – what is known in the industry as a senior business systems analyst or data architect.

It can be a difficult task to identify such an individual from within the technology department, given that most IT staff normally specialize in only one or two business units. Front Office support staff tend to know and understand the idiosyncrasies of working in the trading floor environment, resolving issues at lightning speed, but are not necessarily aware of the impact of change on the Back Office or Settlement. Similarly, Back Office staff understand their domain but are envious of the Front Office's rapidly changing environment. Given this, it may be a good idea to recruit a consultant to undertake the task or to outsource this to a third-party company that specializes in this field. A synopsis of the job description could read:

> *We are urgently seeking a Business Systems Analyst or Data Architect with market data expertise. An essential requirement is a good understanding of financial products (Equity, Fixed Income, static data), with particular emphasis on instrument and counterparty identification. Being able to gather requirements and communicate ideas to senior management is a primary focus. You will possess detailed knowledge of the complete trading lifecycle and deal with business users across all business domains.*

Once identified, this person's first task must be to review the market data usage across the enterprise. Realistically, a minimum of four weeks should be set aside for undertaking this exercise, and if an executive-level report is required then more time should be allotted. Another useful deliverable is the creation of an industry standards assessment report; when used in conjunction with the market data review this can be used to assist in the identification of the appropriate use of industry standards for the particular enterprise. These reports will also help to identify the correct standards for the given business context. It's worth remembering that some industry standards support a limited number of market data elements to meet the specific needs of the business function they perform. It is important to avoid extending a standard beyond its scope – for example, there is little point in using a standard designed to support bilateral communications between parties for securities definitions or reference data management. Most standards limit the identification of instruments to two codings, normally ISIN plus another that has previous been agreed between the two parties.

Identifying the business drivers and obtaining buy-in from business users and operations management is imperative. An organization considering centralizing or updating its reference data management may wish to consider using MDDL. It can also be used as a key component of a program to meet regulatory requirements such as Sarbanes & Oxley and Basel 2, and money-laundering legislation like the Patriot Act. As well as regulation NMS in the United States and the European Union Market in Financial Markets Directive (MiFID), covering market transparency.

Assuming that the decision has been made to go with MDDL, what version of the standard should be used? To minimize the possible use of extensions, the latest available version should normally be adopted. When planning to roll out an MDDL feed, it is also important to be aware of the MDDL roll-out policy. The industry association has opted for a three-stage migration cycle. An initial release is known as the 'beta', three months later it becomes draft, then after a further three months it becomes 'final'. Aligning the roll-out of an interface to coincide with the release cycle of MDDL should considered. It is also advisable to endeavour to use the 'final' version of the roll-out cycle – for example, 'MDDL-2.5-final'.

The business benefits of using MDDL

The benefits outlined below are fairly general, and could apply to any industry standard. It's now worth expanding on the vision and the blueprint further, and examining the specific business benefits to your organization in more detail. Deploying MDDL offers the organization the opportunity to automate operational procedures, resulting in tangible financial benefits. Appropriate use of the standards can result in the reduction of application development time, and the numbers and complexity of interfaces. This in turn reduces the maintenance and support requirements and, ultimately, staffing levels. Other benefits include the ease of deployment and integration of new systems, and greater flexibility in phasing out legacy systems. It enables the business to network effortlessly with its clients, partners and data vendors. The deployment of MDDL also allows an organization to adapt quickly to the needs of the business, enabling it to expand into international markets and outsource business units.

The deployment of MDDL can result in ancillary benefits, such as improved internal information workflow and faster query resolution, thus allowing the organization to meet the requirements of new legislation.

Benefits summary

To ensure alignment of strategy with project-level activities, there is a need to ensure that the business benefits are incorporated within the business case for each program and project. One opportunity that most firms may wish to consider using MDDL for is in the creation of an enterprise-wide market data messaging framework, which is an essential component of the deployment of a centrally managed repository. Some firms may find that using MDDL 'as is' impractical if attempting to undertake run-time validation or using binding tools; in such situations the use of MDDL terms and relationship of terms may be a more viable solution, thus using MDDL-compliant taxonomies to meet specific business functions is an option worth considering. This will entail creating abridged MDDL schemas that meet the requirements of specific business functions – for further information, refer to Chapter 13.

The following list of benefits can form the basis for any program or project; good managers will be able to expand these and include specifics to their organization to ensure stakeholder buy-in to the change (stakeholders include senior management and business users, as well as suppliers):

- the reduced need for expensive, highly-skilled technology professionals
- separation of the dissemination, transportation and acquisition processes, resulting in reduced interface complexity
- better integration times
- improved project planning
- reduction in the change of IT systems and configuration management risk
- a reduction in the number of staff needed to support the systems
- reduced development times and resource usage
- improved information workflow, allowing the organization to meet its regulatory requirements
- improved decision-making
- removal of being tied to data vendors or specific infrastructure
- improved productivity.

MDDL opportunities

There are a couple of opportunities that immediately spring to mind, apart from the creation of a messaging framework based around a Central Repository:

The first is to use MDDL messages in conjunction with XSLT (XML Stylesheet Language for Transformations) to transform the message into a report such as a prospectus; with little effort this could take the form of an elaborate looking document, which can take advantage of the built-in components within Internet browser. A number of examples are provided later in this book, one of which can be seen in Chapter 8 in the section 'Issuance'. XML to HMTL transformation is a fairly simple exercise; however, transforming MDDL into binary, non-mark-up-based data is a little trickier. This is even possible in real time by using proprietary or XSL-FO, an open source initiative which combines XPath+XSLT+XSL-FO all in one. Either can be used to generate high-quality document presentation such as reports in PDF (Portable Document Format).

Another possibility is the use of web services for the delivery of information. Like the layers on an onion, a message can be constructed – an MDDL message is the payload, and information relating to its delivery would normally be in the wrapper or wrappers that surround the content. However, there are exceptions to this rule – when, for example, this data is required by the application, this should be on a need to know basis. Attempts should be made not to duplicate information whenever possible. An example where multiple headers may exist is when the decision is made to use SOAP over an IBM MQ Series transportation layer; here, effectively routing information is duplicated in the MQ Series header as well as the SOAP header.

Chapter 4

The financial standards landscape

Market data plays an important role within every financial institution. Figure 4.1 illustrates the typical internal processes that are dependent upon the supply of market data in a well-structured standardized format. Without this, these are fraught with manual intervention and double entry. Accurate and timely delivered instrument prices are essential, as well as well-maintained reference data. MDDL is designed to support such information.

A market data standard alone cannot support the whole trading process; there is the need for bilateral communications between market participants. An overview of these standards is provided within this section, and of how MDDL's scope fits within the bigger picture.

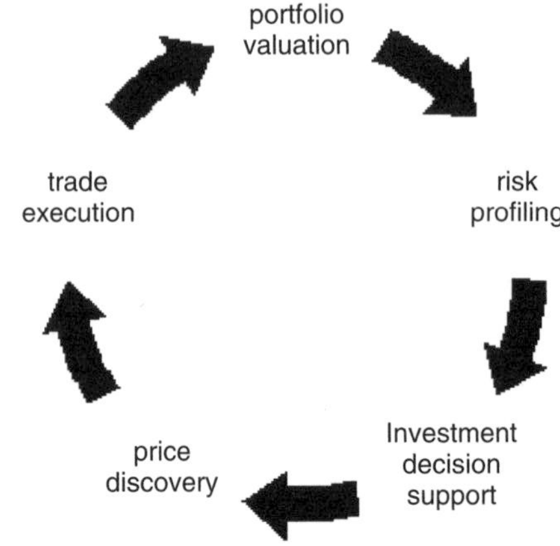

Figure 4.1 Trade lifecycle workflow within a financial institution

Industry standards

Over the past decade, a number of industry standards have emerged to meet the needs of the market. These include RIXML and NewsML to support the information aggregation process, MDDL to support the decision-making and reference data management processes, FIX and FpML to support trade execution, and ISO 15022 to support the settlement process (15022 messages are also used by some organizations in continental Europe to support the trade execution process). More recent developments have seen the creation of ISO 20022, designed to support the entire trade lifecycle, and ISO 19312 – the Securities Data Model.

Figure 4.2 illustrates a number of processes within a typical financial institution, and the industry standards available to support them. In general, each industry standard has been designed to meet the needs of a specific business process. A standard that is broken down by business function into separate taxonomies (or XML schemas) shows a good understanding of the business itself. FIXml, for instance, has separate taxonomies to support the functions of pre-trade, trade, trade confirmation, etc., as well as components to support specific ISDA contract types.

Firms will need to decide which standard or set of standards is appropriate to meet their specific needs. To aid in making this decision, an overview of the standards landscape has been provided. Organizations should adopt a 'plug and play' approach to ensure that their specific business requirements are met. In some instances it may not be suitable to use a standard as is. A company wishing to undertake runtime validation may find it more appropriate to use the terms and relationship of terms of a standard.

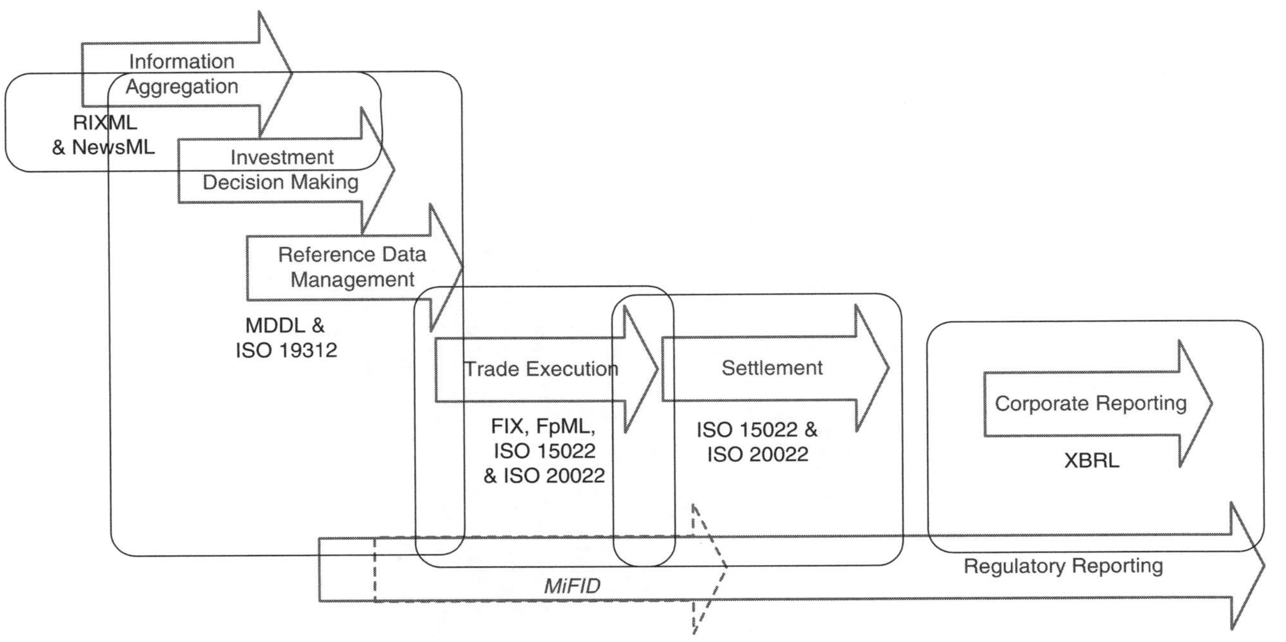

Figure 4.2 Typical processes within a financial institution and industry standards

RIXML is an XML taxonomy for the representation of investment research information. It provides a structure for the publication of instrument (bond, equity, etc.) and industry sector level data.

NewsML is an XML standard designed to provide a structural framework for the dissemination of multi-media news. Each news item may contain photos, graphics, video clips and the same text in different languages. News-service providers may wish to consider this standard for supporting the information aggregation process. The London Stock Exchange, for example, disseminates its RNS service using NewsML.

FIX (Financial Information eXchange protocol) provides a framework to support the trade execution process. It consists of a set of message formats (in both non-XML and XML), as well a transportation (session) layer to allow buy-side and sell-side organizations and stock exchanges to transact effectively.

FpML (Financial products Mark-up Language) is the business information exchange standard for electronic dealing and processing of financial derivatives instruments. It is a protocol for sharing information on, and dealing in, swaps, derivatives and other contracts. From a MiFID perspective, FpML terms should be considered to support exotic financial products.

ISO 15022 is a non-XML standard that provides a set of messages principally to support the settlement process. Some organizations in continental Europe also use 15022 messages to support the trade execution process. These messages are in general transported over the SWIFT network, which provides a reliable backbone for the interaction of industry participants. It incorporates and is upwardly compatible with the previous securities message standards ISO 7775 and ISO 11521.

XBRL (eXtensible Business Reporting Language) supports the financial reporting needs of an organization, including the acquisition and dissemination of data to and from the General Ledger. It is a single language that provides the semantic basis (in terms of natural language) for the creation of taxonomies to meet explicit business requirements. Taxonomies may also be geographically based, thus enabling the language to meet the needs of the specific market in which the business entity exists. Under development in the US are a couple of taxonomies to support the requirements of broker-dealers and investment management organizations.

International Standards Organization (ISO) standards

Bearing in mind the common use of terms by the various industry standards, it soon became apparent that a different approach was required. The solution was to reverse-engineer the existing standards into industry-specific models. Two distinct dimensions were identified; one to support the terms in the trade lifecycle and the other the reference data required to support the lifecycle. This led to the creation of ISO 20022 and ISO 19312 respectively.

ISO 20022 or *UNIFI* (UNIversal Financial Industry message scheme) provides a toolkit for the development of XML financial messages to meet the needs of the financial services industry. The standard has published a set of documents that define the overall methodology, the mechanism for populating the repository, the process to re-engineer existing message standards, the modelling guidelines and the XML schema design rules. The last quarter of 2005 saw ISO approval of a number of 20022-compliant messages to support the bank payment and investment funds distribution processes; in addition, work started on evaluating the Pre-Trade submission others have followed.

ISO 19312 is a securities data model being developed by ISO Working Group 11. The aim of the standard is to cover all financial instruments, standardizing the terms, definitions and relationships throughout the instrument's life. The scope also includes the instrument's maintenance and changes resulting from a corporate announcement, as well as the terms needed to support the corporate action events that may result from an announcement. WG 11 is realistic about the large scope of the standard, and intends to break down the deliverables into manageable chunks. The first task of the group has been to gather the terms for securities (including cash equities and debt instruments, warrants, funds, options and futures products).

ISO 19312 is a logical data model and therefore, by definition, able to support more than one physical implementation or taxonomy, such as an XML schema. MDDL, for example, is a physical implementation as an XML schema, which in future could be generated from the ISO logical model (although with additional content outside the realm of ISO 19312 added). The aim is to integrate ISO 19312 into the ISO 20022 repository.

Statistical Data and Metadata Exchange (SDMX) is an initiative designed to facilitate the exchange of statistical data and metadata using modern information technology, with an emphasis on aggregated data.

Market data is everywhere

As the Ancient Mariner stated, 'Water, water everywhere, nor any drop to drink' (Samuel Taylor Coleridge, *The Rime of the Ancient Mariner*). Standards have tended to be developed in isolated 'language islands', and this has led to the possibility of overlaps occurring and standards being misused outside their intended business context. It may be worth examining one example of this – the distribution of instrument identification. MDDL supports the reference data management process and is able to disseminate a comprehensive set of instrument identifiers. Trade workflow standards like FIX and ISO 15022 also provide the facility to disseminate instrument identifiers, and this information is used to ensure that the participating parties correctly identify the instrument within a particular transaction. It is important to recognize the distinction between the standards and the business function they support; MDDL, reference data management; FIX, trade execution; and 15022, the settlement process. It would be inappropriate, for example, to populate a Front Office system using 15022 settlement messages.

It's important that the business functions and process are supported by a single standard. In the case of reference data management, the standard of choice should be able to support all the possible coding schemes that currently exist as well as being able to support future coding. The only standard, at present, that can meet this requirement is MDDL, which supports the Associated Press, Bloomberg Code, Committee on Uniform Securities Identification Procedures, ComStock Instrument Identifier, Euroclear/Clearstream Common Code, Fannie Mae, Fitch's Rating, Freddie Mac – Federal Home Loan Mortgage Corporation, FT Interactive Data, Ginnie Mae, Reuters Identification Code, Small Business Association, Stock Exchange Daily Official List, and WertpapierKenNummer (WPK), among others. Other standards, on the whole, have instrument identification codings hardwired into the standard, meaning that if it is necessary to add a new instrument identifier then a change to the standard itself must be requested. MDDL uses controlled vocabulary (or look-up tables) for codings that the user may wish to redefine themselves without going back to standard owners to request a change.

Chapter 5

Self-describing data and XML basics

EXtensible Mark-up Language (XML) is a mark-up language for representing structured information, that is, when properly implemented self-describing and human-readable, and allows business functions to effectively communicate without the use of application-specific interfaces. It provides business users with the opportunity to have a better understanding of the flow of information between IT systems, allowing them to play a more active role in the design and selection of technology, and ultimately enabling the organization to make sustainable savings through the simplification of process. It comprises of data as well as the meta data needed to provide meaning and context.

XML has obtained universal acceptance, as it provides the enterprise with a mechanism for simply labelling the structure and content of data. The latest versions of Microsoft's Office suite support XML, and there is the common belief that binary file formats, such as .DOC, .PPT, and .XLS will eventually become obsolete, being replaced by the XML equivalent.

It is not the intention of this book to provide a training course on XML, as there are countless books and websites dedicated to the subject. However, for completeness, the following section summarizes the concepts and constructs of XML.

Elements, attributes and hierarchy

All XML documents comprise of elements and attributes; these are used to define the context of the data represented in the message. Either of these constructs can be used to provide meaning and, according to Elliotte Rusty Harold author of the XML Bible, 'There are no hard-and-fast rules about when to use child elements and when to use attributes'. He goes onto to say, 'one good rule of thumb is that data itself should be stored in elements. Information about data (metadata) should be stored in attributes' (Elliotte Rusty Harold (2004) *THE XML 1.1 Bible*, 3rd edn, Indianapolis: Wiley Publishing Inc., p. 109). However, attributes lack the extensibility and flexibility that are required to support the complex requirements of financial data. For this reason, MDDL's use of attributes has been kept to a minimum. It's also worth noting that MDDL was based on the FpML (Financial products Mark-up Language) model, an XML standard which has obtained wide industry acceptance due to its good structural design.

Elements may contain text or other child elements; these are referred to as containers within the MDDL documentation published on the standard's website (www.mddl.org). Elements provide the user with ability to create deep hierarchical structures within a message.

Elements are delimited by start and end tags. Each tag begins with the 'less-than' character (<) and ends with the 'greater-than' character (>). The end tag differs from a start tag in that the element name is preceded by a forward slash (/). The data itself resides between these two tags.

An attribute is enclosed within the start tag of an element as a name/value pair separated by an equals sign (=), and the attribute value is defined between the single or double quotation marks (see Figure 5.1). There can be more than one attribute defined within the start tag. The element name and attributes are separated by a space. Attributes within MDDL are normally used to qualify the contents of the element.

An illustration of the use of an attribute can be found in Figure 5.2, where *scheme* is used to identify the International Securities Identification Numbering system (ISIN), which is a coding to identify financial instruments (stocks or shares).

The analogy of a railway train can be used to explain the concept of self-describing data. Let's say the train contains information relating to a trade, with each carriage

```
<containeElement>
  <childElement attributeName="attributeValue">text
  </childElement>
</containerElement>
```

Figure 5.1 XML elements and attribute constructs

being labelled to describe the cargo it contains – for example, the stock 'name' is contained in carriage 1, its unique reference 'code' in carriage 2, its traded 'price' in 3, and so on. The contents of the carriages are International Business Machines, US4592001014, \$81.54, 550, 20 and \$44 867.00 respectively (see Figure 5.2).

```
<instrumentIdentifier>
  <name>International Business Machines</name>
  <code scheme=" http://www.mddl.org/ext/scheme/iso6166.xml">
        US4592001014
  </code>
</instrumentIdentifier>

<trade>
   <price> 81.54</price>
   <size>550</size>
   <commission>20</commission>
   <settlement>44867</settlement>
</trade>
```

Figure 5.2 Trade report represented in XML

It can be seen that XML documents are, on the whole, readable, and there is nothing within the sample that ties it to any specific IT application, trading platform or implementation.

Properly written applications do not need to know in advance about the structure of the data, unlike with fixed-length or field-delimited formatted records, that would on the whole be 'hard coded' into applications exchanging the information. Adding a new field to a fixed-length record would result in all applications that use it being recompiled and released back into the production environment.

Generally, with the appropriate use of message versioning, adding a new field to an XML document should not require every application to be recompiled, just the applications that use the new elements of data – thus reducing regression testing requirements and risk of downtime if an application fails.

Chapter 6

Evolution of MDDL

December 2000 saw the formation by the FISD of an XML for Market Data Working Group, with the aim of consolidating the industry's efforts to define the parameters for a standard to meet the market data needs of the industry. Prior to the creation of the working group, Bridge Information Systems initiated the development of Market Data Mark-up Language (MDML) and had released a working draft of the specification earlier that year.

Based on the knowledge obtained by the development of MDML and FpML (prototyping of FpML started in 1998), the XML for Market Data Working Group created MDDL. Version 1 was released at the Fifth World Financial Information Conference in London in November 2001. Its scope was to support common equity and mutual fund securities, as well as the indicators and index terms needed for a vendor to disseminate meaningful information. In early 2002 work started on version 2, which extended the standard to include debt instruments. Even within the first version, flexibility and extensibility was built into the standard with the use of the *other* container, and external controlled vocabulary also meant that there were no hard-coded enumerations within the standard.

In Q1 2002, the Bond Market Association of the USA, working with the FISD/SIIA, hired London Market Systems to coordinate gathering of the requirements for the creation of MDDL version 2. The aim of the engagement was to define the terms needed to support the creation of a portal able to distribute Fixed Income issue data. This analysis formed the basis of MDDL version 2.1.

The main driver for the development of the standard has been the variety of proprietary data formats and the need for the end-user to convert these into a common format for use by desktop applications. Vendors have generally supplied information that makes the best use of their delivery architecture. Even though they have all developed different data models, protocols and symbologies, there is a great deal of commonality of data. This is where MDDL really hits the point; its comprehensive set of common properties and extensible design ensures that each data vendor can include its own value-added information and differentiate its products from others whilst still adhering to the standard itself. The vendor can thus retain its market share whilst attracting new customers!

MDDL versioning

Major releases of the standard are used to introduce new sets of instrument terms. Version 1 introduced equity products, and debt and derivatives were introduced in version 2. April 2007 saw the release of version 3 which consolidated all the security definitions under one domain.

All 'Minor' releases are backward-compatible with earlier versions, and therefore message data formats designed under version 2.1 will still be compliant with version 2.5. Given this fact, messages formats should always be designed based on the latest version released, even if this is a draft or beta. However, when the 'final' version is made available it is important to attempt to validate the messages against the 'final' version and then update the documentation accordingly.

All versions go through a three-stage development process, from beta to draft to final. Migration from one stage to another (beta to draft, draft to final) takes place every quarter, allowing participants to plan ahead. The total time from the initial beta release through to the final stage is therefore 6 months. At least the FISD has endeavoured to adhere to this.

As can be seen from Table 6.1, a three-phase roll-out is deployed by MDDL. Please note that prior to version 2.3 a different roll-out procedure was in place that normally adhered to a two-stage migration approach, going direct from beta to final.

Table 6.1 Version release table

Release date	Version	Content
02 April 2007	3.0-beta	The fundamental change in this edition is that the various instrument domains, such as equity, debt and so on, have been replaced by the *instrumentDomain*, which has been designed to support all instruments under a single nested structure.
14 April 2006	2.5-beta	Originally created 16 June 2005, revised on 20 November 2005, 23 January 2006 and 14 April 2006. It contained further development of the debt domain, business entity support, corporate action event and terms to support Market in Financial Instruments Directive (MiFID). Other changes include the creation of a number of new domains – the 'cashDomain' for describing cash holdings, the 'commodityDomain' for describing physical commodities, and the 'portfolioDomain' for describing portfolios and holdings. A number of new classifications grouping were created to the 'indicatorsDomain', including 'demographicClass', 'economicClass', 'industrySpecificClass' and 'marketClass'.
	2.4-final	Continued development of the debt domain.
20 November 2005	2.4-draft	
01 April 2004	2.4-beta	
31 August 2004	2.3-final	Refinement of debt set-up data and expanded basic pricing support.

(*Continued/*)

Table 6.1 *(/Continued)*

Release date	Version	Content
18 August 2004	2.3-draft	
05 December 2003	2.3-beta	
01 April 2004	2.2-final	Restructured some debt elements, adding basic pricing for all domains and query support containers.
04 December 2003	2.2-beta	
15 May 2003	2.1-beta	Deemed the 'debt set-up' release containing primary reference data for the major asset classes and incorporates 'entity domain' and the foundation for corporate action events.
31 March 2003	2.0-draft	Clarification of the debt domain. Updates to the glossary, schemes, and documentation.
	2.0-beta	Creation of the skeleton structure to support the debt domain and the supporting documentation.
02 November 2001	1.0-final	Common Equities & Collective Instrument Vehicle Funds, pricing and trade reporting associated with those instruments.

The most important concept that was recently adopted by MDDL was the recognition that an instrument could be constructed by a number of underlying properties, and that the constraints of grouping them under headings such as equity, debt and collective investment vehicle domains was inappropriate, given the ever-increasing development of new products that may require a property that has only been defined for use in one of the MDDL instrument domains whilst it is required in another.

The development of more complex structured/hybrid products, which bridge asset classes was the main reason for the change in direction.

Why use schemas?

A number of XML standards were originally supported by two mechanisms for validating the structure and content of an XML document. The first mechanism developed was Document Type Definitions (or DTDs), and the validation dates back to when XML was designed for the publication of manuscripts and books. Since those early days the true capability of XML has been seen, and it is now utilized to interchange data between business functions. The simple validation capabilities of DTDs (for example, it is not possible to state that a date takes the format yyyy-mm-dd), the lack of baseline data types and initiations on combining independent DTDs makes it extremely limiting when defining a complex message standard like MDDL.

The second mechanism, known as a schema, comes from the Greek word meaning form or shape, is a valid XML document in its own right. In complete contrast to DTDs, it does allow the designer to define complex data types, validation and, more importantly, deep hierarchical structures. It provides the ability to combine XML industry standards using what's known as 'namespaces'. For these reasons, most XML standards, including MDDL, no longer support the DTD mechanism (only MDDL version 1 supported both DTD and schema).

An XML schema allows a greater amount of content validation, when compared to a DTD. Taking a date parameter, for example, it is possible to check that the content adheres to the xsd:date data type (yyyy-mm-dd) as defined by W3C (The World Wide Web Consortium, www.w3c.org), which also adheres to the ISO standard, ISO 8601. Using a DTD, all that can be stipulated is that the date element is a string. Where possible, MDDL uses W3C primitive types and ISO standards for content.

Having touched on the subject of DTDs and schemas, there is no intention to dig deeper into this subject or to provide a training manual into how to design schemas; there are countless books and websites that cover this.

Chapter 7

How MDDL works

MDDL has been designed to make the most of XML Schema's deep hierarchical capabilities to provide context and meaning to the information represented within.

Synopsis of the MDDL hierarchy

The data content of an MDDL document is first broken down by domain; instrument, organization, corporate action and so on. Certain domains are further broken down by the use of classes and subclasses. This can be in the *caeDomain*, which can be broken down class (e.g. *corporateActionsClass*) and to subclass level (e.g. *distributionSubclass*).

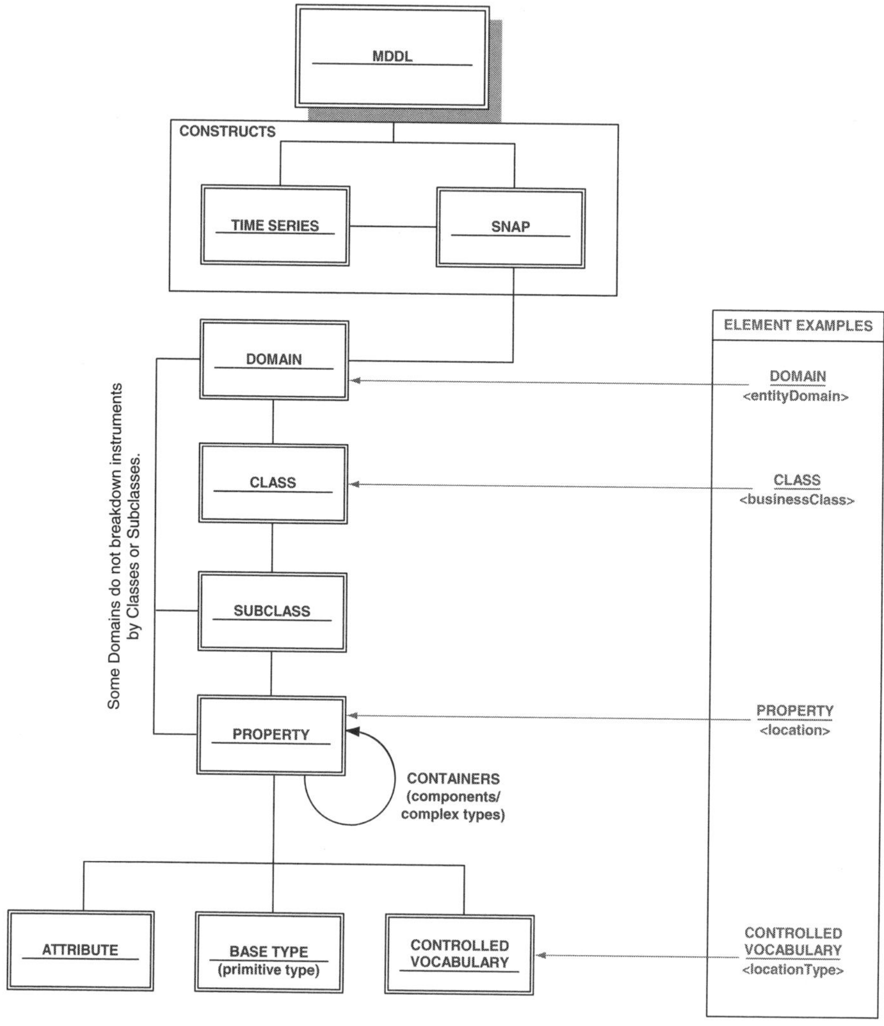

Figure 7.1 MDDL data content hierarchy

Figure 7.1 shows the relationship of terms used in a typical message structure. This structure is encapsulated within a wrapper and does not include the headers within a message; these are discussed later.

Prior to version 3, instrument were domains existed for equities, debt, derivatives and so on, and were based on the traditional breakdown of operations of financial institutions. However, given the development of more complex financial products that bridge these categories, such as structured products, it was recognized that the hierarchical grouping of instrument terms was inappropriate. This is the main reason behind the decision to group the instrument specific containers and properties under the *instrumentDomain*. It's important to recognize that given the removal of the instrument hierarchy, the user of the *instrumentType* term takes on a more significant role. The use of *instrumentType* is explored in Chapter 10 Reference data management.

An MDDL document can contain a number of properties or containers (a property that contain other properties). To help identify the meaning of the content of a property MDDL also uses controlled vocabulary to help define the context – for example, a volume may be classified as the amount bought, the amount sold or the total traded (achieved by the use of the controlled vocabulary property, *volumeType*.

At the lowest level there are a number of MDDL base types; these include constructs to support Boolean, decimal and string information. Attributes are also used to identify schemes that apply to the contents of the element. Figure 7.2 shows how the ISIN (ISO6166) coding scheme would be used to identify the ISIN coding scheme for the instrument, Johnson & Johnson; the ISIN for this instrument is US4781601046. Similarly, the attribute is also used to identify the Reuters (RIC) coding scheme.

```
<instrumentIdentifier>
    <name>Johnson & Johnson</name>
    <code scheme=" http://www.mddl.org/ext/scheme/iso6166.xml ">
            US4781601046
    </code>
    <code scheme="http://www.mddl.org/ext/scheme/symbol?SRC=REUTERS">
            JNJ.N
    </code>
</instrumentIdentifier>
```

Figure 7.2 ISIN and vendor proprietary representation in MDDL

MDDL Domains

A domain is a collection of properties that conveys a specific type of information. The contents of each domain, or an instance, can be visualized as a record of particulars, containing all the information to identify and price a security – such as cash equity, government treasury instruments or swaps. The majority of domains are designed to support specific types of financial products; however, other domains have been created to cater for the requirements of corporate action events and business entities.

Being a market data messaging standard originally designed to support the requirements of data vendors, it was recognized there is a need to disseminate not just securities standing data information (sometimes referred to as static data). Therefore, domains also contain properties to disseminate pricing, transaction reporting, end-of-day reconciliation, and time and sales.

MDDL Domain name	Coverage
caeDomain	Corporate actions and events.
cashDomain	Monetary instruments.
commodityDomain	Physical commodities.
entityDomain	Information about organizations; an issuer of an instrument, a trading counterparty or a business entity.
foreignExchangeDomain	Foreign exchange instruments.
indexDomain	Index domain; statistical composite information, indicating relative change in a particular market or collection of instruments.
indicatorDomain	Indicators domain used to represent non-index indicators that are NOT instruments of their own; rates fall into this domain.
instrumentDomain	Stock and shares, debt products, CIV and derivatives.
portfolioDomain	holdings of more than one stock, bond, commodity, or other asset by an individual or institution.

Classes and subclasses

Due to the complexity of financial instruments, simply grouping all child elements under a domain container is not normally sufficient. A financial instrument such as a cash equity instrument has different properties from a preferred share; this is where the use of classes and subclasses (Figure 7.3) comes into play.

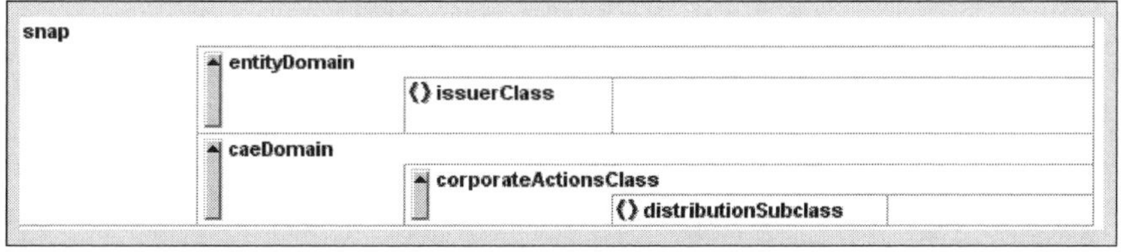

Figure 7.3 Domain/class and subclass relationship

Containers

The term ‘container’ is used in MDDL to refer to an element that ‘contains’ others. The example in Figure 7.4 shows the container <trade> containing <currency> and <last> as well as <settlement>. <settlement> is also a container comprising the elements <mdDecimal> and <currency>.

trade			
	last	mdDecimal	500
		currency	GBP
	size	550	
	settlement	2770.00	

Figure 7.4 MDDL trade report sample

There is also the ‘BooleanContainer’ used within MDDL to indicate whether a financial product is (performance, valuation, or otherwise) linked to another. An example of a ‘linked’ instrument is shown in Figure 7.5 (overleaf), which shows a Treasury Inflation-Protected Security (TIPS) whose coupon is linked to the US Department of Labor Consumer Price Index (CPI).

```
<interestRate>
  <rate>2.5</rate>
  <linked>
    <mdBoolean>true</mdBoolean>
    <instrumentIdentifier>
      <code scheme="http://www.bls.gov/cpi/">
        <mdString>CPI-U (NSA)</mdString>
      </code>
      <name>U.S. Department of Labor Consumer
          Price Indexes (CPI) program</name>
    </instrumentIdentifier>
  </linked>
  <accrual>
    <period>
      <dayRuleType>actual</dayRuleType>
      <duration>semi-annual</duration>
    </period>
    <accrualBasis>
      <accrualBasisType>actual/365</accrualBasisType>
    </accrualBasis>
  </accrual>
</interestRate>
```

Figure 7.5 BooleanContainer example

Properties

An MDDL property is a unit of information, normally an W3C XML element; however, in some instances it may refer to an attribute. When it contains other properties, then it is known as a container. A property may be constrained by a base type and/or a set of the values in an enumerated list specified within an external. Each property is also allocated a classification, which is used to identify its fundamental usage; the classification of properties is discussed later.

MDDL property types

Properties at the atomic level are categorized into a small set of base types, which themselves are based on a subset of the W3C primitive/derived types. These types are used to assist in decoding and in the interpretation of properties by applications. The following table identifies the types used to encode MDDL property values.

Property types	Description
mdBoolean	The mathematical concept of binary-valued logic, the contents of which must be either 'true' or 'false'. A property defined as mdBoolean cannot contain the numerical values 0 or 1, as this can be interpreted differently by each application that encounters the numerical value.
mdDateTime or DateTime	Dates and times based on the Gregorian algorithm, modified to include leap-second.
mdDecimal	A real number.
mdDuration	Duration of time, based on the Gregorian calendar.
mdInteger	A whole number (an integer value) with no decimal point or fraction component.
mdNonNegativeDecimal	Positive decimal values.
mdString	Sequences of characters (the atomic unit as specified by ISO/IEC 10646)
mdURi	A Uniform Resource Identifier, URI (a web page reference).

mdBoolean

The Boolean property is defined as the W3C XML primitive datatype xsd:Boolean, and expects the content to be either 'true' or 'false'. If no content is present within the element, the default is 'true'. A text string is used to represent the two states, thus avoiding any misunderstanding in the interpretation of 0 and 1 by the sending and receiving applications. Figure 7.6 provides an example of the use of mdBoolean.

Figure 7.6 Example of use of mdBoolean

mdDateTime or dateTime

This base type is defined as the union of the W3C XML primitive datatypes xsd:date, xsd:dateTime and xsd:time (see Figure 7.7 overleaf). When a time is specified, the timezone must be present or offset as defined by xsd:time.

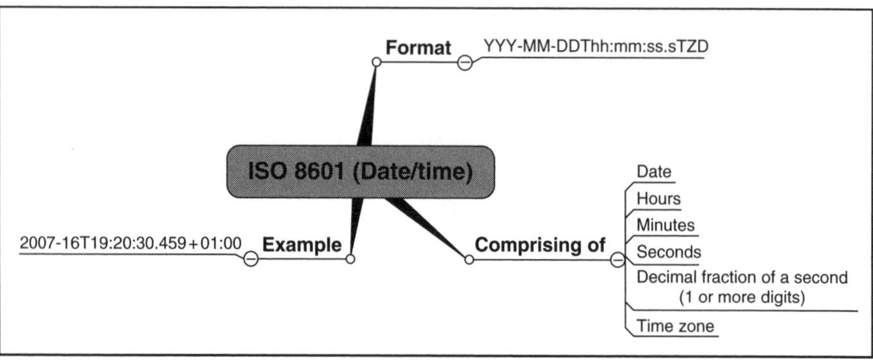

Figure 7.7 Format of DateTime

Example of MDDL representation

Date	<dateTime>2006-03-31</dateTime>
Time	<dateTime>T14:50:10+02:001</dateTime>
Date and Time	<dateTime>2006-03-31T08:20:59Z</dateTime>

mdDecimal

The decimal base type is defined as XML primitive datatype xsd:decimal, and is constrained by this definition. All properties of the type are represented within MDDL by the construct mdDecimal (see Figure 7.8).

{} currency	USD	
Comment	Bond Traded in Ticks, Par+1/4 Tick in Decimal	
open		
	{} mdDecimal	99.00390625
	{} dateTime	2005-12-06T08:30:01Z

Figure 7.8 Example of use of mdDecimal

The aspects of pricing in yields, spreads, basis and ticks are explained in more detail later in this book.

mdDuration

mdDuration is defined as the W3C XML primitive datatype xsd:duration, it's a range of days or time and has no specific starting or ending datetime. The format is defined by ISO 8601, and takes the form PnYnMnDTnHnMnS. MDDL expects the coupon (interestRate) payment period to be represented using mdDuration (Figure 7.9).

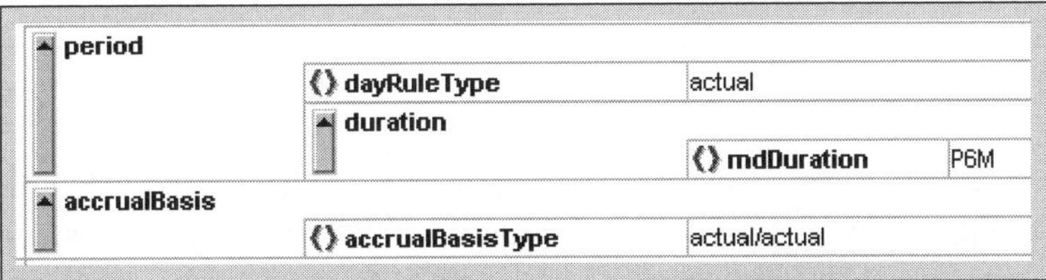

Figure 7.9 A bond with a semi-annual coupon (or duration of 'P6M')

mdInteger or integer

A whole number with no value after the decimal place, mdInteger is defined as the W3C XML derived datatype xsd:integer. It is rarely used within the standard apart from within the 'when' container and a small number of attributes of the element Fraction mdNonNegativeDecimal.

This property is used to enforce the positive value constraint for specific terms, used within <size>, for example.

mdString

Properties defined as a base type 'String' are represented within MDDL by the element mdString. Based on the W3C XML primitive datatype xsd:string, it should support a specific language, using the xml:lang attribute.

The two-digit language code that normally applies includes the following: 'de', German; 'en', English; 'es', Spanish; fr, French; 'it', Italian; 'pt', Portuguese; 'ru', Russian. It is also possible to specify British or American English by setting the attribute's content to 'en-GB' or 'en-US' respectively.

MDDL version 2.5-beta (or earlier) does not support multiple language of text. The specification of the language must therefore be as an attribute at the container level (Figure 7.10 overleaf).

```
<terms xml:lang="en-US">
        <mdString>Withholding Tax applicable if sold outside US jurisdiction</mdString>
</terms>
```

Figure 7.10 Example use of mdString

mdURi

This construct is used to point to reference material to help to provide additional context. The base type URI is defined by the XML primitive datatype xsd:anyURI, and is constrained by this definition. All properties of this type are represented by the element mdURI. This property may include an XLink or XPointer, and in Figure 7.11 two examples are given – the first as an attribute to identify the 'ISIN' coding scheme and the second in the element, nameRef.

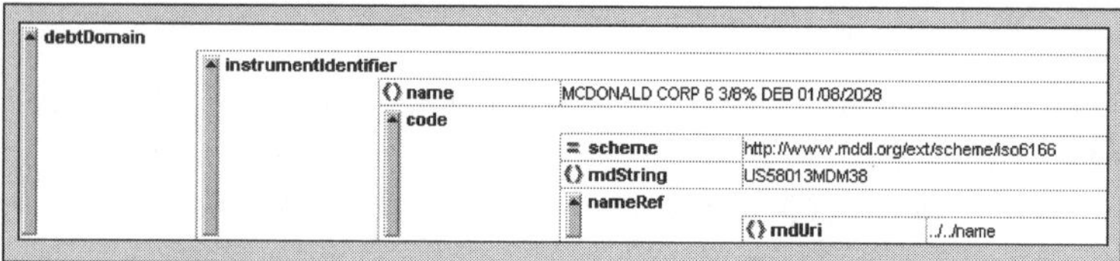

Figure 7.11 Use of mdURi

Industry standards used in content

The contents of fields within MDDL adhere, where possible, to industry standards. Of all standards organizations, the one at the vanguard has been the International Standards Organization (ISO). A voluntary, non-treaty organization founded in 1946, it has been responsible for creating international standards in many areas, including computers and communications. ISO has defined the structure and formats for information used throughout the financial sector. Standards exist for countries, currencies, and the structure and format of dates, times and instruments, among others. Where appropriate, data elements within MDDL adhere to ISO standards.

This section of the book examines some of these 'content' standards and explains their use.

Controlled vocabulary

This is the mechanism used within MDDL to link the contents of a term to an industry standard. There are a number of styles of controlled vocabulary; these take the form of either enumerated lists within the schema, lists defined externally to the schema and maintained by the owner of the schema, or code lists maintained by an overarching organization like the International Standards Organization (ISO).

An enumerated list defined within the XML schema is efficiently 'hard coded' within the schema. This style of controlled vocabulary is not used within MDDL; however, other standards use it to provide context to information such as the instrument code (ISIN, CUSIP, SEDOL etc.) or agency rating.

MDDL has a comprehensive set of controlled vocabulary for providing context and meaning. These are defined outside the schema and, therefore, can be modified without the need to release a new version of the schema. With enumerated lists defined within a schema, any changes to a list would normally result in the need to release a new version of the schema to the market. Every effort has been made to ensure the file listed here encompasses the widest representation of values; however, some of these lists may not be fully populated.

A useful point of reference for further information about MDDL use of ticker symbols can be found by going to the MDDL website (see Figure 7.12).

```
<mddlScheme>
  <head>
    <dateTime>2003-04-04T180000Z</dateTime>
    <title>Code for 'Ticker Symbols'</title>
    <element>code</element>
    <parent wildcard="yes" />
    <definition>A holder for market or source specific 'ticker
       symbols'</definition>
    <uri>http://www.mddl.org/ext/scheme/symbol</uri>

       <uri>http://www.mddl.org/ext/scheme/symbol?MIC=..iso10383
       ..</uri>
    <uri>http://www.mddl.org/ext/scheme/symbol?CC=...NNA
       cc..</uri>
```

Figure 7.12 MDDL symbols http://www.mddl.org/ext/scheme/symbol.xml (Continued/)

```
      <uri>http://www.mddl.org/ext/scheme/symbol?SRC=..source..
      </uri>
    <note>The 'ticker' is the code assigned to instrument by the
      market or source.</note>
    <note>The first parameterized URI (..?MIC=) specifies
      market(exchange) ticker symbols. The market is identified by
      the ISO 10383 Market Identifier Code.</note>
    <note>The second parameterized URI (..?CC=) specifies the ISO
      3166 country code for national numbering agency assigned
      symbols. See http://www.anna-web.com/anna-
      web/ANNA_Directories/ANNA_Directories.php.</note>
    <note>The third parameterized URI (..?SRC=) is for third-party
      assigned symbology. See
      http://www.mddl.org/ext/scheme/thirdparty.xml.</note>
  </head>
</mddlScheme>
```

Figure 7.12 (Continued/)

The *scheme* attribute within the *code* element makes use of the thirdparty (http://www.mddl.org/ext/scheme/thirdparty.xml) scheme, to identify the source of the identifier (Figure 7.13).

```
<code scheme="http://www.mddl.org/ext/scheme/SYMBOL?SRC=Bloomberg">
```

Figure 7.13 Use of the *scheme* attribute with *<code>*

Controlled vocabulary	**Scheme location (URI)**
accrualBasisType	www.mddl.org/mddl/scheme/accrualBasisType.xml
accrualConventionType	www.mddl.org/mddl/scheme/accrualConvention Type.xml
agentType	www.mddl.org/mddl/scheme/agentType.xml
amortizationType	www.mddl.org/mddl/scheme/amortizationType.xml
amountOutstandingType	www.mddl.org/mddl/scheme/amountOutstanding Type.xml
caeType	www.mddl.org/mddl/scheme/caeType.xml
calculationType	www.mddl.org/mddl/scheme/calculationType.xml
callableType	www.mddl.org/mddl/scheme/callableType.xml

callConditionType	www.mddl.org/mddl/scheme/callCondition Type.xml
capitalizationType	www.mddl.org/mddl/scheme/capitalizationType.xml
changeType	www.mddl.org/mddl/scheme/changeType.xml
closeType	www.mddl.org/mddl/scheme/closeType.xml
closingDateType	www.mddl.org/mddl/scheme/closingDateType.xml
codeType	www.mddl.org/mddl/scheme/codeType.xml
collateralType	www.mddl.org/mddl/scheme/collateralType.xml
convertibleType	www.mddl.org/mddl/scheme/convertibleType.xml
creditEnhancementType	www.mddl.org/mddl/scheme/creditEnhancement Type.xml
dayOfWeek	www.mddl.org/mddl/scheme/dayOfWeek.xml
dayRuleType	www.mddl.org/mddl/scheme/dayRuleType.xml
debtIndicatorsType	www.mddl.org/mddl/scheme/debtIndicators Type.xml
deliveryType	www.mddl.org/mddl/scheme/deliveryType.xml
deviationType	www.mddl.org/mddl/scheme/deviationType.xml
direction	www.mddl.org/mddl/scheme/direction.xml
distributionType	www.mddl.org/mddl/scheme/distributionType.xml
earningsType	www.mddl.org/mddl/scheme/earningsType.xml
entityType	www.mddl.org/mddl/scheme/entityType.xml
eventType	www.mddl.org/mddl/scheme/eventType.xml
exerciseRightsType	www.mddl.org/mddl/scheme/exerciseRights Type.xml
fundStrategyType	www.mddl.org/mddl/scheme/fundStrategyType.xml
incomeType	www.mddl.org/mddl/scheme/incomeType.xml
indicatorsType	www.mddl.org/mddl/scheme/indicatorsType.xml
instrumentFormType	www.mddl.org/mddl/scheme/instrumentForm Type.xml
instrumentStatusType	www.mddl.org/mddl/scheme/instrumentStatus Type.xml
instrumentType	www.mddl.org/mddl/scheme/instrumentType.xml
issueFeesType	www.mddl.org/mddl/scheme/issueFeesType.xml
issueMarketType	www.mddl.org/mddl/scheme/issueMarketType.xml
issueStatusType	www.mddl.org/mddl/scheme/issueStatusType.xml
jurisdictionType	www.mddl.org/mddl/scheme/jurisdictionType.xml
liquidationStatusType	www.mddl.org/mddl/scheme/liquidationStatus Type.xml
locationType	www.mddl.org/mddl/scheme/locationType.xml
marketStatusType	www.mddl.org/mddl/scheme/marketStatus Type.xml

marketType	www.mddl.org/mddl/scheme/marketType.xml
maturityType	www.mddl.org/mddl/scheme/maturityType.xml
nonFixedRateType	www.mddl.org/mddl/scheme/nonFixedRate Type.xml
objectiveType	www.mddl.org/mddl/scheme/objectiveType.xml
offerType	www.mddl.org/mddl/scheme/offerType.xml
openType	www.mddl.org/mddl/scheme/openType.xml
orderbookType	www.mddl.org/mddl/scheme/orderbookType.xml
partyStatusType	www.mddl.org/mddl/scheme/partyStatusType.xml
peRatioType	www.mddl.org/mddl/scheme/peRatioType.xml
periodType	www.mddl.org/mddl/scheme/periodType.xml
programType	www.mddl.org/mddl/scheme/programType.xml
putableType	www.mddl.org/mddl/scheme/putableType.xml
putConditionType	www.mddl.org/mddl/scheme/putCondition Type.xml
quantityType	www.mddl.org/mddl/scheme/quantityType.xml
rateChangeType	www.mddl.org/mddl/scheme/rateChangeType.xml
ratingType	www.mddl.org/mddl/scheme/ratingType.xml
redemptionType	www.mddl.org/mddl/scheme/redemptionType.xml
registrationStatusType	www.mddl.org/mddl/scheme/registrationStatus Type.xml
relationshipType	www.mddl.org/mddl/scheme/relationshipType.xml
role	www.mddl.org/mddl/scheme/role.xml
rulesType	www.mddl.org/mddl/scheme/rulesType.xml
salesRestrictionsType	www.mddl.org/mddl/scheme/salesRestrictions Type.xml
scheduleEventType	www.mddl.org/mddl/scheme/scheduleEvent Type.xml
scopeType	www.mddl.org/mddl/scheme/scopeType.xml
segmentType	www.mddl.org/mddl/scheme/segmentType.xml
sessionStatusType	www.mddl.org/mddl/scheme/sessionStatus Type.xml
settlementType	www.mddl.org/mddl/scheme/settlementType.xml
sinkableComputation Type	www.mddl.org/mddl/scheme/sinkableComputation Type.xml
sinkableType	www.mddl.org/mddl/scheme/sinkableType.xml
snapType	www.mddl.org/mddl/scheme/snapType.xml
stripType	www.mddl.org/mddl/scheme/stripType.xml
targetMarketType	www.mddl.org/mddl/scheme/targetMarketType.xml
taxType	www.mddl.org/mddl/scheme/taxType.xml
timeseriesType	www.mddl.org/mddl/scheme/timeseriesType.xml

tradingHaltedType	www.mddl.org/mddl/scheme/tradingHalted Type.xml
tradingRestrictionsType	www.mddl.org/mddl/scheme/tradingRestrictions Type.xml
tradingStatusType	www.mddl.org/mddl/scheme/tradingStatusType.xml
trancheIDType	www.mddl.org/mddl/scheme/trancheIDType.xml
underwritingFeesType	www.mddl.org/mddl/scheme/underwritingFees Type.xml
unitType	www.mddl.org/mddl/scheme/unitType.xml
valuationType	www.mddl.org/mddl/scheme/valuationType.xml
volatilityCalculationType	www.mddl.org/mddl/scheme/volatilityCalculation Type.xml
volatilityType	www.mddl.org/mddl/scheme/volatilityType.xml
volumeType	www.mddl.org/mddl/scheme/volumeType.xml
votingRightsType	www.mddl.org/mddl/scheme/votingRights Type.xml
yieldType	www.mddl.org/mddl/scheme/yieldType

Finally, there is external controlled vocabulary; this consists of standards maintained by other organizations. In some cases a copy of these code lists may be kept and maintained on the MDDL website. The external vocabularies maintained on the MDDL website include:

- ISO 3166 (two-alpha) Country codes
- ISO 3166 (three-alpha) Country codes
- ISO 4217 (three-alpha) Currency codes.

Others that are not maintained include:

- ISO 6166 – Securities Identification Numbering system (ISIN)
- ISO 10962 – Classification of Financial Instruments (CFI)
- ISO 10383 – Market Identifier Code (MIC).

There is the occasional exception where it may be considered inappropriate to use a list – for example, where a code list is a superset of one or more smaller lists. An example of this is ISO 10962, the Classification of Financial Instruments, where each digit of the six characters is used to represent a characteristic of a financial instrument, and the meaning of each digit is affected by the setting of another.

Use of country codes (ISO 3166)

The International Standards Organization has defined a standard for country codes; the financial industry has adopted the two-alpha code created by the United Nations. The standard also supports three-digit numeric and three-digit letter codes.

Country	Two-alpha code	Three-alpha code	Three-numeric code
United States	US	USA	840
United Kingdom	GB	GBR	826

(With regard to these codes, Great Britain (GB) is an island off continental Europe comprising England, Scotland and Wales. The United Kingdom is a superset comprising Great Britain and Northern Ireland. Given that Northern Ireland does not have a country code in its own right, it can be argued that the ISO country code of GB, GBR is incorrect.)

The default schema in MDDL is the two-alpha coding; this can be overridden by specifying a different scheme (see Figure 7.14).

```
<country scheme=" http://www.mddl.org/ext/scheme/iso3166-alpha-3.xml">USA</country>
```

Figure 7.14 Country code example

Use of currency codes (ISO 4217)

The ISO standard for currency codes is allocated by the maintenance agency under an international identification scheme as described in the latest edition of the international standard ISO 4217. These currency codes may be used within other industry standards. The standard comprises three alphabetic characters, and has been universally adopted as the *de facto* standard; however, it also provides the industry with the little known alternative, a three-digit numeric coding. It's also worth noting that some countries require more than one currency code to support their requirements. The following table provides examples of ISO currency codes.

Currency	Three-alpha code	Three-numeric code
Swiss Franc	CHF	756
WIR Franc	CHW	948
WIR Euro	CHE	947
US Dollar	USD	840
US Dollar	(Same Day) USS	998
US Dollar	(Next day) USN	997

The MDDL default scheme is the 3-Alpha code; however, this can be overridden (please refer to the Country Code example as to how to achieve this by specifying an alternative scheme).

Instrument identification

MDDL has been designed to support multiple instrument codes, from those defined by the market (that are allocated by a specific exchange), those at national level (normally allocated by one of the Association of National Numbering Agencies, 'ANNA'), or those at international level. The following table provides an example of instrument identification.

Instrument	Local market identifier	US ANNA (CUSIP) ISIN
Advanced Micro Devices, Inc.	AMD (NYSE) 007903107	US0079031078

For uniquely identifying an instrument, where possible the International Securities Identification Numbering system (ISIN) is used. This standard is defined by ISO 6166 and is composed of a two-character prefix representing the country of issue, followed by the national security number (if one exists) and a check digit. Each country has a national numbering agency that assigns ISIN numbers for securities in that country. The format is therefore defined as [A-Z]{2,2}[A-Z0-9]{9,9}[0-9]{1,1}.

Describing the attributes of a financial instrument

Where there is uncertainty regarding precise instrument coding or type, organizations may wish to use financial instrument classifications such as ISO 10962 CFI

(Classification of Financial Instruments, which can be purchased at www.iso.ch) or the ESA 95 Instrument classifications (statistical classifications of financial markets instruments, ©European Central Bank, July 2005). In MDDL, the classification of an instrument can be represented by using the term 'instrument type'.

The default scheme associated with the instrument type does not provide the user with sufficient granularity, in every case, to correctly identify an instrument – for example, the type of instrument is limited to: 'equityCommon', 'equityDepositary', 'equityPartnershipLimited' and so on. ISO 10962, on the other hand, uses six digits (alphabetic) to define the attributes of an instrument, thus providing organizations with a more precise description.

```
<instrumentIdentifier>
  <name>International Business Machines</name>
  <code
scheme="http://www.mddl.org/ext/scheme/iso6166.xml">US4592001014</code>
  <instrumentData>
    <!-- CFI Code for IBM -->
    <instrumentType scheme="http://www.mddl.org/ext/scheme/iso10962.xml">
       ESVUFR
    </instrumentType>
    <instrumentType scheme="http://www.lms.eu.com/ext/scheme/iso18773-2">
       Sh $0.20
    </instrumentType>
  </instrumentData>
</instrumentIdentifier>
```

Figure 7.15 Describing the attributes of an exchange traded equity

The instrument in the MDDL sample shown in Figure 7.15 is defined as being 'ESVUFR', where

E = An equity product,
S = comprising common/ordinary shares,
V = with voting rights,
U = with unrestricted, no ownership or transfer restrictions,
F = fully paid, and
R = registered.

The ISO CFI standard defines the instrument 'International Business Machines' as being common shares, with unrestricted voting rights, fully paid.

ISO 10962 (Classification of Financial Instruments) is based on a six alpha digit hierarchical structured enumerated list. At the highest level an instrument (the first character) represents the category of the instrument, eight in all (see Figure 7.16).

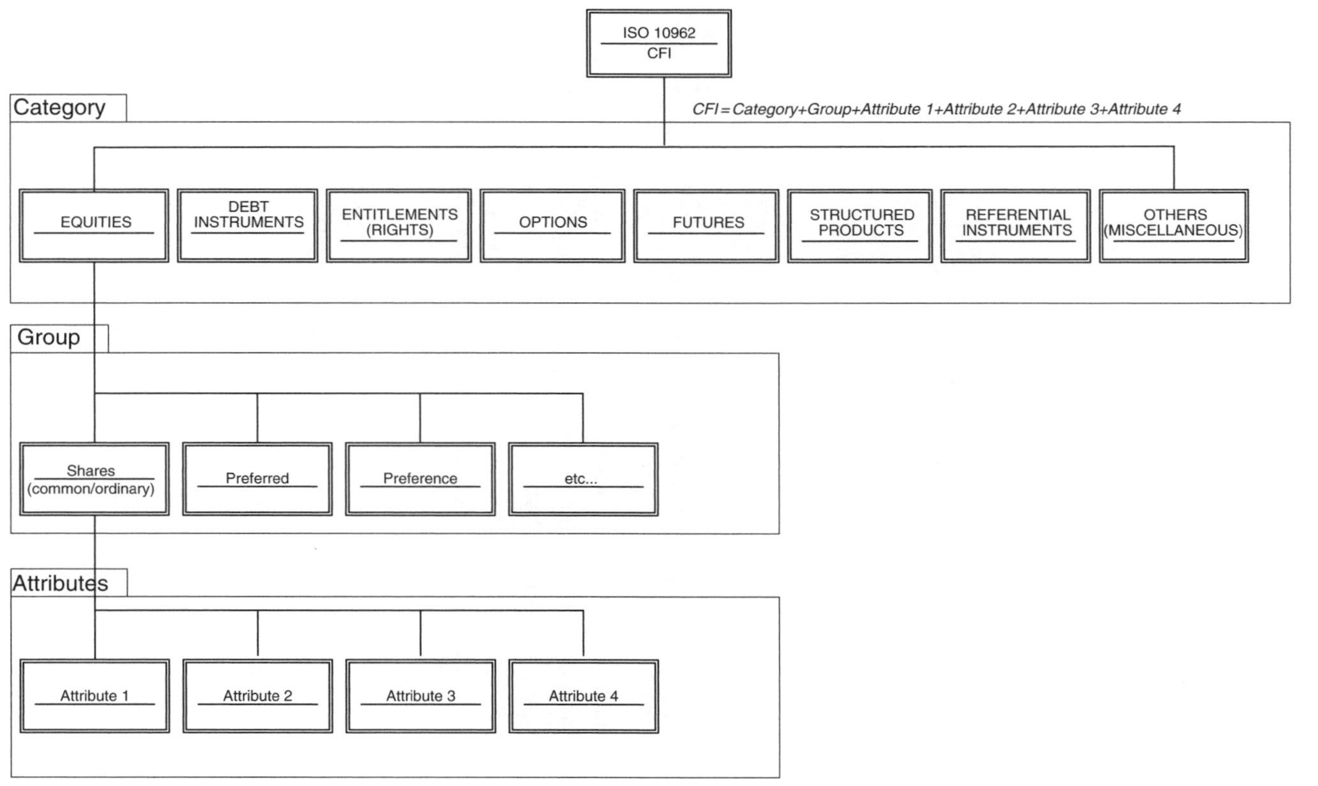

Figure 7.16 ISO 10962 (CFI) represented in a visual hierarchical form

Next, the instrument is broken down into groups. For example, equities are categorized by common/ordinary, preference and convertible shares and so on. The remaining four characters, based on enumerated lists, define the characteristics (attributes) associated with that financial product. All in all, this standard comprises of over 70 enumerated lists.

There are other codings that organizations may wish to consider, such as ISO 18774 (Securities and Related Financial Instruments – Financial Instrument Short Name, FISN), or the CFI coding in conjunction with another ISO, 18773-2, which defines the 'Abbreviations of Financial Instruments'. An example of ISO attribute codings is provided in the table.

Instrument full name	Local market identifier	ISO 10962	ISO 18773-2
International Business Machines	IBM	ESVUFR	Sh $0.20

ISO 18774 AND ISO 18773 – PARTS 1 AND 2

Having introduced ISO 18773-2, which defines the 'Abbreviations of Financial Instruments', now let's examine how it can be used in conjunction with Part 1 of the standard to identify an instrument and its issuer.

ISO 18774 is a Financial Instrument Short description Name (FISN) comprising the issuer short name (up to 15 alphanumeric, as defined by ISO 18773 – Part 1) and the abbreviated characteristics for the financial instrument (19 alphanumeric characters as defined by ISO 18773 – Part 2). The delimiter '/' is used between the two pieces of information. If the Issuer short name does not use all 15 characters, those remaining may be used by the characteristics of the financial instrument. The total length of the FISN is 35 alphanumeric characters.

ISO 18773 – Part 1 comprises the abbreviation of the issuer name, allocated and maintained by the Association of Numbering Agencies (ANNA), along with the ISIN (International Security Identification Number) as defined in ISO 6166. It is up to 15 alphanumeric characters in length.

ISO 18773 – Part 2 is the abbreviation of financial instrument types and characteristics taken from an international directory of Financial Instrument Short Names that is maintained by the Registration Authority and made available to users. It is up to 19 alphanumeric characters in length.

For example:

The standard	Full description	Abbreviation example
ISO 18774: FISN	NEWS AMER INC 7.300%,04/30/2028 ISIN: US652482AH30	News Amer/7.3 Deb 20280430 SrGtd AI
ISO 18773 – Part 1	Citigroup Inc	CIT GROUP INC
ISO 18773 – Part 2	A Future, maturing March 2008	F 03 2008

Identification of the trading venue

The ISO standard ISO 10383 MIC (or Market Identification Code) is a four alphanumeric code list used in MDDL to identify the trading venue. From an issuance perspective, the MDDL terms placeOfListing and placeOfTrade can be populated with the markets in which the instrument is listed and traded respectively (Figure 7.17).

```
<instrumentIdentifier>
  <name>REUTERS GROUP</name>
  <scopeType>International</scopeType>
  <code scheme="http://www.mddl.org/ext/scheme/iso6166.xml">
          <mdString>GB0002369139</mdString>
  </code>
  <scopeType>market</scopeType>
  <code scheme="http://quotes.nasdaq.com">
          <mdString>RTRSY</mdString>
  </code>
</instrumentIdentifier>
<issueData>
  <!-- Country of Register -->
  <location>
    <country>GB</country>
    <locationType>register</locationType>
  </location>
  <!-- OPOL based on Market Identifier Code (MIC) -->
  <placeOfListing>
     <code scheme=
"http://www.mddl.org/ext/scheme/iso10383.xml">XNAS</code>
  </placeOfListing>
  <!-- Place of trade based on Market Identifier Code (MIC) -->
  <placeOfTrade>
     <code scheme=
"http://www.mddl.org/ext/scheme/iso10383.xml">XNAS</code>
  </placeOfTrade>
</issueData>
```

Figure 7.17 Official Place of Listing (OPOL) and Place of Trade (POT)

As shown in the previous sample, the scheme used for the MIC is defined within the <code> child element of <placeOfTrade>, and therefore if the user wishes to override this scheme it will need to be specified within this element attribute (scheme).

From pre-trade (quote/order) and trade (trade reporting) perspectives the MDDL term 'marketCenter' would normally take the form of a MIC too (Figure 7.18).

```
<trade>
  <last>....
    <marketCenter>
      <code scheme=
"http://www.mddl.org/ext/scheme/iso10383.xml">XNAS
      </code>
    </marketCenter>
  </last>
</trade>
```

Figure 7.18 Trade report with trading venue specified as being the Nasdaq

To summarize ISO standards of interest:

Applicable ISO standard	Description	Pattern	Examples
ISO 16372: International Business Entity Identification **(Awaiting Implementation)**	Business Entity Identifier Code allocated by the Registration Authority (to be confirmed)	The format expected to be: [A-Z]{2,2}[A-Z0-9]{7,7}[0-9]{0,1}	US based Citigroup Asset Management could be represented as **USCITAMLE9**
ISO 9362: Banking Telecommunication Messages – Bank Identifier Codes	Valid BICs are registered with the ISO 9362 Registration Authority, and consist of eight or eleven contiguous characters comprising the first three or all four of	pattern [A-Z]{6,6}[A-Z2-9][A-NP-Z0-9]([A-Z0-9]{3,3}){0,1}	**VOLKGB21**

	the following components: BANK CODE, COUNTRY CODE, LOCATION CODE, BRANCH CODE. The bank code, country code and location code are mandatory, while the branch code is optional		
ISO 13616: Banking and Related Financial Services – International Bank Account Number (IBAN)	An identifier used internationally by financial institutions to uniquely identify the account of a customer, as described in the latest edition of the international standard ISO 13616 'Banking and Related Financial Services – International Bank Account Number (IBAN)'	[a-zA-Z]{2,2}[0-9]{2,2}[a-zA-Z0-9]{1,30}	**GB97MIDL 40010921212818**

Creation of new types

As base types are fundamental to the receiving application's understanding of the message content, it is recommended new types are not created without going through the formal review process. Advice should be sought before taking this course of action.

Classification of properties

Classifications are used to identify the use of an MDDL property and its relationship to others. Each property is allotted one of the following classifications:

Classification	Description
Amount	A quantity in a specific unit of currency.
BooleanContainer	A BooleanContainer is a wrapper for a Boolean property, plus other elements such as an instrument identifier to qualify the logical value.
Container	An MDDL property that may contain other MDDL containers and/or properties.
DateTime	A date, time or 'date and time' property, the format that adheres to the industry standard, ISO 8601.
Enumeration	An enumerated list, known as controlled vocabulary; normally this property is suffixed with 'type' – for example, accrualBasisType. The underlying base type for enumerations is 'string'.
Price	A single item in a specific unit of currency.
Quantity	A value without being associated with a unit of currency – for example, the number of shares traded.
Rate	A value, normally represented as a percentage relative to a specific period of time. A bond's annual coupon is an example of a 'Rate'.
Simple	A property that adheres to the constraints and facets of one of the underlying base types (Boolean, decimal string).

Controlled vocabulary

A property that is defined as a controlled vocabulary means that the contents of this element should be limited to the values identified by the associated enumerated list. It is defined as an mdString, and the MDDL schema specifies the location of the list of possible values, which are defined within specific schemas – one for each controlled vocabulary. Constraining the contents to these values is not mandated by the MDDL schema, and therefore it is up to the application to verify the contents. The norm is for a controlled vocabulary property to be suffixed with 'type' – for example, settlementType. Each controlled vocabulary term has a default scheme that applies to the content of the term; this can be overridden by the user.

Top-level wrappers

At the highest level, MDDL has two main data content wrappers. Earlier versions of the MDDL documentation published on www.mddl.org refer to them as MDDL constructs. This term is not used within this book so as to avoid any confusion with the XML term construct, which normally refers to low-level base types.

A wrapper can contain one or more domain containers within which all other elements and attributes reside. The wrappers are 'snap' and 'timeseries'.

'Snap' is used to group the properties of financial product information and other market data information under a common heading (Figure 7.19). It is a snapshot of the market at a specific point within the trade lifecycle. It may contain data about the instrument, changes resulting from a corporate action event, or reference data material such as business entity information. It can be used for bulk or flat file interfaces.

```
<snap>
    <instrumentDomain>... </instrumentDomain>
</snap>
```

Figure 7.19 A snap wrapper

A 'timeseries' wrapper is used to support real-time events and comprises of one or more snap events (Figure 7.20).

```
<timeseries>
  <event>
    <dateTime>2007-04-01T09:00:00Z</dateTime>
    <snap>
      <instrumentDomain> ... </instrumentDomain>
    </snap>
  </event>
  <event>
    <dateTime>2007-04-01T09:00:01Z</dateTime>
    <snap>
      <instrumentDomain> ... </instrumentDomain>
    </snap>
  </event>
</timeseries>
```

Figure 7.20 A timeseries wrapper

If further MDDL wrappers are required, in addition to snap and timeseries, then it is recommended that the user seeks advice.

Instance headers

Each MDDL document instance, as a rule, should comprise of an XML document header (declarations within the root element) and an MDDL header.

XML DOCUMENT HEADER

The XML instance header must always be present, starting with the prolog (<?XML...>), the header is used to declare the locations of the schemas used by the document. Multiple namespaces (or vocabularies) are defined by using the xmlns attribute. These declarations taking the form of URIs are nothing more than formal identifiers that assist the user in distinguishing between elements from different taxonomies. The default namespace is the MDDL schema itself.

The xsi:schemaLocation attribute is used to provide 'hints' as to the physical location of the schemas themselves. The contents of this attribute take the form of Namespace URI and physical schema location pairs, space separated. These are normally used by document editors and validators to ensure that the document is MDDL-compliant. The URI can be either an absolute or a relative location, and it is recommended that these locations are accessible to both the sender and receiving applications.

For course, XML doesn't care where namespaces are declared, though for consistency it is recommended that they are defined within the root element (Figure 7.21).

```
<?xml version="1.0" encoding="UTF-8" ?>
<mddl xmlns="http://www.mddl.org/mddl/3.0-beta"
    xmlns:ext="http://www.yourCompany.com/mddl/exte
    nsions"
    xmlns:mdref="http://www.mddl.org/mddl/3.0-beta/ref"
    xmlns:xlink="http://www.w3.org/1999/xlink"
    xmlns:xsi="http://www.w3.org/2001/XMLSchema-
    instance"


    xsi:schemaLocation="http://www.mddl.org/
    3.0-beta http://www.mddl.org/mddl/3.0-
    final/mddl-3.0-final.xsd
    http://www.yourCompany.com/mddl/extensions
    http://www.yourCompany.com/mddl/extensions/ext-
    mddl.xsd" />
....
```

Figure 7.21 MDDL root element declaration

MDDL HEADER

In addition to the XML document header, it is good practice to include the MDDL header (Figure 7.22).

```
...
  <header>
    <dateTime>2006-01-
       07T00:00:00.000Z</dateTime>
    <source>London Market Systems
       Limited</source>
  </header>
</mddl>
```

Figure 7.22 An MDDL header

The MDDL header is used to identify the source, date/time of the data and other information that is required to ensure the effective routing of the data content (contained within the snap and timeseries wrappers). If the MDDL header is present, the only mandatory property is date/time.

Header property	Description (as described within the schema)
DateTime	Date (and/or time) of the event.
Query	Information about the query (if any) from which this MDDL document was produced.
References	Placeholder for relatively static content that can be referenced within the document.
SchemeInfo	A pointer to additional descriptive information about the MDDL document itself.
Sequence	An indication from the provider of the relative sequence.
Source	The source of the data provided; this is normally the organization name that disseminated the information, i.e. the vendor's name (e.g. Reuters) rather than the originator of the data itself (the LSE). If within the enterprise, the source may contain the application name.

Inheritance

The principle intent of inheritance within any standard is to reduce message size, and this is the main driver for its use within MDDL. The majority of properties can either be inherited or inherit others. As a general rule of thumb, the higher a property is up the hierarchical structure, the more properties it can inherit. As a user, it's important to appreciate how this facility has been deployed. Even though MDDL makes the best of what XML inheritance can offer, it does not include any default values.

A simple example of how a property is inherited can be shown using the property 'Currency'. If a price or amount property does not have a currency specified within, then the price will inherit the currency of the nearest ancestor with one specified. However, the existence of a currency within the child overrides any inherited currency. In addition to a property classified as Price, Amount also allows for a currency to be present.

Figure 7.23 shows an example of inheritance, with <open>, <last>, <low> and <high> all inheriting the currency of US dollars (USD) from their parent <trade>, whilst the <settlement> price is in pounds sterling (GBP), overriding the inherited currency.

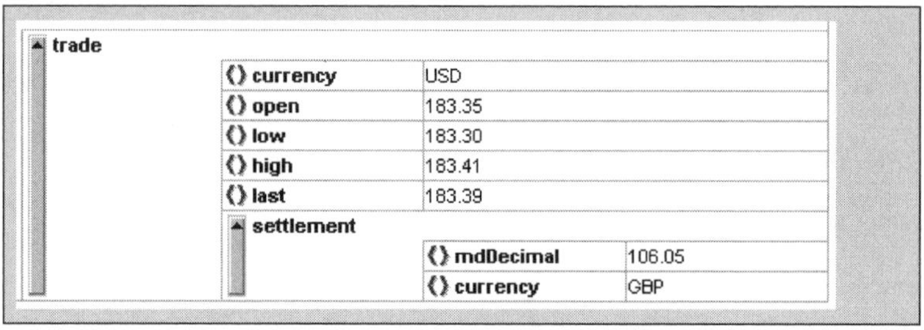

trade			
	() currency	USD	
	() open	183.35	
	() low	183.30	
	() high	183.41	
	() last	183.39	
	settlement		
		() mdDecimal	106.05
		() currency	GBP

Figure 7.23 Inheritance example, default currency, 'USD' unless specified

There is another inheritance mechanism built into the standard, and this is known as XML 'shorthand'. There are two ways that shorthand can be applied. The first style is where the parent element (or container) is removed – for example, Figure 7.24(a) is shortened to Figure 7.24(b).

This is only valid as long as '<child>' is the only element of '<container>'. Figure 7.24(c) shows an example where the container <trade> has been removed.

(a)

```
<container>
        <child>183.39</child>
</container>
```

(b)

```
<child>183.39</child>
```

(c)

```
<instrumentDomain>
        <last>183.39</last>
</instrumentDomain>
```

Figure 7.24 Shorthand inheritance example (style 1)

The second shorthand style can be used when there is more than one child element. With this style, the user throws away the opening tag of a container and uses a modified closing tag to indicate this. Figure 7.25 shows the use of the trade container, where the opening tag which would normally be present after the instrumentDomain opening tag has been removed and the forward slash within the closing tag becomes a suffix to the tag itself. This is a technique normally used to indicate an empty tag.

```
<instrumentDomain>
                <currency>USD</currency>
                <open>183.35</open>
                <low>183.30</low>
                <high>183.41</high>
                <last>183.39</last>
                <settlement>

          <mdDecimal>106.05</mdDecimal>
              <currency>GBP</currency>
            </settlement>
          <trade />
</instrumentDomain>
```

Figure 7.25 Shorthand inheritance example (style 2)

Though both shorthand styles are valid MDDL, it is not recommended policy to use these as it could result in a receiving application misunderstanding the information sent. It also requires additional processing by the receiving application, as it will need to normalize the information before being able to process it.

Just a final point regarding the use of inheritance: whenever possible, always err on the side of simplicity rather than reducing message size, just because it's possible. It's far better to reduce bandwidth using data compression techniques, examined later in this book.

MDDL extensions

One of MDDL's biggest strengths is its extensibility. This is provided by use of the other container, which is designed so that firms using MDDL could add terms to meet their specific requirements and that could, at a later stage, easily be migrated into the standard when the subsequent release was available. The extension process is easy to use, and it allows for the inheritance of properties and the use of property types that are defined within the standard itself – for example, it's possible to specify mdDecimal within an extension. Overall, when compared to other standards in the market, it scores top marks for extensibility.

So, why do you need to extend? Even though MDDL contains a comprehensive set of terms, there is always the need to add vendor or end-user specific terms; these are the icing on the cake, the value-add a vendor can offer.

Polymorphism

Polymorphism is the ability to assign a different meaning or usage to something in different contexts. This technique is used within MDDL, and an example can be seen in the use of the property, *code*. It is used to represent the code relating to an instrument when used within the *instrumentIdentifier*, or the code of a trading venue when used within *placeOfTrade*. It can be also used in the following containers:

- *agent*
- *collateralType*
- *componentIdentifier*
- *industryIdentifier*
- *issuerClass*
- *issuerRef*

- *marketCenter*
- *marketIdentifier*
- *municipality*
- *placeOfListing*
- *ranking*
- *rating*
- *region*
- *segmentIdentifier*
- *source*
- *stateOrProvince*.

Similarly, the property '*name*' takes on a different meaning based on its context within an MDDL document.

Naming convention

Prior to creating your required first extension, it is worth having an appreciation of the naming convention used by MDDL.

Major XML consortia such as OASIS, Universal Business Language (UBL), UN/CEFACT, RosettaNet, Biztalk and ebXML have all adopted the camel case convention for XML component naming, with ebXML differentiating between upper and lower camel case for different aspects of the standard.

MDDL has adopted the convention of using lowerCamelCase across the board, for elements, attributes and controlled vocabulary (also referred to as code list).

Are element names comprising of underscore ('_') delimited words acceptable? The answer is, 'No'.

Similarly, acronyms and abbreviations are not used in element or attribute names *and* in the contents of controlled vocabulary (code lists) too!

When creating extensions, it is recommended that the user adheres to the naming convention.

MDDL has adopted the KISS philosophy (or Keep It Simple Stupid!) to naming convention – something I've attempted to adhere to within this book.

Figure 7.26 (overleaf) shows the naming conventions that should be adopted when creating an extension. It shows an example of a return on investment type code list (or controlled vocabulary). The code list, known as roiType, comprises three possible enumerated entries (netReturn, grossReturn and cashFlow), which also adhere to the lowerCamelCase convention. The enumerated values contained within the short element are meaningful, NOT abbreviated or numerical values (such as 1 to represent 'net' and 2 'gross', and so on).

mddlScheme

head

dateTime	2006-01-11T110000Z
title	Types of Returns
element	returnOnInvestmentType
parent wildcard=yes	
definition	The type of period specified.

value (3)

	short	full
1	net	Net Return = (Net Income+Interest-Tax)/Book Value of Assets
2	gross	Gross Return = Net Income / Book Value of Assets
3	cashFlow	Cash Flow Return On Investment (CFROI) = Cash Flow / Market (Economic) Value of Capital Employed

Figure 7.26 Code list (controlled vocabulary) sample

So how is it possible to identify properties that are extensions to the standard? This is fairly simple, as all new properties are placed with the <other> container. MDDL will accept the use of the <other> container in the majority of MDDL containers.

The namespace prefix (or short code), in this case 'ext:', is used to identify within which schema the new element resides. This prefix is replaced by tools with the actual namespace value specified with the attribute. In Figure 7.27, the ext: prefix will be replaced by the URI 'http://www.yourCompany.com/mddl/extensions'. This is required by the schema validation and binding tools to ensure that the document is schema-compliant.

```
<other>
    <ext:returnOnInvestment>
        <mdDecimal>1012398</mdDecimal>
     <ext:returnOnInvestmentType >net</ext:returnOnInvestmentType>
    </ext:returnOnInvestment >
</other>
```

Figure 7.27 Sample of the extension

That, of course, is not the whole story; all extension properties will need to be declared within an extension schema.

Prior to using an extension property it will need to be declared within an extension schema, which is identified in the document header (Figure 7.28).

```
<?xml version="1.0" encoding="UTF-8" ?>
<mddl xmlns="http://www.mddl.org/mddl/2.5-final"
xmlns:ext="http://www.yourCompany.com/mddl/extensions"
xmlns:mdref="http://www.mddl.org/mddl/2.5-final/ref "
xmlns:xlink="http://www.w3.org/1999/xlink"
xmlns:xsi="http://www.w3.org/2001/XMLSchema-instance"

  xsi:schemaLocation="http://www.mddl.org/mddl/2.5-beta
http://www.mddl.org/mddl/2.5-final/mddl-2.5-final.xsd
http://www.yourCompany.com/mddl/extensions
http://www.yourCompany.com/mddl/extensions/ext-mddl.xsd" />
....
<other>
    <ext:returnOnInvestment>
        <mdDecimal>1012398</mdDecimal>
      <ext: returnOnInvestment ype >net</ext:
returnOnInvestmentType>
    </ext:returnOnInvestment >
</other>
```

Figure 7.28 Declaring the extension schema within the header

Creating an extension schema

Having previously stated that the creation of schemas is not covered within this book, let's examine how to create an XML schema to extend the terms of MDDL.

In the instance of a document, Figure 7.29 shows the contents of a container *returnOnInvestment* (i.e. return on investment), which comprises of an amount plus a code list indicating how to interpret this value. So we need to create an extension to MDDL to support this. Figure 7.30 (overleaf) shows the relationship of terms. It's

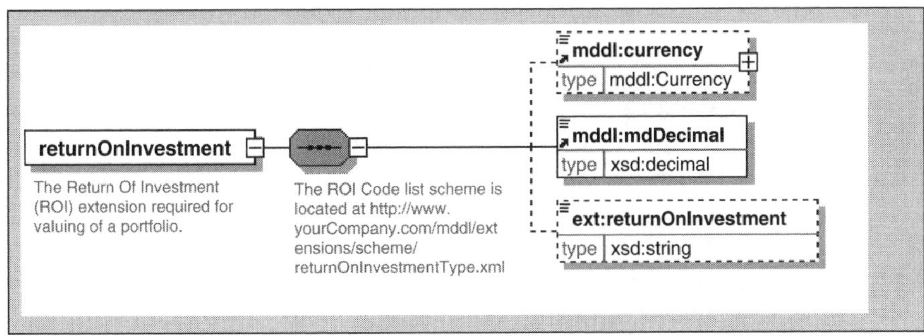

Figure 7.29 Definition of a structure to Return On Investment (ROI)

```
<?xml version="1.0" encoding="UTF-8" ?>
<!-- edited with XMLSpy v2007 sp1 (http://www.altova.com) by Martin Sexton (London
  Market Systems limited)-->
<xsd:schema xmlns:mddl="http://www.mddl.org/mddl/3.0-beta"
    xmlns:xsd="http://www.w3.org/2001/XMLSchema"
    xmlns:ext="http://www.yourCompany.com/mddl/extensions"
    targetNamespace="http://www.yourCompany.com/mddl/extensions"
    elementFormDefault="qualified" attributeFormDefault="unqualified">
   <xsd:import namespace="http://www.mddl.org/mddl/3.0-beta"
      schemaLocation="../../schemas/3.0-beta/mddl-3.0-beta-full.xsd" />
  <!-- Feed extension elements -->
  <xsd:element name="returnOnInvestment" type="ext:ReturnOnInvestment">
    <xsd:annotation>
      <xsd:documentation>The Return Of Investment (ROI) extension required for valuing
          of a portfolio.</xsd:documentation>
    </xsd:annotation>
  </xsd:element>
  <xsd:complexType name="ReturnOnInvestment">
    <xsd:sequence>
      <xsd:annotation>
          <xsd:documentation>The ROI Code list scheme is located at http://www.
            yourCompany.com/mddl/extensions/scheme/
            returnOnInvestmentType.xml</xsd:documentation>
      </xsd:annotation>
      <xsd:element ref="mddl:currency" minOccurs="0" />
      <xsd:element ref="mddl:mdDecimal" />
      <xsd:element name="returnOnInvestment" type="xsd:string" minOccurs="0" />
    </xsd:sequence>
  </xsd:complexType>
  </xsd:schema>
```

Figure 7.30 Extension schema to support the *returnOnInvestment* structure

worth noting that as *returnOnInvestment* is classified as an amount, it comprises a currency and a value.

How can this relationship be represented as an XML schema? Once the MDDL extension header has been created, then the schema design itself adheres to W3C design conventions. Though the structure and content of the schema extension header is not mandated, for consistency it should include a reference (via a namespace declaration) to the directory wherein the extension and the actual MDDL schemas are defined. The MDDL schema declaration is required if existing MDDL properties are used within the extension schema.

Defining code lists (controlled vocabulary)

To assist the user with the creation of an enumerated (code) list, MDDL recommends that a structure comprising of couple mandatory elements; these are:

Element	Description
short	The enumerated value in lowerCamelCase, with no abbreviations or numerical values
full	A note describing the short code entry

The enumerated list is contained within a simple *mddlScheme* wrapper. Figure 7.31 provides an example of the *returnOnInvestmentType* code list.

```
<?xml version="1.0" encoding="utf-8" ?>
<mddlScheme>
  <head>
    <dateTime>2006-01-11T110000Z</dateTime>
    <title>Types of Returns</title>
    <element>returnOnInvestmentType</element>
    <parent wildcard="yes" />
    <definition>The type of period specified.</definition>
  </head>
  <value>
     <short>net</short>
    <full>Net Return = (Net Income+Interest-Tax)/Book Value of
        Assets</full>
  </value>
  <value>
    <short>gross</short>
    <full>Gross Return = Net Income / Book Value of
        Assets</full>
  </value>
  <value>
    <short>cashFlow</short>
    <full>Cash Flow Return On Investment (CFROI) = Cash Flow
        / Market (Economic) Value of Capital Employed</full>
  </value>
</mddlScheme>
```

Figure 7.31 MDDL code list

Chapter 8

The life of a financial instrument

Market data plays an important role supporting a financial instrument from its inception through its life as a traded entity, and finally to its maturity. This chapter examines real-life scenarios in which MDDL can be used to support the instrument throughout its existence. Processes of particular interest include birthright, issuance, reference data management, pricing and portfolio valuation, corporate action management, end-of-day pricing and reconciliation, and regulatory reporting.

Issuance

After the initial release of MDDL version 1 at the Fifth World Financial Information Conference (WFIC) show in London in October/November 2001, debate started regarding what area of interest MDDL should tackle next. The minutes of the October's MDDL Working Group minutes states, 'The only open question is to determine the priority of the data products and constructs to be addressed within MDDL.'

At the January meeting in New York, London Market Systems presented its thoughts on the subject; what followed was a heated debate that culminated in the question being raised, 'Do we do convertibles or debt?' Someone pointed out that a convertible is a form of debt, so the decision was made: 'Let's do fixed income.' The seed was planted; however, given the complexity of some debt products, consensus was still required on the precise business area to be tackled. Shortly afterwards the business driver came in the form of the Bond Market Association (BMA) examining the possibility of creating the Securities Master Database, which would lend itself to the subsequent development of an online portal (or hub) used for disseminating bond issuance data (Securities Master Database – Request for Proposals, dated 12 September 2002).

London Market Systems was hired by the FISD to integrate the BMA new issue data requirements into the MDDL. LMS coordinated the working groups' efforts, and what resulted was a set of terms and relationship of terms that subsequently led to the creation of MDDL version 2. The aim of the assignment was to define the vocabulary required to support the creation of a portal able to distribute fixed income issue data. The next step was the creation of the BMA's New Issues Portal based around the standard. Unfortunately, consensus within the BMA was not achieved, and the appropriate vendor was not found to create the portal; therefore to this day the issuance process continues to be a non-automated process, with all the inevitable errors associated with manual entry!

From the time of inception, information about an instrument is disseminated to potential buyers and salespeople in the form of a prospectus and announcements. If properly managed, a portal would allow for this process to be completely automated. This was the forward-thinking idea behind the BMA's project.

The basic workflow of the issuance process is shown in Figure 8.1. From a market data perspective, there are three main documents that can be represented in MDDL: the advanced notification, the prospectus (or term sheet) and the allocation announcement. These are not prescriptive, and are dependent upon the type of product being issued. Large issues normally make use of all three, smaller issues may only require the release of a prospectus and an allocation announcement, whilst some instruments (such as covered warrants) only require the publication of the terms sheet.

It is worth examining the issuance process of US Treasuries and how MDDL could be deployed in the creation of a portal to support the US Bureau of Public Debt with the issuance of bonds. The example that follows shows how the issuance process of a 182-day US Treasury Bill CUSIP: 912795 XW 6 could be represented in MDDL throughout the whole issuance process.

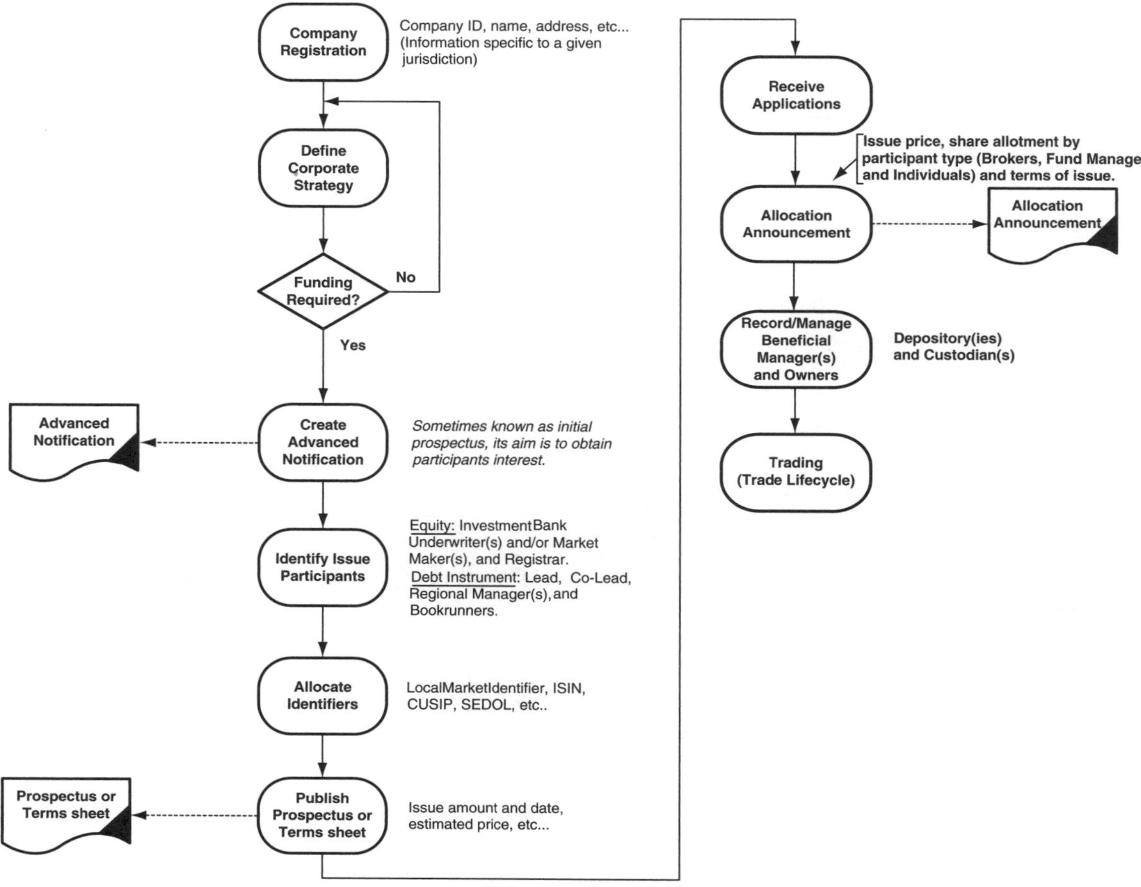

Figure 8.1 Issuance process flow diagram

```
<PendingAuction>
   <SecurityTermWeekYear>26-
      WEEK</SecurityTermWeekYear>
   <SecurityTermDayMonth>182-
      DAY</SecurityTermDayMonth>
   <SecurityType>BILL</SecurityType>
   <CUSIP>912795XW6</CUSIP>
   <AnnouncementDate>2006-03-
      16</AnnouncementDate>
   <AuctionDate>2006-03-20</AuctionDate>
   <IssueDate>2006-03-23</IssueDate>
   <MaturityDate>2006-11-21</MaturityDate>
   <OfferingAmount>17.0</OfferingAmount>
</PendingAuction>
```

Figure 8.2 Pending Auction in XML

The first step in the process is the pre-auction announcement; this currently takes the form of an XML document that is located at: www.publicdebt.treas.gov/xml/PendingAuctions.xml.

The PendingAuction structure within this document is used to supply the pre-auction information for each instrument (Figure 8.2).

The mapping and transformation from the Treasury format to MDDL is described in Figure 8.3.

Pre-auction Term	**MDDL Representation**	**Meaning**
Announcement Date	<announcementDate>**2006-03-16**</announcementDate>	March 16, 2006
Offering Amount	<issueAmount>**17000000000**</issueAmount>	$17,000 million
Term and type of security (SecurityTerm WeekYear)	<duration>**P26W**</duration>	26-week bill
Term and type of security (SecurityTerm DayMonth)	<duration>**P182D**</duration>	182-day bill
CUSIP number	<instrumentIdentifier> <code scheme="**http://www.mddl.org/ext/scheme/SYMBOL?SRC=CUSIP**"> <mdString>**912795XW6**</mdString> </code> </instrumentIdentifier>	912795 XW 6
Auction date	<auctionDate>**2006-03-20**</auctionDate>	March 20, 2006
Issue date	<issueDate>**2006-03-23**</issueDate>	March 23, 2006
Maturity date	<maturityDate>**2006-09-21**</maturityDate>	September 21, 2006

Figure 8.3 MDDL auction terms mapping

```
<snap>
  <instrumentDomain>
      <instrumentIdentifier>
        <code
          scheme="http://www.mddl.org/ext/scheme/SYMBOL?SRC=CUSIP">
          <mdString>912795XW6</mdString>
        </code>
      </instrumentIdentifier>
      <debtIssueData>
        <maturity>
          <maturityDate>2006-09-21</maturityDate>
        </maturity>
      </debtIssueData>
      <issueData>
        <announcementDate>2006-03-16</announcementDate>
        <issueAmount>17000000000</issueAmount>
        <auctionDate>2006-03-20</auctionDate>
        <issueDate>2006-03-23</issueDate>
      </issueData>
  </instrumentDomain>
</snap>
```

Figure 8.4 Pre-auction announcement in MDDL

This information can be disseminated in MDDL to support Front, Middle and Back Office applications, and takes the form shown in Figure 8.4.

Some may ask, why are there two containers, debtIssueData and issueData? Terms that are common to all instruments reside within issueData, whilst debt specific issuance terms live within debtIssueData.

The next step in the process is the publication of the prospectus associated with the issue (Figure 8.5, overleaf). It is possible to construct an MDDL document to support this information and effectively automate the process to deliver to the information to trading system application, and with a little bit of effort the prospectus can be transformed into the PDF. Organizations contemplating this route should take a look at the open source Apache XML Graphics Project, and in particular FOP (the Formatting Objects Processor), or contact a vendor offering a proprietary equivalent.

To create the prospectus, the MDDL pre-auction announcement document will need to be supplemented with some addition information:

- minimum bid amount and multiples, supported by the *denomination* definition within MDDL
- maximum award (35% of offering amount)
- maximum recognized bid, and
- NLP exclusion amount.

OFFICE OF PUBLIC AFFAIRS • 1500 PENNSYLVANIA AVENUE, N.W. • WASHINGTON, D.C. • 20220 • (202) 622-2960

EMBARGOED UNTIL 12:30 P.M.
March 16, 2006

CONTACT: Office of Financing
March 16, 2006 202/504-3550

TREASURY OFFERS 13-WEEK AND 26-WEEK BILLS

The Treasury will auction 13-week and 26-week Treasury bills totaling $37,000 million to refund an estimated $32,375 million of publicly held 13-week and 26-week Treasury bills maturing March 23, 2006, and to raise new cash of approximately $4,625 million. Also maturing is an estimated $19,000 million of publicly held 4-week Treasury bills, the disposition of which will be announced March 20, 2006.

The Federal Reserve System holds $16,005 million of the Treasury bills maturing on March 23, 2006, in the System Open Market Account (SOMA). This amount may be refunded at the highest discount rate of accepted competitive tenders either in these auctions or the 4-week Treasury bill auction to be held March 21, 2006. Amounts awarded to SOMA will be in addition to the offering amount.

Up to $1,000 million in non-competitive bids from Foreign and International Monetary Authority (FIMA) accounts bidding through the Federal Reserve Bank of New York will be included within the offering amount of each auction. These non-competitive bids will have a limit of $100 million per account and will be accepted in the order of smallest to largest, up to the aggregate award limit of $1,000 million.

Treasury Direct customers have scheduled purchases of approximately $1,135 million into the 13-week bill and $931 million into the 26-week bill.

The allocation percentage applied to bids awarded at the highest discount rate will be rounded up to the next hundredth of a whole percentage point, e.g., 17.13%.

This offering of Treasury securities is governed by the terms and conditions set forth in the Uniform Offering Circular for the Sale and Issue of Marketable Book-Entry Treasury Bills, Notes, and Bonds (31 CFR Part 356, as amended).

Details about each of the new securities are given in the attached offering highlights.

oOo

Attachment

Figure 8.5 Published prospectus

```
                HIGHLIGHTS OF TREASURY OFFERINGS OF BILLS
                       TO BE ISSUED MARCH 23, 2006
March 16, 2006
Offering Amount ..........................  $17,000 million
Maximum Award (35% of Offering Amount) ....  $ 5,950 million
Maximum Recognized Bid at a Single Rate ....  $ 5,950 million
NLP Reporting Threshold ...................  $ 5,950 million
NLP Exclusion Amount ......................  None
Description of Offering:
Term and type of security .................  182-day bill
CUSIP number ..............................  912795 XW 6
Auction date ..............................  March 20, 2006
Issue date ................................  March 23, 2006
Maturity date .............................  September 21, 2006
Original issue date .......................  March 23, 2006
Currently outstanding .....................  ---
Minimum bid amount and multiples ..........  $1,000
The following rules apply to all securities mentioned above:
Submission of Bids:
Noncompetitive bids:
Accepted in full up to $5 million at the highest discount rate of
accepted competitive bids.
Foreign and International Monetary Authority (FIMA) bids:
     Non-competitive bids submitted through the Federal Reserve Banks
     as agents for FIMA accounts. Accepted in order of size from
     smallest to largest with no more than $100 million awarded per
     account. The total non-competitive amount awarded to Federal
     Reserve Banks as agents for FIMA accounts will not exceed $1,000
     million. A single bid that would cause the limit to be exceeded
     will be partially accepted in the amount that brings the
     aggregate award total to the $1,000 million limit. However, if
     there are two or more bids of equal amounts that would cause the
     limit to be exceeded, each will be prorated to avoid exceeding
     the limit.
Competitive bids:
     (1) Must be expressed as a discount rate with three decimals in
     increments of .005%, e.g., 7.100%, 7.105%.
     (2) Net long position (NLP) for each bidder must be reported
     when the sum of the total bid amount, at all discount rates,
     and the net long position equals or exceeds the NLP reporting
     threshold stated above.
     (3) Net long position must be determined as of one-half hour
     prior to the closing time for receipt of competitive tenders.
     (4) Competitive bids from Treasury Direct customers are not
     allowed.
Receipt of Tenders:
Noncompetitive tenders:
Prior to 12:00 noon eastern standard time on auction day
Competitive tenders:
Prior to 1:00 p.m. eastern standard time on auction day
```

Figure 8.5 (/Continued)

Apart from the *denomination*, all the other terms will need to be placed in an extension schema. For completeness, these terms can be added as extension elements defined in an extension schema (please refer to 'Creating an extension schema', in Chapter 7). The MDDL instance to support the prospectus would look like Figure 8.6; however, to convert this into the printable form shown in Figure 8.5, an XSLT style sheet is required.

```
<snap>
    <instrumentDomain>
        <debtIssueData>
            <instrumentIdentifier>
                <name>182-DAY BILL 2006-06-29</name>
                <code scheme=" http://www.mddl.org/ext/scheme/SYMBOL?SRC=CUSIP ">
                    <mdString>912795XW6</mdString>
                </code>
            </instrumentIdentifier>
            <denomination>1000</denomination>
            <maturity>
                <maturityDate>2006-09-21</maturityDate>
            </maturity>
            <other>
                <ext:thresholds>
                    <ext:maximumAwardAmount>595000000</ext:maximumAwardAmount>
                    <ext:maximumRecognizedBid>5950000000</ext:maximumRecognizedBid>
                    <ext:nlpReportingThreshold>5950000000</ext:nlpReportingThreshold>
                </ext:thresholds>
            </other>
        </debtIssueData>
        <issueData>
            <announcementDate>2006-03-20</announcementDate>
            <auctionDate>2006-03-21</auctionDate>
            <issueDate>2006-03-23</issueDate>
            <issueAmount>17000</issueAmount>
            <settlementDate>2006-03-23</settlementDate>
        </issueData>
    </instrumentDomain>
</snap>
```

Figure 8.6 MDDL document to support the parameters within the prospectus

Another situation where MDDL can play a part is where fund managers or brokers detail with retail clients. In such circumstances the MDDL pre-announcement document can be supplemented with addition information, including the full descriptive name and derived information such as the estimated yield (Figure 8.7).

Using an XSLT style sheet, it is then possible to reformat the MDDL for use on a website. Figure 8.8 shows how the MDDL document can be transformed into an HTML representation using the XSLT style sheet in Figure 8.9.

Upon completion of the auction, the results will need to be published. MDDL can again be used to disseminate this information. There are a small number of additional terms required to support this part of the process. For each bidder (*submitterType*) there are two amounts, the tendered (*tenderedAmount*) and accepted amounts (*acceptedAmount*). There is also the requirement to add a *note* definition. These definitions are repeated for each of the types of submitters – primary dealer, direct bidder and indirect bidder – and therefore the extension schema will need to be created to include the above definitions within the container, *auctionBid*. A code list for *submitterType* is also required to support the possible val-

```
<snap>
  <instrumentDomain>
    <instrumentIdentifier>
      <name>US TSY BILLS 0.000% 09/21/2006</name>
      <code
        scheme="http://www.mddl.org/ext/scheme/SYMBOL?SRC=CUSIP">
        <mdString>912795XW6</mdString>
      </code>
    </instrumentIdentifier>
    <debtIssueData>
      <interestRate>
        <rate>4.770</rate>
      </interestRate>
      <maturity>
        <maturityDate>2006-09-21</maturityDate>
      </maturity>
    </debtIssueData>
    <issueData>
      <auctionDate>2006-03-20</auctionDate>
      <issueDate>2006-03-23</issueDate>
      <settlementDate>2006-03-23</settlementDate>
    </issueData>
  </instrumentDomain>
</snap>
```

Figure 8.7 MDDL document enriched with the instrument name, settlement date and estimated yield

MDDL Sample of a US Treasury Auction Announcement

Name	CUSIP	Expected Yield	Maturity Date	Auction Date	Issue Date	Settlement Date
US TSY BILLS ZERO CPN 09/21/2006	912795XW6	4.770	2006-09-21	2006-03-20	2006-03-23	2006-03-23

Figure 8.8 MDDL document transformed by the XSLT style sheet

ues. (Refer to the sections titled 'Creating an extension schema' and 'Defining code lists (controlled vocabulary)', in Chapter 7, for further information on these subjects.)

The result announcement document (Figure 8.10 overleaf) can now be populated, and all that remains is to transform this MDDL into the readable allocation announcement normally seen. This can be achieved by using a XSLT style sheet (see Figure 8.11 on page 82).

```
<?xml version="1.0" encoding="ISO-8859-1"?>
<xsl:stylesheet version="1.0"
xmlns:xsl="http://www.w3.org/1999/XSL/Transform">
<xsl:template match="/">
 <html>
 <body>
  <b><center>MDDL Sample of a US Treasury Auction Announcement</center></b>
  <p>
  <table border="1">
   <tr bgcolor="grey">
        <th align="left"><small>Name</small></th>
        <th align="center"><small>CUSIP</small></th>
        <th align="center"><small>Expected Yield</small></th>
        <th align="center"><small>Maturity Date</small></th>
        <th align="center"><small>Auction Date</small></th>
        <th align="center"><small>Issue Date</small></th>
        <th align="center"><small>Settlement Date</small></th>
   </tr>
   <tr>
   <xsl:for-each select="mddl">
    <td><small><xsl:value-of select="snap/debtDomain/instrumentIdentifier/name" /></small></td>
    <td align="center"><small><xsl:value-of select="snap/debtDomain/nstrumentIdentifier/code" /></small></td>
    <td align="center"><small><xsl:value-of select="snap/debtDomain/debtIssueData/interestRate" /></small></td>
    <td align="center"><small><xsl:value-of select="snap/debtDomain/debtIssueData/maturity" /></small></td>
    <td align="center"><small><xsl:value-of select="snap/debtDomain/issueData/auctionDate" /></small></td>
    <td align="center"><small><xsl:value-of select="snap/debtDomain/issueData/issueDate" /></small></td>
    <td align="center"><small><xsl:value-of select="snap/debtDomain/issueData/settlementDate" /></small></td>
   </xsl:for-each>
   </tr>
  </table>
  </p>
 </body>
 </html>
</xsl:template>
</xsl:stylesheet>
```

Figure 8.9 XSLT style sheet sample for US Treasury Auction Announcement

```
<mddl>
  <header>
    <dateTime>2006-03-20T10:20:00Z</dateTime>
    <source>Martin Sexton of London Market Systems</source>
  </header>
  <snap>
    <instrumentDomain>
      <debtIssueData>
        <instrumentIdentifier>
          <name>182-DAY BILL 2006-06-29</name>
          <code
              scheme="http://www.mddl.org/ext/scheme/SYMBOL?
              SRC=CUSIP">
            <mdString>912795XW6</mdString>
          </code>
        </instrumentIdentifier>
      </debtIssueData>
      <issueData>
        <other>
```

Figure 8.10 Result announcement in MDDL

```
          <ext:auctionBid>
            <ext:note>(Note-1)</ext:note>
            <ext:tenderedAmount>
              <mdDecimal>42321500</mdDecimal>
              <ext:submitterType>Primary
                  Dealer</ext:submitterType>
            </ext:tenderedAmount>
            <ext:acceptedAmount>
              <mdDecimal>21375669</mdDecimal>
            </ext:acceptedAmount>
          </ext:auctionBid>
          <ext:auctionBid>
            <ext:note>(Note-2)</ext:note>
            <ext:tenderedAmount>
              <mdDecimal>2175000</mdDecimal>
              <ext:submitterType>Direct Bidder</
                </ext:submitterType>
            </ext:tenderedAmount>
            <ext:acceptedAmount>
              <mdDecimal>1163570</mdDecimal>
            </ext:acceptedAmount>
          </ext:auctionBid>
          <ext:auctionBid>
            <ext:note>(Note-3)</ext:note>
            <ext:tenderedAmount>
              <mdDecimal>3670554</mdDecimal>
              <ext:submitterType>Indirect
                  Bidder</ext:submitterType>
            </ext:tenderedAmount>
            <acceptedAmount>
              <mdDecimal>3170554</mdDecimal>
            </ext:acceptedAmount>
          </ext:auctionBid>
          <ext:auctionBid>
            <ext:tenderedAmount>
              <mdDecimal>48167054</mdDecimal>
              <ext:submitterType>Total
                  Competitive</ext:submitterType>
            </ext:tenderedAmount>
            <ext:acceptedAmount>
              <mdDecimal>25709793</mdDecimal>
            </ext:acceptedAmount>
          </ext:auctionBid>
        </other>
      </issueData>
    </instrumentDomain>
  </snap>
</mddl>
```


Figure 8.10 (Continued/)

```
<?xml version="1.0" encoding="ISO-8859-1" ?>
<xsl:stylesheet version="1.0"
xmlns:xsl="http://www.w3.org/1999/XSL/Transform">
<xsl:template match="/">
<html>
<body>
<font face="Courier New">
<center>
<table>
<tr>
<td align="left">
<center>
<img
src="http://www.londonmarketsystems.com/mddl/ustNewsHdr.gif"
alt="US Treasury News" />
</center>
</td>
</tr>
</table>
<p />
<p />
 Bureau of the Public Debt - Office of Financing
<br />
 Addendum to Press Release(s) dated March 21 2006
<br />
<p />
<p />
<xsl:value-of
select="mddl/snap/debtDomain/debtIssueData/instrumentIdentifier
/name" />
<br />
 CUSIP:
<xsl:value-of
select="mddl/snap/debtDomain/debtIssueData/instrumentIdentifier
/code" />
<br />
 (amounts in thousands)
<br />
<p />
<p />
</center>
<table>
<tr>
<th width="180" align="left">Tender Type</th>
<th width="60" />
<th width="40" />
<th width="140">Tendered</th>
<th width="40" />
<th width="150">Accepted</th>
</tr>
<xsl:for-each
select="mddl/snap/debtDomain/issueData/other/auctionBid">
<tr>
<td>
<xsl:value-of select="tenderedAmount/submitterType" />
</td>
```

Figure 8.11 The style sheet for transforming into the result announcement

```
<td align="right">
<xsl:value-of select="note" />
</td>
<td align="right">$</td>
<td align="right">
<xsl:variable name="ta"> <xsl:value-of select="tenderedAmount
/mdDecimal"/> </xsl:variable>
<xsl:value-of select='format-number($ta, "###,###,###")' />
</td>
<td align="right">$</td>
<td align="right">
<right>
<xsl:variable name="aa"> <xsl:value-of select="acceptedAmount
/mdDecimal"/> </xsl:variable>
<xsl:value-of select='format-number($aa, "###,###,###")' />
<xsl:value-of select="acceptedAmount/mdDecimal" />
</right>
</td>
</tr>
</xsl:for-each>
</table>
<p>
<br />
</p>
<p>
<br />
</p>
<left>
 Notes:
br />
 1: Primary dealers as submitters bidding for their own house
accounts.
br />
 2: Non-Primary dealer submitters bidding for their own house
accounts.
<br />
 3: Customers placing competitive bids through a direct submitter,
including foreign and
<br />
 international monetary authorities placing bids through the New
York Federal Reserve Bank.
<br />
</left>
</font>
</body>
</html>
</xsl:template>
</xsl:stylesheet>
```

Figure 8.11 (Continued/)

The transformed document now looks like a result announcement (Figure 8.12, page 84). It is worth noting that the MDDL definitions are merged with the text in the style sheet plus the logo, which is a graphic specified as a URI.

PUBLIC DEBT NEWS

Department of the Treasury • Bureau of the Public Debt • Washington, DC 20239

Bureau of the Public Debt - Office of Financing
Addendum to Press Release(s) dated March 21 2006

182-DAY BILL 2006-06-29
CUSIP: 912795XW6
(amounts in thousands)

Tender Type			Tendered		Accepted
Primary Dealer	(Note-1)	$	42,321,500	$	21,375,669
Direct Bidder	(Note-2)	$	2,175,000	$	1,163,570
Indirect Bidder	(Note-3)	$	3,670,554	$	3,170,554
Total Competitive		$	48,167,054	$	25,709,793

Notes:
1: Primary dealers as submitters bidding for their own house accounts.
2: Non-Primary dealer submitters bidding for their own house accounts.
3: Customers placing competitive bids through a direct submitter, including foreign and international monetary authorities placing bids through the New York Federal Reserve

Figure 8.12 Result announcement created from MDDL

Pricing and reporting

MDDL version 1 was essentially designed to support the pricing and reporting requirements for equity instruments; this was expanded in version 2 to support a greater range of asset classes. The fundamental pricing terms bid, ask, high, low, close and last traded price are supported, as well as various trade reporting terms. Real-life examples of how MDDL can be used to maintain the decision-making process have been provided, across various asset classes. These including trading summaries, historical pricing, order book representation (top of book and market depth), and an example of a retail style of stock portfolio.

General pricing and volumes

The simplest way of showing how to represent pricing and trading volumes in MDDL is to construct a trading summary, as shown in Figure 8.13, the associated MDDL is supplied in Figure 8.14.

It's worth noting that the *bid* and *ask* prices of DCXAJ.X are displayed as 'N/A' (Not available). It is not valid MDDL to put the 'N/A' in these fields; however a 0 or a negative value can be converted by the style sheet or receiving application to display the string 'N/A'.

Strike	Symbol	Last	Chg	Bid	Ask	Volume	Open Interest
20.00	DCXAD.X	31.9	0	N/A	N/A	20	181
22.50	DCXAS.X	27.1	0	N/A	N/A	15	102
30.00	DCXAF.X	24.4	0	N/A	N/A	10	141
35.00	DCXAG.X	14.7	0	N/A	N/A	10	67
40.00	DCXAH.X	12.9	0	N/A	N/A	10	347
42.50	DCXAV.X	10.5	0	N/A	N/A	10	45
45.00	DCXAI.X	6.4	0	N/A	N/A	1	754
47.50	DCXAW.X	4.3	0.25	4.28	4.35	249	531
50.00	DCXAJ.X	3.3	0	N/A	N/A	15	1626
52.50	DCXAX.X	1.8	0	N/A	N/A	5	92
55.00	DCXAK.X	1.15	0	N/A	N/A	11	1897
57.50	DCXAY.X	0.8	0	N/A	N/A	10	258
60.00	DCXAL.X	0.45	0	N/A	N/A	21	1551
65.00	DCXAM.X	0.55	0	N/A	N/A	2	238
70.00	DCXAN.X	0.1	0	N/A	N/A	10	118

Figure 8.13 Daimler Chrysler AG (DCX) Jan 2007 20.0000 calls

```
<snap>
  <instrumentDomain>
    <instrumentIdentifier>
      <code scheme="www.phlx.com">
        <mdString>DCXAW.X</mdString>
      </code>
    </instrumentIdentifier>
    <exercisePrice>47.50</exercisePrice>
    <bid>
      <last>4.28</last>
    </bid>
    <ask>
      <last>24.35</last>
    </ask>
    <trade>
      <last>4.35</last>
      <change>0.25</change>
      <volume>
        <last>249</last>
        <volumeType>total</volumeType>
      </volume>
      <volume>
        <last>531</last>
        <volumeType>openInterest</volumeType>
      </volume>
    </trade>
  </instrumentDomain>
```

Figure 8.14 Equity option trading summary intraday snapshot (Continued/)

```
    <instrumentDomain>
      <instrumentIdentifier>
        <code scheme="www.phlx.com">
          <mdString>DCXAW.X</mdString>
        </code>
      </instrumentIdentifier>
      <exercisePrice>50.00</exercisePrice>
      <!-- No best bids or asks are available, therefore
        contents set to 0. -->
      <bid>
        <last>0</last>
      </bid>
      <ask>
        <last>0</last>
      </ask>
      <trade>
        <last>3.3</last>
        <change>0</change>
        <volume>
          <last>15</last>
          <volumeType>total</volumeType>
        </volume>
        <volume>
          <last>1626</last>
          <volumeType>openInterest</volumeType>
        </volume>
      </trade>
    </instrumentDomain>
  </snap>
```

Figure 8.14 (/Continued)

Exchange traded futures can also supported in MDDL, and it's possible to support the investment decision process in a similar way to options.

Taking a trading summary screen for the Dow Jones Industrial Average (see Figure 8.15), it is possible to support each contract (Cash, Dec 06...) using the MDDL instrumentDomain.

A decision needs to be made as how to represent a dash '–' in MDDL. The value of minus 1 (−1) in an MDDL element (open, high, low, settlement, or change) could be transformed into a '–' quite easily using XSLT style sheets; similarly, the MDDL date times will need to be transformed from the mdDateTime (or xsd:datetime ('YYYY-MM-DDTHH:MM') to 'DD-Mon-YYYY' and 'HH:MM'.

DJX Future	Dow Jones Industrial Average Session Date: 21-Sep-2006								Previous Day	
	Open	High	Low	Last	Time	Settlement	Change	Volume	Settlement	Open Interest
Cash	11613.12	11648.17	11586.70	11589.90	09:16	-	−3.29	0	11613.19	0
Dec 06	11715	11720	11670	11670	09:17	-	−27	4169	11697	55006

Figure 8.15 Dow Jones Industrial Average

Finally, the developer/designer will use colour to indicate the change since the start of day (the convention is green for an increase and red for a negative price change).

Figure 8.16 shows the equivalent MDDL that represents the screen shown in Figure 8.15.

```
<snap>
  <instrumentDomain>
    <instrumentIdentifier>
      <name>Cash</name>
    </instrumentIdentifier>
    <open>11613.12</open>
    <high>11648.17</high>
    <low>11586.70</low>
    <trade>
      <last>
        <mdDecimal>11589.90</mdDecimal>
      </last>
      <change>-3.29</change>
       <volume>
         <last>0</last>
         <volumeType>total</volumeType>
       </volume>
       <volume>
         <last>0</last>
         <volumeType>openInterest</volumeType>
      </volume>
      <settlement>
        <mdDecimal>-1</mdDecimal>
      </settlement>
      <settlement>
        <mdDecimal>11613.19</mdDecimal>
        <dateTime>2006-09-20</dateTime>
      </settlement>
    </trade>
  </instrumentDomain>
  <instrumentDomain>
    <instrumentIdentifier>
      <name>Dec 06</name>
    </instrumentIdentifier>
    <!-- No best bids or asks are available, therefore contents set to 0. -->
    <open>11715</open>
    <high>11720</high>
    <low>11670</low>
    <trade>
      <last>11670</last>
      <change>-27</change>
       <volume>
         <last>4169</last>
```

Figure 8.16 DJIA futures trading summary represented in MDDL (Continued/)

```
        <volumeType>total</volumeType>
      </volume>
      <volume>
        <last>55006</last>
        <volumeType>openInterest</volumeType>
      </volume>
      <settlement>
        <mdDecimal>-1</mdDecimal>
      </settlement>
      <settlement>
        <mdDecimal>11697</mdDecimal>
        <dateTime>2006-09-20</dateTime>
      </settlement>
    </trade>
  </instrumentDomain>
</snap>
```

Figure 8.16 (/Continued)

A business requirement for firms that have exposures across multiple currencies is the question of valuation of positions to meet their corporate reporting requirements. The treasury department within most organizations will need to apply a daily fix, a snapshot of the FX rates, normally at the same time of day, from the same source, (Figure 8.17) – for example, one organization I worked for always took the FX rate fix at 10 am London time.

From a securities definitions perspective, FX on the surface seems fairly simple. An FX rate comprises of a currency pairs represented by the ISO 8601 3 character code, normally separated by a forward slash (/). Given that this market is very fluid and prices change in a blink of an eye, the dateTime associated with any transaction (bid, ask, mid, or deal) is very significant. It is possible to specify a time to milliseconds, if required.

```
<foreignExchangeDomain>
  <instrumentIdentifier>
    <code scheme="http://www.mddl.org/ext/scheme/
      iso3166-alpha-3.xml">EURUSD</code>
    <name>EUR/USD</name>
  </instrumentIdentifier>
  <mid>
    <last>
      <mdDecimal>1.2791</mdDecimal>
      <dateTime>2006-09-25T10:00:00+01:00</dateTime>
    </last>
  </mid>
</foreignExchangeDomain>
```

Figure 8.17 The daily FIX represented in MDDL

```
<foreignExchangeDomain>
  <instrumentIdentifier>
    <code scheme="http://www.mddl.org/ext/scheme/
      iso3166-alpha-3.xml">GBPUSD</code>
    <name>GBP/USD</name>
  </instrumentIdentifier>
  <mid>
    <last>
      <mdDecimal>1.9003</mdDecimal>
      <dateTime>2006-09-25T10:00:00+01:00</dateTime>
    </last>
  </mid>
</foreignExchangeDomain>
```

Figure 8.17 The daily FIX represented in MDDL (Continued/)

Historical pricing

Another application where MDDL can be used is in historical pricing. Figure 8.18 shows the current FX rate alongside that of the previous day's close, the close of a week ago and of a month ago.

MDDL has a term that allows the closing prices to be associated with a particular previous date/time (Figure 8.19). A small irritation is that in the version of MDDL (2.5-beta) used to create the example, the *previousDateTime* only supports absolute and not relative dates (-P1D, -P1W, -P1M, representing minus 1 day, 1 week and 1 month respectively) as required in this real-life scenario. In such situations the user may wish

Ccy Pair	Current Rate	24 Hours Ago	1 Week Ago	1 Month Ago
USD/EUR	0.7818	0.7818	0.7913	0.7840
USD/GBP	0.5260	0.5260	0.5324	0.5297

Figure 8.18 Historical FX example

```
<foreignExchangeDomain>
  <instrumentIdentifier>
    <code
        scheme="http://www.mddl.org/ext/schem
        e/iso3166-alpha-3.xml">USDEUR</code>
    <name>USD/EUR</name>
  </instrumentIdentifier>
  <close>
    <mdDecimal>0.7818</mdDecimal>
```

Figure 8.19 Historical FX pricing sample (Continued/)

```
    </close>
    <close>
      <mdDecimal>0.7818</mdDecimal>
      <previousDateTime>-P1D</previousDateTime>
    </close>
    <close>
      <mdDecimal>0.7913</mdDecimal>
      <previousDateTime>-P1W</previousDateTime>
    </close>
    <close>
      <mdDecimal>0.7840</mdDecimal>
      <previousDateTime>-P1M</previousDateTime>
    </close>
  </foreignExchangeDomain>
          scheme="http://www.mddl.org/ext/scheme/
          iso3166-alpha-3.xml">USDGBP</code>
      <name>USD/GBP</name>
    </instrumentIdentifier>
    <close>
      <mdDecimal>0.5260</mdDecimal>
    </close>
    <close>
      <mdDecimal>0.5260</mdDecimal>
      <previousDateTime>-P1D</previousDateTime>
    </close>
    <close>
      <mdDecimal>0.5324</mdDecimal>
      <previousDateTime>-P1W</previousDateTime>
    </close>
    <close>
      <mdDecimal>0.5297 </mdDecimal>
      <previousDateTime>-P1M </previousDateTime>
    </close>
  </foreignExchangeDomain>
```

Figure 8.19 (/Continued)

to either ignore the validation or go the route of creating an abridged MDDL adherent schema, a stand-alone taxonomy to support this specific business function.

Book management

There are various levels of orders book information that can be represented in MDDL. In its simplest form known as the 'top of book', it comprises of the best prices for a stock, both the bid and ask (if available), and the volume available at these prices.

The classic view of the top of book is what's known as the 'yellow strip'. Certain LSE trading screens containing quotes from market makers are shown in two columns, one containing bid prices and the other offer prices. A yellow strip (seen in

Figure 8.20 shaded grey) runs across the screen, highlighting the best bid and offer prices. In addition, to the best price spread it contains the volume at the given price as well as the number of market makers, represented by the figures directly under the BUY and SELL column headings.

The yellow strip would normally form the basis of a screen consisting of a portfolio of instruments and in some instances this material may be supplemented with information about the participating market-maker at the given price. The MDDL bid and ask containers are used to represent the best prices and to associate each stock with its volumes and number of market-makers participating; all this information needs to be wrapped with the domain class (commonClass) container itself to distinguish the information specific to each instrument (Figure 8.21).

Further examples of top of book (level 1) and depth of market can be found in Chapter 9, as well as in the section titled 'MDDL to FIX, FIX to MDDL' in Chapter 11.

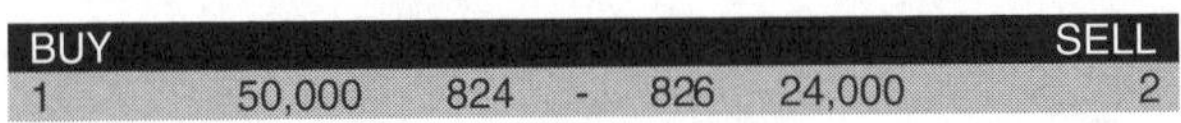

Figure 8.20 Top of book display

```
<instrumentDomain>
    <instrumentIdentifier>
      <code
          scheme="http://www.lms.eu.com/schemes/localMarke
          tIdentifers">
        <mdString>ABC</mdString>
      </code>
    </instrumentIdentifier>
    <bid>
      <last>
        <mdDecimal>824</mdDecimal>
      </last>
      <size>50000</size>
      <rank>1</rank>
      <other>
        <ext:numberOfParticipants>1</ext:numberOfParticipants>
      </other>
    </bid>
    <ask>
      <last>
        <mdDecimal>826</mdDecimal>
      </last>
      <size>24000</size>
      <rank>1</rank>
      <other>
        <ext:numberOfParticipants>1</ext:numberOfParticipants>
      </other>
    </ask>
  </instrumentDomain>
```

Figure 8.21 Top of book in MDDL (Continued/)

```
<instrumentDomain>
  <instrumentIdentifier>
    <code
       scheme="http://www.lms.eu.com/schemes/localMarke
       tIdentifers">
      <mdString>XYZ</mdString>
    </code>
  </instrumentIdentifier>
  <bid>
    <last>
      <mdDecimal>125</mdDecimal>
    </last>
    <size>50000</size>
    <rank>1</rank>
    <other>
      <ext:numberOfParticipants>4</ext:numberOfParticipants>
    </other>
  </bid>
  <ask>
    <last>
      <mdDecimal>125.50</mdDecimal>
    </last>
    <size>46000</size>
    <rank>1</rank>
    <other>
      <ext:numberOfParticipants>2</ext:numberOfParticipants>
    </other>
  </ask>
</instrumentDomain>
```

Figure 8.21 (/Continued)

Depth of market (level 2)

The yellow strip is normally not the only information to be displayed on a trader's screen; other decision-making information also appears, such as offers near the best price. These are known as market depth or level 2 information, and normally come with other useful information such as daily highs/lows, consolidated prices (VWAP), trade history and so on (Figure 8.22).

Figure 8.23 shows the equivalent in MDDL.

	ABC					Close		817.5
	High	830	Open	820				
	Low	818	VWOP	822				
	Volume	485m	VWAP	827				
	BUY							SELL
	1	50,000	824	-	826	24,000		2
823.62	128,000	78,000	823.5		825.5	21,500	45,500	825.34
823.40	188,000	60,000	823		826	50,000	95,500	835.75

Figure 8.22 Trader's screen

```
<instrumentDomain>
  <instrumentIdentifier>
    <code
      scheme="http://www.lms.eu.com/schemes/loca
      lsecurityIdentifiers">
      <mdString>ABC</mdString>
    </code>
  </instrumentIdentifier>
  <close>817.50</close>
  <trade>
    <high>830</high>
    <low>818</low>
    <volume>
      <last>485000000</last>
    </volume>
  </trade>
  <open>820</open>
  <vwop>822</vwop>
  <vwap>827</vwap>
  <orderbook>
    <bid>
      <last>
        <mdDecimal>824</mdDecimal>
      </last>
      <size>50000</size>
      <rank>1</rank>
      <other>
        <ext:numberOfParticipants>1</ext:numberOfParticip
          ants>
      </other>
    </bid>
    <ask>
      <last>
        <mdDecimal>826</mdDecimal>
      </last>
      <size>24000</size>
      <rank>1</rank>
      <other>
        <ext:numberOfParticipants>1</ext:numberOfParticip
          ants>
      </other>
    </ask>
```

Figure 8.23 Depth of market for ABC Plc in MDDL (Continued/)

```
        <bid>
          <last>
            <mdDecimal>823.50</mdDecimal>
          </last>
          <size>78000</size>
          <rank>2</rank>
          <other>
            <ext:cumulativeOrderbookPrice>823.62</ext:cumul
                ativeOrderbookPrice>
            </other>
        </bid>
        <ask>
          <last>
            <mdDecimal>826</mdDecimal>
          </last>
          <size>21500</size>
          <rank>2</rank>
          <other>
            <ext:cumulativeOrderbookPrice>825.34</ext:cumul
                ativeOrderbookPrice>
          </other>
        </ask>
        <bid>
          <last>
            <mdDecimal>823</mdDecimal>
          </last>
          <size>60000</size>
          <rank>3</rank>
          <other>
            <ext:cumulativeOrderbookPrice>823.40</ext:cumul
                ativeOrderbookPrice>
          </other>
        </bid>
        <ask>
          <last>
            <mdDecimal>826</mdDecimal>
          </last>
          <size>50000</size>
          <rank>3</rank>
          <other>
            <ext:cumulativeOrderbookPrice>826</ext:cumulativ
                eOrderbookPrice>
          </other>
        </ask>
      </orderbook>
    </instrumentDomain>
```


Figure 8.23 (/Continued)

Trade reporting

Trade reporting in the context of market data normally refers to the immediate post trade, and as such it comprises a fairly limited set of terms that includes the report date/time, ticker symbol, execution time, the price and size of the trade and the market centre identifier. Each market has its own particular requirements. For example the Nasdaq trade data supplied as part of the NASTRAQ® Nasdaq Trade and Quote Data service uses terms such as *trade modifier*, indicators to represent the trade source and UTP traded security (Figure 8.24). The *tradeModifier* (or saleConditionType, to give it a more descriptive name) and *sourceIndicator* can be supported via the creation MDDL controlled vocabulary (Figure 8.25).

```
<snap>
  <!-- Entry Date/Time -->
   <dateTime>2006-09-29T14:37:00+05:00</dateTime>
  <instrumentDomain>
      <instrumentIdentifier>
        <name>USA Truck, Inc.</name>
        <code scheme="http://quotes.nasdaq.com">
          <mdString>USAK</mdString>
        </code>
      </instrumentIdentifier>
      <trade>
        <marketIdentifier>
            <marketCenter>
              <code
                  scheme="http://www.mddl.org/ext/scheme/iso10383.x
                  ml">XPAR</code>
            </marketCenter>
          </marketIdentifier>
          <last>
            <mdDecimal>19.05</mdDecimal>
            <dateTime>2006-09-29T14:36:48+05:00</dateTime>
          </last>
          <size>10000</size>
          <other>
            <!-- trade modifier -->
            <ext:saleConditionType>nextDaySettlement</ext:saleConditionType>
            <!-- source indicator: SOES trade or SelectNet trade -->
            ext:systemSource>SOES</ext:systemSource>
            <!-- UTP traded security (true or false) -->
            <ext:utpTraded>true</ext:utpTraded>
          </other>
        </trade>
    </instrumentDomain>
  </snap>
```

Figure 8.24 NASTRAQ® Nasdaq trade file layout equivalent in MDDL

```
<mddlScheme>
  <head>
    <dateTime>2006-09-16T181000Z</dateTime>
    <title>NASTRAQ(r) Nasdaq Trade and Quote Data
        service - trade modifier</title>
    <element>tradeModifierType</element>
    <definition>Qualifies the trade report</definition>
  </head>
  <value>
    <short>acquisition</short>
    <full>ACQ = acquisition</full>
  </value>
  <value>
    <short>bunched</short>
    <full>B = bunched</full>
  </value>
  <value>
    <short>cashSale</short>
    <full>C= cash sale</full>
  </value>
  <value>
    <short>rule155Trade</short>
    <full>K = Rule 155 trade</full>
  </value>
  ...........
  <value>
    <short>nextDaySettlement</short>
    <full> ND = next day delivery</full>
  </value>
</mddlScheme>
```

Figure 8.25 A snippet of the saleConditionType control vocabulary

Similarly, other historical trade reporting and quotation services, such as the NYSE's TAQ Web or the London Stock Exchange's LMIL Market Data feed, can easily be represented too using the same MDDL containers. Further information regarding reporting has been provided in Chapter 9, under the heading 'Regulatory reporting'.

Time and sales

Exchanges and Multilateral Trading Facilities, that have consolidated to obtain a greater market presence in the new global market may find it useful, if not imperative, to disseminate the time and sales to its various market centres. This can be achieved as a variant on the trade report. The *timeseries* construct should be considered for the purpose, with the *snapType* element set to eodHistory (Figure 8.26).

```
<timeseries>
  <timeseriesType>eodHistory</timeseriesType>
  <event>
    <dateTime>1698-01-01</dateTime>
    <snap>
      ....
```

Figure 8.26 End-of-day time and sales

Reconciliation

The normal business-to-business reconciliation takes the form of three distinct phases. The first is a three-way transaction-by-transaction (or trade-by-trade) reconciliation between the fund manager, the investment bank and the custodian. The next is the flow or asset servicing events (cash flows and instrument deliveries, as part of complying with the contractual obligation of the trade, normally associated with OTC deals), and the final is by netted position.

Let's examine one of these scenarios, the matching of the daily net positions and the associated cash flow between a fund manager (or requesting entity) and the matching entity (a counterparty). These entities could be business entities or system applications, which by their nature may be internal IT systems.

The example MDDL document used to explain the scenario is based on the exchange of 50 000 ordinary shares in IBM with a settlement (value) date of today's date +1 business day (or T + 1).

The flow of information between the two actors is based on just a single instrument.

In step 1, the requesting entity populates what it believes to be the net total of the transactions in IBM for T + 1 (Figure 8.27). The fund manager expects to receive 50 000 shares in exchange for the compensation of $3,788,000 USD. If the fund manager were selling the shares rather than purchasing them, the <volume> would be negative and the compensation (*turnover*) would be positive. The requesting entity will also populate all the other fields in the record apart from the *matchID* and the *returnStatus*, which are specifically populated by the matching entity.

In step 2, the matching firm receives the MDDL record and attempts to match it with its records. If there is 100% agreement by both firms, then the *returnStatus* is set to matched accordingly.

If there is any piece of information in dispute, then the disputed value or values will be overwritten by the matching firm with what it has on its records and the *returnStatus* set to mismatched (Figure 8.28 overleaf). If the matching firm believes it's found the match, then it will populate the *matchId with its reference*. The matching entity found a couple of discrepancies; the settlementType it believes is T + 2 and not T + 1, and the turnover is (3 789 005) and not (3 788 000).

```
<?xml version="1.0" ?>
- <mddl xmlns="http://www.mddl.org/mddl/3.0-beta"
  xmlns:ext="http://www.yourCompany .com/mddl/extensions"
  xmlns:mdref="http://www.mddl.org/mddl/3.0-beta/ref"
  xmlns:xlink="http://www.w3.org/1999/xlink"
  xmlns:xsi="http://www.w3.org/2001/XMLSchema-instance"
  xsi:schemaLocation="http://www.mddl.org/mddl/3.0-beta ../../schemas/3.0-
  beta/mddl-3.0-beta-full.xsd http://www.yourCompany.com/mddl/extensions
  ../../extensions/3.0-beta/8-29ext-mddl.xsd">
  <header>
    <dateTime>2006-04-01</dateTime>
    <source>London Market Systems</source>
  </header>
  <snap>
    <instrumentDomain>
      <trade>
        <currency>USD</currency>
            <!-- 50,000 shares purchased by the Requesting Firm for
            compensation of $3,788,000 USD to the Matching Firm -->
        <settlement>
          <mdDecimal>74.75</mdDecimal>
          <settlementType>t1</settlementType>
        </settlement>
        <volume>
          <volumeType>total</volumeType>
          <last>50000</last>
        </volume>
        <turnover>-3788000</turnover>
        <other>
          <ext:reconcile>
            <ext:requestorsId>123456</ext:requestorsId>
          </ext:reconcile>
        </other>
      </trade>
    </instrumentDomain>
  </snap>
</mddl>
```


Figure 8.27 Requestor's reconciliation message


```
<?xml version="1.0" encoding="UTF-8" ?>
<mddl xmlns:xsi="http://www.w3.org/2001/XMLSchema-instance"
    xmlns:xlink="http://www.w3.org/1999/xlink"
    xmlns:mdref="http://www.mddl.org/mddl/3.0-beta/ref"
    xmlns="http://www.mddl.org/mddl/3.0-beta"
    xmlns:ext="http://www.londonmarketsystems.com/mddl/extensio
    ns" xmlns:xsd="http://www.w3.org/2001/XMLSchema"
    xmlns:mddl="http://www.mddl.org/mddl/3.0-beta"
    xsi:schemaLocation="http://www.mddl.org/mddl/3.0-beta
    D:\mddl\3.0-beta\mddl-3.0-beta.xsd
    http://www.londonmarketsystems.com/mddl/extensions
    D:\mddl\3.0-beta\extMddl.xsd">
```


Figure 8.28 Reconciliation response (mismatched)

```
  <header>
    <dateTime>2006-04-01</dateTime>
    <source>London Market Systems</source>
 </header>
 <snap>
  <equityDomain>
   <commonClass>
    <instrumentIdentifier>
      <name>International Business Machines</name>
      <code
          scheme="http://www.mddl.org/ext/scheme/iso6166.xml
          ">US4592001014</code>
    </instrumentIdentifier>
   </commonClass>
   <trade>
    <currency>USD</currency>
    <!--
    50,000 shares purchased by the Requesting Firm for
      compensation of $3,788,000 USD  to the Matching Firm, else
      the matching Firm believes the figure to be  $3,789,005 USD,
      also the settlement is T+2 and not T+1.
    -->
    <settlement>
      <mdDecimal>74.75</mdDecimal>
      <settlementType>t2</settlementType>
    </settlement>
    <volume>
      <volumeType>total</volumeType>
      <last>50000</last>
    </volume>
    <turnover>-3789005</turnover>
    <other>
      <ext:reconcile>
      <ext:requestorsId>123456</ext:requestorsId>
      <ext:matchId>10001</ext:matchId>
      <ext:resultStatus
          scheme="www.londonmarketsysytems.com/scheme/re
          conciliationStatusType">mismatched</ext:resultStatus>
      </ext:reconcile>
    </other>
   </trade>
  </equityDomain>
 </snap>
</mddl>
```

Figure 8.28 (Continued/)

Alternatively, if the matching firm cannot identify the transaction at all, then it will set the *returnStatus* to unmatched.

In step 3, the requesting firm receives back the MDDL document from the matching firm. If there is a 100% match within the record or the requesting firm accepts the changes, then the reconciliation process is complete. Alternatively, by mutual agreement both parties may correct the figures and then the document is resubmitted for matching – and thus the process is repeated from step 1.

In the sample MDDL documents, there are three definitions which are not part of standard MDDL: requestorsId, matchId and the resultStatus. These are defined within an extension (schema) to MDDL, and the resultStatus is expected to contain one of the values defined within the coding list reconciliationStatType, which is based on the FpML reconciliation *returnStatus* scheme (Figure 8.29) the contents of the scheme is specified in Table 8.1.

This example could easily be extended to include FpML definitions within the MDDL *other* container, or any other XML, if the user so wishes.

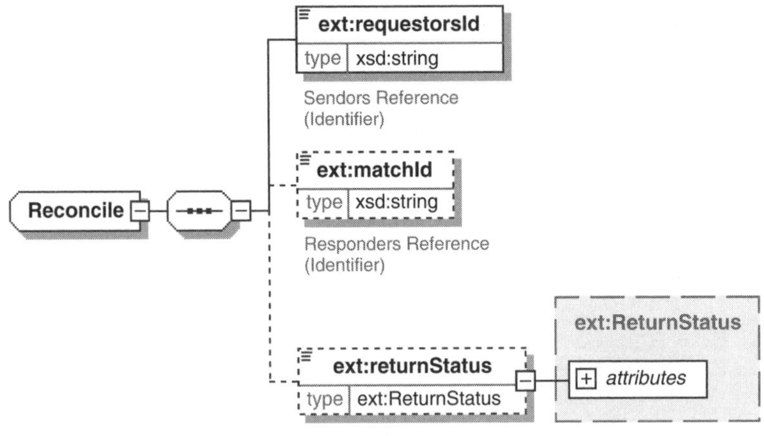

Figure 8.29 The MDDL extension schema (visual representation)

Table 8.1 The reconciliation StatType code list

	Code	Full
1	alleged	Populated by the requesting firm. Matching firm expected to validate record against its position. The document will be populated by the matching firm and the reconciliationStatus is populated with (matched, mismatched, unmatched).
2	matched	Both sides have the same information, positions match. matchID is populated by the matching firm.
3	mismatched	A near match position; for example, there is a mismatch in turnover. The definition in error is supplied placed in the mismatchedProperty element.
4	unmatched	Mismatch, where two or more definitions do not match.

Portfolio valuation

The container to support portfolios was added in version 2.5 with the inclusion of the *portfolioDomain*. Such a business context requires the ability to support multiple currencies of each security, any cash positions, as well as the base currency of the overall portfolio. There is a requirement to support the cash component totals as well as the account identification itself (Figure 8.30).

The FX rate(s) are supported by the foreignExchangeDomain, and the cash component via the use of the cashDomain. The final bit of the equation is to link the terms within the portfolio. The information associated with each stock is contained in the underlying container; there is one for each instrument (Figure 8.31). An extension schema will be required to support the positionValuation and profitAndLoss containers.

Account: JDoh		Number: 12345			1:26:48 PM Sep 27			USDGBP 1.89	
Security Name	Symbol .Market	Qty.	Local Mkt. Price	Security CCY	Book Cost	Market Value	P&L (Security CCY)	P&L (GBP)	Market Value (GBP)
ITV Plc.	ITV.LSE	15,000	98.50	GBP	14,881.90	14,775.00	−106.90	−106.90	14,775.00
Ford Motor Co.	F.NYSE	10,000	8.31	USD	82,100.00	83,100.00	1000.00	524.10	43,968.26
Securities Total								417.20	58,743.26
Cash									23,000.00
Total Value									81,743.26

Figure 8.30 Portfolio screen

```
<header>
  <dateTime>2006-09-27T09:36:48+05:00</dateTime>
  <other>
    <ext:account>
      <code scheme="http://www.lms.eu.com/schemes">
        <mdString>12345</mdString>
      </code>
      <name>Jon Doh</name>
    </ext:account>
  </other>
```

Figure 8.31 Portfolio information represented in MDDL (Continued/)

```
    </header>
    <snap>
      <dateTime>2006-09-27T09:36:48+05:00</dateTime>
      <foreignExchangeDomain>
        <instrumentIdentifier>
          <code scheme="http://www.mddl.org/ext/scheme/iso3166-
              alpha-3.xml">
            <mdString>USDEUR</mdString>
          </code>
          <name>USD/GBP</name>
        </instrumentIdentifier>
        <last>
          <mdDecimal>1.89</mdDecimal>
        </last>
      </foreignExchangeDomain>
      <portfolioDomain>
        <currency>GBP</currency>
        <underlyingCount>2</underlyingCount>
        <underlying>
          <instrumentIdentifier>
            <code scheme="www.lms.eu/schemes">
              <mdString>ITV.LSE</mdString>
            </code>
              <name>ITV Plc.</name>
          </instrumentIdentifier>
          <other>
            <ext:performance>
        <size>15000</size>
        <last>
          <mdDecimal>98.50</mdDecimal>
          <currency>GBX</currency>
        </last>
        <ext:positionValuation>
          <mdDecimal>14881.90</mdDecimal>
          <currency>GBP</currency>
          <sequence>1</sequence>
        </ext:positionValuation>
        <ext:positionValuation>
          <mdDecimal>14775.00</mdDecimal>
          <currency>GBP</currency>
          <dateTime>2006-09-
              27T09:36:48+05:00</dateTime>
          <sequence>2</sequence>
        </ext:positionValuation>
        <ext:positionValuation>
          <mdDecimal>14775.00</mdDecimal>
          <currency>GBP</currency>
          <dateTime>2006-09-
              27T09:36:48+05:00</dateTime>
          <sequence>3</sequence>
        </ext:positionValuation>
```

Figure 8.31 (/Continued)

```
          <ext:positionValuation>
            <mdDecimal>82100.00</mdDecimal>
            <currency>USD</currency>
            <sequence>1</sequence>
          </ext:positionValuation>
          <ext:positionValuation>
            <mdDecimal>83100.00</mdDecimal>
            <currency>USD</currency>
            <dateTime>2006-09-
                27T09:36:48+05:00</dateTime>
            <sequence>2</sequence>
          </ext:positionValuation>
          <ext:positionValuation>
            <mdDecimal>43968.26</mdDecimal>
            <currency>GBP</currency>
            <dateTime>2006-09-
                27T09:36:48+05:00</dateTime>
            <sequence>3</sequence>
          </ext:positionValuation>
          <ext:profitAndLoss>
            <mdDecimal>-106.90</mdDecimal>
            <currency>GBP</currency>
            <dateTime>2006-09-
                27T09:36:48+05:00</dateTime>
            <sequence>1</sequence>
          </ext:profitAndLoss>
          <ext:profitAndLoss>
            <mdDecimal>-106.90</mdDecimal>
            <currency>GBP</currency>
            <dateTime>2006-09-
                27T09:36:48+05:00</dateTime>
            <sequence>2</sequence>
          </ext:profitAndLoss>
          <ext:profitAndLoss>
            <mdDecimal>1000</mdDecimal>
            <currency>USD</currency>
            <dateTime>2006-09-
                27T09:36:48+05:00</dateTime>
            <sequence>1</sequence>
          </ext:profitAndLoss>
          <ext:profitAndLoss>
            <mdDecimal>524.10</mdDecimal>
            <currency>GBP</currency>
            <dateTime>2006-09-
                27T09:36:48+05:00</dateTime>
            <sequence>2</sequence>
          </ext:profitAndLoss>
        </ext:performance>
      </other>
    </underlying>
```


Figure 8.31 (/Continued)

```
<underlying>
  <instrumentIdentifier>
    <code scheme="www.lms.eu/schemes">
      <mdString>F.NYSE</mdString>
    </code>
      <name>Ford Motor Co.</name>
  </instrumentIdentifier>
  <other>
    <ext:performance>
      <size>10000</size>
      <last>
        <mdDecimal>8.31</mdDecimal>
        <currency>USD</currency>
      </last>
      <ext:positionValuation>
        <mdDecimal>14881.90</mdDecimal>
        <currency>GBP</currency>
        <sequence>1</sequence>
      </ext:positionValuation>
      <ext:positionValuation>
        <mdDecimal>14775.00</mdDecimal>
        <currency>GBP</currency>
        <dateTime>2006-09-
            27T09:36:48+05:00</dateTime>
        <sequence>2</sequence>
      </ext:positionValuation>
      <ext:positionValuation>
        <mdDecimal>14775.00</mdDecimal>
        <currency>GBP</currency>
        <dateTime>2006-09-
            27T09:36:48+05:00</dateTime>
        <sequence>3</sequence>
      </ext:positionValuation>
      <ext:positionValuation>
        <mdDecimal>82100.00</mdDecimal>
        <currency>USD</currency>
        <sequence>1</sequence>
      </ext:positionValuation>
      <ext:positionValuation>
        <mdDecimal>83100.00</mdDecimal>
        <currency>USD</currency>
        <dateTime>2006-09-
            27T09:36:48+05:00</dateTime>
        <sequence>2</sequence>
      </ext:positionValuation>
      <ext:positionValuation>
        <mdDecimal>43968.26</mdDecimal>
        <currency>GBP</currency>
        <dateTime>2006-09-
            27T09:36:48+05:00</dateTime>
        <sequence>3</sequence>
      </ext:positionValuation>
```


Figure 8.31 (/Continued)

```
            <ext:profitAndLoss>
              <mdDecimal>-106.90</mdDecimal>
              <currency>GBP</currency>
              <dateTime>2006-09-
                  27T09:36:48+05:00</dateTime>
              <sequence>1</sequence>
            </ext:profitAndLoss>
            <ext:profitAndLoss>
              <mdDecimal>-106.90</mdDecimal>
              <currency>GBP</currency>
              <dateTime>2006-09-
                  27T09:36:48+05:00</dateTime>
              <sequence>2</sequence>
            </ext:profitAndLoss>
            <ext:profitAndLoss>
              <mdDecimal>1000</mdDecimal>
              <currency>USD</currency>
              <dateTime>2006-09-
                  27T09:36:48+05:00</dateTime>
              <sequence>1</sequence>
            </ext:profitAndLoss>
            <ext:profitAndLoss>
              <mdDecimal>524.10</mdDecimal>
              <currency>GBP</currency>
              <dateTime>2006-09-
                  27T09:36:48+05:00</dateTime>
              <sequence>2</sequence>
            </ext:profitAndLoss>
          </ext:performance>
        </other>
      </underlying>
    </portfolioDomain>
    <cashDomain>
      <other>
        <currency>GBP</currency>
        <ext:amount>23000.00</ext:amount>
      </other>
    </cashDomain>
  </snap>
```


Figure 8.31 (/Continued)

Chapter 9

Regulatory adherence

Two major pieces of legislation are having a real impact on firms providing financial services. In the United States there is the 'Regulation Nation Market System' (or REG NMS), formulated by the Securities and Exchange Commission, and in Europe there is the European Commission's Markets in Financial Instruments Directive (MiFID). There is a great deal of overlap between the two, and they compel organizations to re-examine their corporate governance and business practices. They will provide firms with proactive forward-thinking leadership, the opportunity to implement new innovative business models.

In addition to regulated (exchanges), unregulated (MTFs) and sell-side organizations, buy-side firms also fall into the net of the initiatives as they too have a responsibility to their investors.

Reference data terms

Realistically, the only way to ensure that both pieces of legislation have been adhered to is by the use of industry standards – how is it possible to be sure that like is being compared with like, without using industry standards? It is apparent that the use of existing industry standards and market conventions is a key to the success of the regulations.

This was the primary driver behind the creation of the MiFID Reference Data Subject Group, which was founded in June 2005 by four of the major 'global' industry associations – FIX Protocol Ltd, ISITC, the Reference Data User Group (RDUG) and SIIA/FISD. The Reference Data Subject Group identified the need to examine the reference data implications of the directive. Work immediately started on writing a discussion paper that examined the processes within the trade lifecycle, and an evaluation of how instruments and parties are identified. It provided recommendations regarding the terms needed to support the directive's requirements. The paper seeks to address the issues of identification of financial instruments, investment firms and trading venues. The publication is broken down into two discrete sections, 'Unique (Unambiguous) Instrument Identification' and 'Business Entity Identification'. It also includes an annex that explores the industry messages standards and the terms coverage supported by each. Even though the paper is European-centric, the subject matter discussed relates to all markets and the recommendations are also relevant to REG NMS.

To identify an instrument unambiguously, the group recommends the adoption of the ISO 10383 MIC (Market Identification Code) to identify the Place of Listing (POL), Place of Trade (POT) and Place of Quote (POQ) for both instrument and trading venue. When these codings are combined with the local market identifier or ISIN, it is possible to uniquely to identify an instrument throughout the life of a trade.

MDDL's instrument identification (instrumentIdentifier) container was, from the start designed to be flexible; there is no hardwiring of enumerated source identifiers within the schema itself, which is prevalent in other industry standards. Therefore there is no restriction to using one of the top ten codings – CUSIP, SEDOL, ISIN, Bloomberg, RIC, QUIK, Valoren, IBES, ThomsonPermId or CommonCode. In fact, as most standards are based on bilateral communication, the instrument codings for each transaction are normally limited to two – the ISIN plus another previously agreed by both parties.

Unlike other message standards, MDDL can support multiple instrument identifiers. Figure 9.1 provides an example of how to construct a message to support a CUSIP, ISIN, SEDOL and the local (Nasdaq) market identifier. Also shown is the use of the controlled vocabulary term, scopeType, which is used to identify the scope of the identifier. An ISIN is the international identifier, CUSIP is the country-level identifier, whilst the local market identifier is specific to the Nasdaq.

```
<instrumentIdentifier>
  <name>REUTERS GROUP</name>
  <scopeType>country</scopeType>
  <code scheme="http://www.mddl.org/ext/scheme/symbol?SRC=CUSIP">
        <mdString>G7540P109</mdString>
  </code>

  <scopeType>International</scopeType>
  <code scheme="http://www.mddl.org/ext/scheme/iso6166.xml">
        <mdString>GB0002369139</mdString>
  </code>

  <scopeType>listing</scopeType>
  <code
scheme="http://www.mddl.org/ext/scheme/symbol?SRC=SEDOL">
        <mdString>0065805</mdString>
  </code>

  <scopeType>market</scopeType>
  <code scheme="http://quotes.nasdaq.com">
        <mdString>RTRSY</mdString>
  </code>
</instrumentIdentifier>

<issueData>
  <!-- Country of Register -->
  <location>
    <country>GB</country>
    <locationType>register</locationType>
  </location>
  <!-- OPOL based on Market Identifier Code (MIC) -->
  <placeOfListing>
     <code scheme=
"http://www.mddl.org/ext/scheme/iso10383.xml">XNAS</code>
  </placeOfListing>
  <!-- Place of trade based on Market Identifier Code (MIC) -->
  <placeOfTrade>
     <code scheme=
"http://www.mddl.org/ext/scheme/iso10383.xml">XNAS</code>
  </placeOfTrade>
</issueData>
```

Figure 9.1 Unique (unambiguous) instrument identification

In addition to instrument identifiers, MDDL can also support the requirement to identify the Official Place of Listing (OPOL) as well as the Place of Trade (POT), both of which use the ISO MIC coding. These elements of reference data are published at time of issue.

The paper's recommendation is 'to press ahead with the development and subsequent adoption of the ISO 16372 IBEI standard, including (if necessary) an interim BEI solution.' It is believed that the use of the existing ISO standard, 9362: Bank Identifier Codes (BIC), is not a workable solution, as there is not always a one-to-one relationship between entities and BICs; some firms use one BIC to cover multiple entities, and others assign more than one BIC to the same entity. It is also worth differentiating the purpose of BICs: they are used to route transactions between financial organizations and are NOT identifiers of business entities. It would be inappropriate for BICs to be used to identify the complex hierarchies of legal/business entities and ownership structures. Figure 9.2 shows the proposed ISO 16372 IBEI format.

Country of Registration	IBEI Core	Check Digit
2a	7c[1]	1n[2]

[1]Alphanumeric excluding vowels
[2]Mod 10

Figure 9.2 Proposed ISO 16372 IBEI

MDDL can be used to disseminate information relating to an organization. The entity domain was enhanced in version 2.5 to support business entities as well as trading counterparties. Prior to this release, the entity domain was designed to support the issuance process only. Figures 9.3, 9.4 and 9.5 show how MDDL can be used to represent an issuer, a business entity and a transaction routing code (Figure 9.5 shows an illustration based on a BIC).

The need to agree on a mechanism to identify unregulated markets and systematic internalizers (algorithmic trading facilities/internal orderbooks) was identified. To support this requirement, the use of an 'extended' MIC and the business entity identifier has been debated. Both are viable solutions; however, the requirement to identify both the systematic internalizer (SI) and the market will result in the creation

```
<entityDomain>
      <issuerClass>
         <name>UBS AG, Jersey Branch</name>
         <location>
            <address>PO Box 35024, Union Street, St. Helier</address>
            <country>JERSEY</country>
            <postalCode scheme="http://www.royalmail.co.uk">
               JE4 8UT</postalCode>
         </location>
      </issuerClass>
      <industryIdentifier>
         <name>Long-Short SUPER Notes Series No. 6</name>
      </industryIdentifier>
</entityDomain>
```

Figure 9.3 An issuer

```
<entityDomain>
    <businessClass>
        <name>UBS AG, Jersey Branch</name>
        <location>
            <address>PO Box 35024, Union Street, St. Helier</address>
            <country>JERSEY</country>
            <postalCode scheme="http://www.royalmail.co.uk">JE4
                8UT</postalCode>
        </location>
        <comment>ISO 16372: (Dummy) International
            Business Entity Identifier </comment>
        <code scheme="
            http://www.mddl.org/ext/scheme/iso106372.xml">JEUBSNIBH9
            </code>
    </businessClass>
</entityDomain>
```

Figure 9.4 A business entity

```
<entityDomain>
        <counterpartyClass>
            <name>UBS AG Global Asset Management</name>
            <location>
                <address>Bahnhofstrasse 45, CH-8098 Zurich</address>
                <country>SWITZERLAND</country>
                <postalCode
                    scheme="http://www.swisspost.ch">8098</postalCode>
            </location>
            <comment>ISO 9362: Bank identifier example</comment>
            <code scheme="http://www.iso.org">UBSACHZZ</code>
        </counterpartyClass>
</entityDomain>
```

Figure 9.5 A counterparty, an example of a BIC

of hundreds (if not thousands) of new codes. Figure 9.6 (overleaf) is an illustration of how an SI could be represented as a business entity as well as a market centre within a trade report.

The publication also encourages the use of ISO 10962 CFI (Classification of Financial Instrument) codes for the classification of instruments where there is uncertainty regarding the unique identification of an instrument. The CFI can be used to eliminate this ambiguity by defining the properties of the instrument.

The ISO 10962 standard defines the properties of a financial product, and therefore it can be used to assist in unambiguously identifying an instrument – for example, the distribution policy attribute can be used to distinguish an investment fund (profits

```
<trade>
  <marketIdentifier>
    <marketCenter>
    <code scheme=
"http://www.mddl.org/ext/scheme/iso10383.xml">NYSE</code>
    </marketCenter>
 </marketIdentifier>
  <last>
   <mdDecimal>13.35</mdDecimal>
     <!-- Systematic Internaliser -->
     <source>
     <mdString>Lehman Brothers London - SI</mdString>
     <code scheme="
http://www.mddl.org/ext/scheme/iso106372.xml">LEBOSI001</code>
     </source>
   </last>
</trade>
```

Figure 9.6 Systematic internalizer and market centre identified within a transaction

```
<snap>
 <instrumentDomain>
      <instrumentIdentifier>
           <name>International Business Machines</name>
           <code scheme=
"http://www.mddl.org/ext/scheme/iso6166.xml">US4592001014</code>
           <code scheme=
"http://www.mddl.org/ext/scheme/iso10962.xml">ESVUFR</code>
      </instrumentIdentifier>
  </instrumentDomain>
</snap>
```

Figure 9.7 MDDL supports ISO 10962

reinvested into the fund) from an income fund (with profits being distributed to its bearer). Under certain circumstances, both may share the same International Securities Identification Numbering system (ISIN) number. The Classification of Financial Instruments (CFI) – ISO 10962 – can be represented in MDDL as shown in Figure 9.7.

For a fuller explanation of CFI, please refer to the section entitled 'Describing the attributes of a Financial Instrument' in Chapter 7.

Finally, many organizations may wish to examine the use of reference data terms by industry message standards. Some may feel it is impractical to use industry message standards as they stand, as there is always a risk in aligning to a standard over which the organization has no direct control of (in terms of scope and roll-out schedule). Therefore, some may consider that using the terms and relationship of terms defined by an industry standard is a viable alternative. Table 9.1 shows the key reference terms identified as being important to REG NMS and MiFID. In addition to MDDL, other standards have been included within the table as a point of reference. However, ISO 19312 is a securities data model and is not a message standard, and the other standards are for bilateral communications.

Table 9.1 Reference data terms supported by industry standards

Identifier	Term	MDDL	FIX	ISO 19312	ISO 15022 & ISO 20022
Instrument	ISIN (ISO 6166)	Yes	Yes	Yes	Yes
	Local market identifier	Multiple	Yes	Multiple	Yes
	CFI (ISO 10962)	Yes	Yes	Yes	Yes
	Official place of listing	Yes	Yes	Yes	Yes
	Place of quote	No	Change required for MiFID	No	No
	Place of trade	Yes	Yes	Yes	Yes
	Place of settlement	Change required for MiFID	Yes	Not within scope	Yes
Business Entity	IBEI or BEI	Yes	Change required for MiFID	Not within scope	Yes
	BIC (ISO 9362)	Yes	Yes	Not within scope	Yes

Without the use of industry standards, it's difficult to see how the REG NMS and MiFID best execution requirements can be adhered to. This is a real opportunity for the financial sector to appreciate the importance of industry standards, and in particular how MDDL can be appropriately used to meet the challenge.

Best execution

To effectively adhere to the REG NMS trade-through rule, firms must be able to show that they have achieved the 'best price' for the investor. The example given examines the trade-through rule from a European exchange context to provide a near-to-life case study that could be applied to any regulatory environment. The German market centres (XETRA, Stuttgart, Munich, Berlin-Bremen, Frankfurt), in this scenario, could be substituted with the US equivalent.

A chain of responsibility exists between the investor, the trader and the market. The trader has to ensure that he achieves best execution for the client, and, similarly, under the trade-through rule the market (exchange or multilateral trading facility) will need to prove it has achieved the best price for the trader, and thus the investor. The trade-through rule provides the industry with the motivation to develop a best execution engine (Figure 9.8).

REG NMS states that an exchange cannot execute an order at a price that is inferior to one listed on another, even if it results in the fulfilment of an order at multiple centres. Many online brokers have implemented 'smart order routing' technology which scans the markets and finds the best place to execute a customer's order, based on price and liquidity. Extending the regulation means that this innovation will most likely be negated with much of the work being undertaken by exchanges and MTFs to meet their regulatory requirements.

Examining the key functions of the best execution engine, as outlined within the use case diagram (Figure 9.8), it is possible to show how market data would be used to support such a system. Using an example based on an actual instrument traded on multiple German exchanges, it is possible to develop a scenario that shows how the trade-through rule would work. The US stock, 'Duke Energy Corporation', whose local market identifier is DUK (across all exchanges), this has been used to illustrate this walkthrough.

An investor places an order to purchase 35 000 shares in DUK through his broker. Working on the assumption that the broker is only authorized to trade on the Berlin–Bremen bourse, the order is placed on that market. To achieve the 'best price' for the investor, it is NOT appropriate for the order to be fully filled by the Berlin–Bremen bourse. For the purpose of this example, it is assumed that all exchanges are automated.

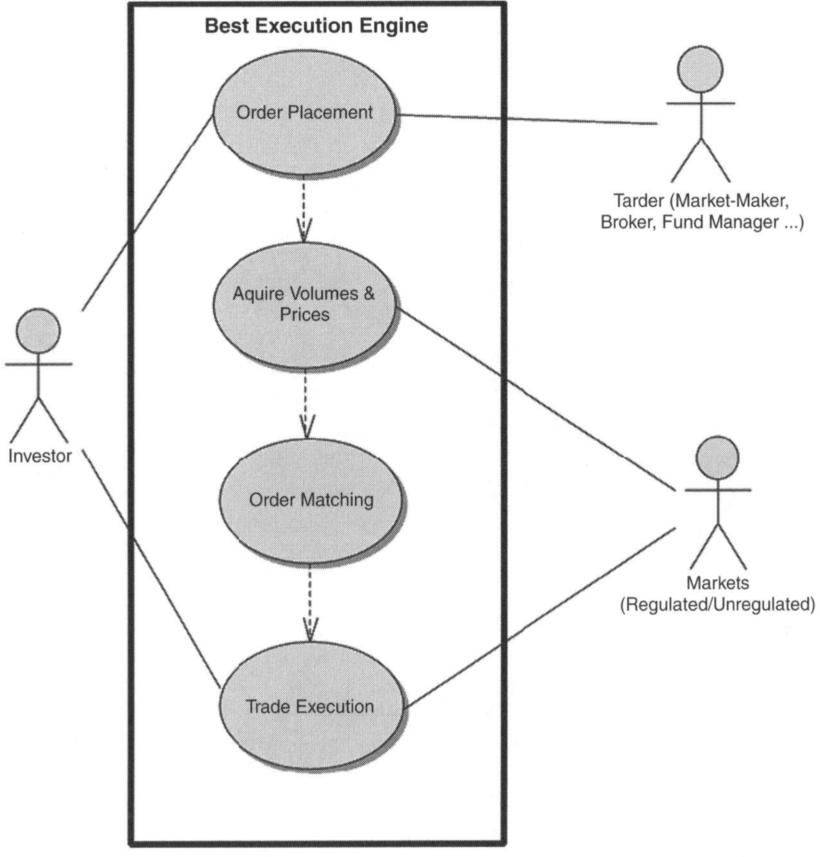

Figure 9.8 Best execution engine use case diagram

Order

The order is captured and disseminated to interested parties using MDDL; the purchase of 35 000 DUK shares at 24.50 would be represented as shown in Figure 9.9 (overleaf).

Consolidated orderbook

The exchange, upon receipt of the order, is responsible for ensuring that the best price is achieved; therefore all other exchanges trading the same instrument must be

```
<instrumentDomain>
        <industryIdentifier>
          <name>Duke Energy Corporation</name>
           <code
             scheme="http://www.mddl.org/ext/scheme/sym
             bol?SRC=WKN">
            <mdString>9858649</mdString>
          </code>
           <scopeType>Market</scopeType>
           <code scheme="http://deutsche-boerse.com">
             <mdString>DUK</mdString>
          </code>
        </industryIdentifier>
          <bid>
          <last>
             <mdDecimal>24.50</mdDecimal>
          </last>
          <size>35000</size>
        </bid>
</instrumentDomain>
```

Figure 9.9 Buy order

examined to assess the volumes and prices of sellers of the instrument. The volumes and prices on the sell-side across all exchanges are as follows:

Exchange	Price	Size
XETRA	23.46	9 000.00
Stuttgart	23.86	5 000.00
Munich	24.05	8 000.00
Berlin–Bremen	24.06	35 000.00
Frankfurt	24.42	10 000.00

From this information a consolidated orderbook can be constructed by the 'acquire prices and volumes' process within the best execution engine, and the 'order matching' can then take place. To adhere to MiFID and the concentration rules, under which some member states require investment firms to route all transactions through central stock exchanges, the same mechanism and method of representing data can be used by data vendors, to aggregate data from multiple sources in a single stock. This consolidated 'sell-side' orderbook can be represented as in Figure 9.10.

```
<orderbook>
  <ask>
  <!-- XETRA -->
  <marketIdentifier>
     <marketCenter>
     <code scheme= "http://www.mddl.org/ext/scheme/iso10383.xml ">XETR</code>
     </marketCenter>
 </marketIdentifier>
     <last>23.46</last>
     <size>9000</size>
   </ask>
   <ask>
   <!-- Stuttgart -->
  <marketIdentifier>
     <marketCenter>
     <code scheme= "http://www.mddl.org/ext/scheme/iso10383.xml ">XSTU</code>
     </marketCenter>
 </marketIdentifier>
       <last>23.86</last>
       <size>5000</size>
   </ask>
    <ask>
    <!-- Munich -->
  <marketIdentifier>
     <marketCenter>
     <code scheme= "http://www.mddl.org/ext/scheme/iso10383.xml">XMUN</code>
     </marketCenter>
 </marketIdentifier>
        <last>24.05</last>
        <size>8000</size>
  </ask>
   <ask>
   <!-- Berlin-Bremen -->
     <marketIdentifier>
       <code scheme=
"http://www.mddl.org/ext/scheme/iso10383.xml ">XBER</code>
     </marketIdentifier>
     <last>24.06</last>
     <size>35000</size>
  </ask>
  <ask>
  <!-- Frankfurt -->
  <marketIdentifier>
     <marketCenter>
     <code scheme= "http://www.mddl.org/ext/scheme/iso10383.xml"> XBER</code>
     </marketCenter>
 </marketIdentifier>
     <last>24.42</last>
     <size>10000</size>
  </ask>
</orderbook>
```

Figure 9.10 Consolidated order book

Trade executions

Though the order was sent to the Berlin–Bremen market centre, the best offer ('ask') price and volume is on the XETRA exchange, where it is partially fulfilled. It is then sent on to the other exchanges (Stuttgart and Munich) in best price order. In total, there are three transactions executed before the original exchange that received the order satisfies the final partial fulfilment of the order – that being the remaining 13 000 shares.

The trade execution process would result in the following transactions:

- buy 9 000 shares from XETRA
- buy 5 000 shares from Stuttgart
- buy 8 000 shares from Munich
- buy 13 000 shares from Berlin-Bremen

This would be represented in MDDL as shown in Figure 9.11.

The best execution engine has now successfully filled the order at the best possible price for the investor. However, given the increased complexity of processing and increased transactional throughput required to meet the new regulations, it can be seen that the investor is likely to be paying for this service in the form of increased commission fees!

Regulatory reporting

MiFID will result in some European member states removing the contraction rules that force investment firms to report all trades through a central stock exchange. This will expose regulated markets to competition from unregulated trading platforms, such as MTFs and systematic internalizers (SIs). Financial institutions may wish to report transactions direct to a competent authority in any one of the member states; this does not need to be the state in which the transaction took place.

In late 2005 I provided a report to the MiFID JWG – Standard Protocols Subject Group that listed the proposed set of terms (see Appendix B) required to meet the transaction reporting requirements for MiFID. In February 2006 the report, entitled *MiFID Gap Analysis – MDDL*, was published. Within this report James Hartley, the author, identified the MDDL terms needed to support this process. Table 9.2 (see page 120) is based on this analysis and can be used to construct the appropriate MDDL transaction/trade report. This set of terms will also support the interchange of data between competent authorities.

```
<trade>
  <!-- XETRA -->
  <marketIdentifier>
    <marketCenter>
    <code scheme= "http://www.mddl.org/ext/scheme/iso10383.xml">XETR</code>
    </marketCenter>
  </marketIdentifier>
  <last>23.46</last>
    <volume><last>9000</last></volume>
</trade>
<trade>
  <!-- Stuttgart -->
  <marketIdentifier>
    <marketCenter>
    <code scheme= "http://www.mddl.org/ext/scheme/iso10383.xml">XSTU</code>
    </marketCenter>
  </marketIdentifier>
  <last>23.86</last>
    <volume><last>5000</last></volume>
</trade>
<trade>
  <!-- Munich -->
  <marketIdentifier>
    <marketCenter>
    <code scheme= "http://www.mddl.org/ext/scheme/iso10383.xml">XMUN</code>
    </marketCenter>
  </marketIdentifier>
  <last>24.05</last>
    <volume><last>8000</last></volume>
</trade>
<trade>
  <!-- Berlin-Bremen -->
  <marketIdentifier>
    <marketCenter>
    <code scheme= "http://www.mddl.org/ext/scheme/iso10383.xml">XBER</code>
    </marketCenter>
  </marketIdentifier>
  <last>24.06</last>
    <volume><last>13000</last></volume>
</trade>
```

Figure 9.11 Trade execution transactions

Data vendors and end of concentration rules

MiFID lays down the gauntlet to data vendors, who will be required to aggregate data from multiple sources for a single stock. This is as a direct result of the end of concentration rules, under which some member states require investment firms to route all transactions through central stock exchanges. Organizations will be able to choose where reports are published. Data vendors will need to aggregate data from multiple sources for a single stock at the time of pre-trade and immediate post-trade.

Table 9.2 MDDL terms needed to meet the transaction reporting requirements for MiFID

Term	MDDL equivalent
Buy/sell indicator	*<buyer>/<seller>* is expected to be used
Cancellation flag	*IndicatorsType* is used, with the value of cancelled; the default code list is located at: http://www.mddl.org/mddl/scheme/IndicatorsType.xml
CFI instrument type	ISO 10962, Classification of Financial Instruments (CFI) to fill the role of <InstrumentType>; the revised version 10962:2006 for planned release early 2007 will provide better coverage than the current version: <instrumentData> <instrumentType scheme="http://www.mddl.org/ext/scheme/iso10962.xml"> ESVUFR </instrumentType> </instrumentData>.
Counterparty name and code	*<buyer>* and *<seller>* elements allow the counterparty to be identified in the appropriate location
Customer/client identification	*<buyer>/<seller>* is expected to be used
Derivative type	The default scheme for *<instrumentType>* does not define the instruments to the granularity expected, therefore it is appropriate to use an alternative code list
Instrument identification	*<instrumentIdentifier>* can be used to supply the ISIN, Local market identifier (exchange code) as well as the market identifier, as: <instrumentIdentifier> <code scheme="http://www.mddl.org/ext/scheme/iso6166.xml"> <mdString>GB00B16GWD56</mdString>

Table 9.2

Term	MDDL equivalent
	< /code> <code scheme=“http://www.mddl.org/ext/scheme/ symbol? SRC=SEDOL”> <mdString>B16GWD5</mdString> </code> <code scheme=“http://www.mddl.org/ext/scheme/symbol? SRC=RIC”> VOD < /code> <name>Vodaphone Grp. ORD USD0.11 3/7</name> < /instrumentIdentifier>
Instrument type	<instrumentType> can be used to support this term; the default scheme is: http://www.mddl.org/mddl/scheme/ instrumentType.xml. If CESR or the Regulatory Authority requires a different list, the scheme can be specified as an attribute of *instrumentType* <instrumentData> <instrumentType>equityCommon</instrumentType> < /instrumentData>
Maturity date	Supported by *<maturityDate>*, schema modified so that it can be used within a transaction report rather than as purely issuance information
Price	Price can be defined within *<last>*, *<currency>* may also need to be supplied; this is possible as a property of *<last>* too
Price multiplier	Normally used for derivative products; support by contractValueMultiplier
Price notation	<valuationType> can be used to support this requirement; if the default code list (http://www.mddl.org/mddl/ scheme/valuationType.xml) does not meet the directive's requirements, a different scheme can always be specified

(Continued/)

Table 9.2 *(/Continued)*

Term	MDDL equivalent
Put/call	Flags added to MDDL version 2.5 onwards
Quantity	<size> within <trade>
Quantity notation	<quantityType> can be used, with the appropriate schema to support the codes identified
Reporting party name and identification Strike price	Covered in the <source> element within the mddl <header>; the ability to specify a code is required <exercisePrice>
Time identifier	DateTime can be specified within the< trade>
Trading capacity	A new term to support the requirement – own account, customer/client account etc.
Trading day	DateTime can be specified within the< trade>
Trading time	DateTime can be specified within the< trade>
Trading venue	<marketIdentifier> can be used. "BIC"= ISO 9362 - SWIFT/Bank Identifier code (BIC) 'BEI' = ISO XXXX - Business Entity Identifier <marketIdentifier> <marketCenter> <code scheme="http://www.mddl.org/ext/scheme/iso10383.xml"> XLON</code> < /marketCenter> </marketIdentifier>
Transaction reference number	New term identified as being required, <referenceIdentifier>
Underlying instrument identification	<underlying>
Authority key	New terms required; country code + sequence number

Chapter 10

Reference data management

More and more organizations are re-examining their securities definitions systems and reference data management process. The timely and accurate delivery of this data is key to the success of any financial firm. It plays an important role throughout the organization, from investment decision-making for market-makers, brokers and fund managers through to valuations on the general ledger.

This chapter concentrates on the business entity security definitions management, including non-tradable information that takes the form of indices, indicators and rates, as well as corporate actions affecting the aforementioned.

A comprehensive selection of examples has been supplied to show how terms can be represented and, given the development of structured products, these will hopefully allow the reader to construct new and interesting products from them.

MDDL version 2 onwards has been specifically designed to support the reference data terms needs of financial institutions. This is broken down into number of broad categories to cover business entities, indicators, corporate action events and financial instruments. In MDDL, these are represented by the use of discrete domains (entityDomain, indicatorDomain and caeDomain domains).

Business entities

Business entities are supported by the entityDomain, which is broken down into the key categories (or classes in MDDL-speak) to meet the requirements of the industry (see Figure 10.1). These include issuer, counterparty and business entity (a general container used for venue and client identification).

To help the reader understand how each of these can be represented in MDDL, a number of entity samples have been supplied in Chapter 9, in the section entitled 'Reference data terms'. The main categories (or classes) within the *entityDomain* these are the *issuerClass, counterpartyClass* and the *businessClass.*

The issuerClass contains information about the issuer of a financial instrument, this includes contact details, its market capitalization and status, among others.

The counterpartyClass class is used to identify a parties which are taking part of a transaction. This would normally include routing information, such as the party's BIC (the ISO 9632 Bank Identification Code.)

The businessClass is a category used for information that does not fit under the categories of either an issuer or a counterparty, this includes trading venue and

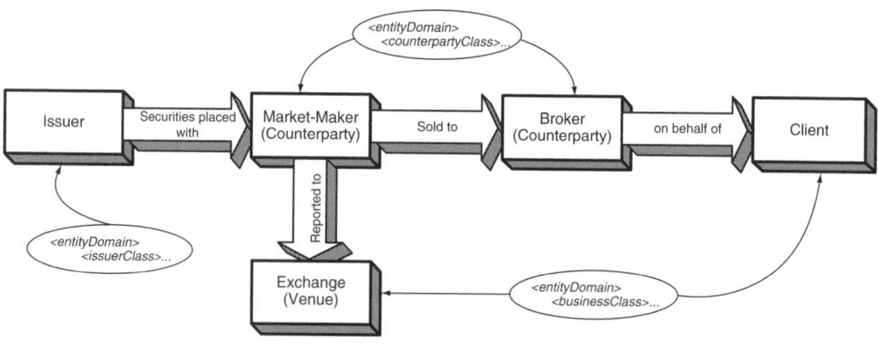

Figure 10.1 Business entities within the trade lifecycle

client identification. An indentification scheme that would be appropriate under this heading would be ISO 16372, the International Business Entity Indentification (IBEI) standard. The MiFID Reference Data Subject Group has however proposed extending BIC to include venue and client indentification to meet the requirement of MiFID. If the BIC is adopted for this use, it is imperative that it is used in conjunction a mechanism to indicate its activity, otherwise there is a risk that processes and IT systems will have difficulty in identifiying the correct BIC in a given activity and thus the organization may fall foul of its regulatory obligations. In addition to the broad entity classifications (issuerClass, counterpartyClass and businessClass) it may be appropriate to extend them to include a term to support the role.

Indices, rates and indicators

These are items of data that are not tradable instruments in their own rights; however, they are used to calculate the value of specific instruments, positions and/or exposures. Instruments are effectively linked to an underlying index or an interbank rate in the case of floating rate instruments.

US Treasury Inflation Protected Securities (TIPS) are linked for example, to the Consumer Price Index (CPI) (see Figure 10.2); similarly in the United Kingdom the UK Government Debt Management Office (DMO) issues bonds linked to the UK equivalent inflation index, the Retail Price Index (RPI).

```
<snap>
  <indicatorDomain>
    <interestRateClass>
      <description>U.S. Department of Labor
          Consumer Price Indexes (CPI)
          program. July 06 All Items Un-
          adjusted 12 months
          ended</description>
      <code
          scheme="http://www.bls.gov/cpi/">
        <mdString>July 06 - All
            Items</mdString>
      </code>
      <rate>4.1</rate>
      <dateTime>2006-08-16</dateTime>
    </interestRateClass>
  </indicatorDomain>
</snap>
```

Figure 10.2 July 2006 Consumer Price Index represented in MDDL

Another example of an indicator is an interbank rate. Floating Rate Notes (FRNs) are variable coupon bonds whose income is typically based on a margin over an interbank rate (also known as reference rate). These interbank rates (the rates fixes) can be disseminated via MDDL using the indicatorsDomain. Each interbank rate is split into three types:

1. IBID (Interbank BID), the rate at which banks offer to take deposits
2. IBOR, the rate at which banks offer (ask) to make deposits – therefore this is higher than the BID
3. IMEAN, the average of IBID and IBOR.

The above abreviations are normally prefixed with up to a two-alpha code that denotes the city – NY for New York, L for London, F for Frankfurt, and so on.

```
<snap>
  <indicatorDomain>
    <dateTime>2006-08-19</dateTime>
    <interestRateClass>
      <description>London InterBank Offer Rate 1
      month</description>
      <code scheme="http://www.bls.gov/cpi/">
        <mdString>1 month LIBOR</mdString>
      </code>
      <rate>5.33</rate>
    </interestRateClass>
    <interestRateClass>
      <description>London InterBank Offer Rate 3
months</description>
      <code scheme="http://www.bls.gov/cpi/">
        <mdString>3 month LIBOR</mdString>
      </code>
      <rate>5.40</rate>
    </interestRateClass>
    <interestRateClass>
      <description>London InterBank Offer Rate 6
months</description>
      <code scheme="http://www.bls.gov/cpi/">
        <mdString>6 month LIBOR</mdString>
      </code>
      <rate>5.45</rate>
    </interestRateClass>
  </indicatorDomain>
</snap>
```

Figure 10.3 July 2006 LIBOR Rates (1,3 and 6 months) represented in MDDL

Corporate action events

The domain of Corporate Action Events (CAEs) is extremely complex; a single corporate announcement may result in multiple event transactions affecting the issuer and/or the issue. In the SEDOL (Stock Exchange Daily Official List, i.e. security identification numbers issued by the London Stock Exchange) Masterfile™ Technical Specifications Version 5.7 dated 21 December 2005, there are 14 corporate action events identified that have an impact on SEDOLs; similarly, there are 73 corporate action events (corporate action event indicator (:22F:) within the MT564 message) in the ISO 15022 MT564 (non XML) message.

MDDL uses the corporate action event domain, *caeDomain*, to support the myriad event messages. As with the SEDOL Masterfile project, the majority of the corporate action terms are supported via an extension schema.

There are two categories of corporate action events supported within this MDDL domain; the *corporateEventsClass* is used for announcements and events related to the issue, whilst the *corporateActionsClass* is for events relating to the instrument. It's worth appreciating that corporate announcements that are verbose and textual (such as press releases) fall within the remit of XBRL.

These two classes are further broken down into distinct groupings (or subclasses).

The corporateEventsClass, which concentrates on the organizational aspects, breaks down the attributes further into the following subclasses:

Subclass	**Description of contents**
corporateSubclass	Relating to an issuer or other organization affected
meetingSubclass	Used to contain information relating to meetings, Annual General, extraordinary, special or board meetings

The *corporateActionsClass*, which relates to instrument related material, similarly has a number of *subclasses*:

Subclass	**Description of contents**
corporateChangeSubclass	Change as a result of an acquisition/merger, de-merger, spin-off or takeover.
dataChangeSubclass	Change in the underlying data, change in name or other information that does not directly affect the value of an issue.
distributionSubclass	Distribution of a benefit to the holder, including dividends and other bonuses.

issuanceSubclass	New, tap and other issuance related material.
holderActionSubclass	Contains information where an action is expected to be undertaken by the holder (exercise rights to purchase additional shares).
paymentActionSubclass	Non-dividend payments, such as coupons, excludes redemptions (see *redemptionSubclass*).
redemptionSubclass	A container for the redemption of a debt by either issuer or holder. Calls and puts are a form of redemption, however a repurchase due to change in corporate strategy is considered as a Restructure (see *restructureSubclass*).
restructureSubclass	Restructure subclass – Corporate Actions class – CAE domain. Restructure type corporate action. A restructuring of the capital and/or debt structure as a result of change in corporate strategy.
statusChangeSubclass	A change that directly affects the value or capital of the issue. A change in market capitalization resulting from a tap issue is an example of this.

An announcement will, in the majority of cases, result in multiple distinct events that, on the whole, are not necessarily sent consecutively.

Corporate Action Event (CAE) – special dividend

To help crystallize how to use the caeDomain, let's examine a special dividend, which is used to return value to the shareholders. The assumption is made that the Extraordinary General Meeting has taken place and that the resolution has been approved by the shareholders. This means that the announcement of the meeting, the request for approval and the approval notification messages have already been disseminated.

The next message in the sequence is the special dividend notification message itself. The example message in Figure 10.4 is based on the London Stock Exchange listed stock 'Cable & Wireless Ordinary 25p share' special dividend declared in November 2001. The information represented within the message includes the dividend of 11.50p, to be paid on 3 September 2001 to registered shareholders on 20 July 2001. The shares will go ex-dividend on 18 July 2001.

Some readers who may be used to seeing corporate actions in the form of ISO 15022 MT 564 messages will see that the sample has be annotated with the ISO 15022 syntax. However, to retain the appropriate context, the MDDL elements do not necessarily match the field order in the ISO 15022 message. Similarly, the use

```
<header>
  <dateTime>20070911</dateTime>
  <! ISO15022=":20C::SEME//" Senders Reference >
  <sequence>2007189012</sequence>
</header>
<snap>
  <! ISO15022 = ":23G:NEWM" New Message >
  <snapType>new</snapType>
  <caeDomain>
    <corporateActionsClass>
      <! ISO15022=":22F::CAEV//">DVSE" >
      <caeType>specialDividend</caeType>
      <instrumentIdentifier>
        <name>CABLE AND WIRELESS ORD 25P</name>
        <! ISO 15022=":16R:USECU :35B:ISIN" Underlying Security >
        <code scheme="http://www.mddl.org/ext/scheme/iso6166">
          <mdString>GB0001625572</mdString>
        </code>
        <marketIdentifier>
          <marketCenter>
            <! ISO 15022=":94B::PLIS//EXCH/XLON" >
            <code
              scheme="http://www.mddl.org/ext/scheme/iso10383.xml">XLON</code>
          </marketCenter>
        </marketIdentifier>
      </instrumentIdentifier>
      <distributionSubclass>
        <! ISO15022=":20C::CORP//" Corporate Action Reference >
        <caeIdentifier>SDIVCW001</caeIdentifier>
        <! ISO15022=":98A::XDTE//" >
        <entitlementDate>20020130</entitlementDate>
        <recordDate>20020130</recordDate>
        <deadlineDate>20020123</deadlineDate>
        <other>
          <ext:corporateActionOptions>
            <! ISO15022=":16R::CAOPTN" 2 options are available to the holder. Cash
              Dividend (the defauilt) and the reinvestment option is the second. >
            <ext:corporateActionOption>
              <! ISO15022=":13A::CAON//001" CA Option 1 >
              <sequence>001</sequence>
              <! ISO15022=":17B::DFLT//Y" This is the default >
              <ext:defaultOption>true</ext:defaultOption>
              <! ISO15022=":22F::CAOP//CASH" Cash Option >
              <ext:corporateActionOptionType>CASH</ext:corporateActionOptionType>
              <ext:mandatoryVoluntaryType>CHOS</ext:mandatoryVoluntaryType>
              <! ISO15022=":98A::PAYD//" >
              <paymentDate>20020301</paymentDate>
              <! Gross dividend payable per share,
                ISO15022=":92F::GRSS//GBP0,3300" >
              <dividend>
                <mdDecimal>0.33</mdDecimal>
                <currency>GBP</currency>
              </dividend>
```


Figure 10.4 An entitlement message (special one-time dividend) (Continued/)

```
            <! ISO15022=":16S::CAOPTN" >
          </ext:corporateActionOption>
          <ext:corporateActionOption>
            <! ISO15022=":13A::CAON//002"  CA Option 2 >
            <sequence>002</sequence>
            <! ISO15022=":17B::DFLT//N" >
            <ext:defaultOption>false</ext:defaultOption>
            <! ISO15022=":22F::CAOP//DRIP" Reinvestment Option >
            <ext:corporateActionOptionType>DRIP</ext:corporateActionOptionType>
            <! ISO15022=":22F::CAMV//"  Mandatory instructions with owners
              choice. >
            <ext:mandatoryVoluntaryType>CHOS</ext:mandatoryVoluntaryType>
            <! ISO15022=":98A::PAYD//" >
            <paymentDate>20020308</paymentDate>
          </ext:corporateActionOption>
        </ext:corporateActionOptions>
      </other>
    </distributionSubclass>
  </corporateActionsClass>
 </caeDomain>
</snap>
```

Figure 10.4 (/Continued)

of start/end fields (in the 15022 message) are replaced in MDDL by the container start/end tags. For example, ':16R::CAOPTN' becomes *<corporateActionOption>*, and ':16S::CAOPTN' becomes *</corporateActionOption>*.

Table 10.1 will assist the reader in understanding the transformation between MT564 notification and the MDDL equivalent.

Table 10.1 The transformation between MT564 notification and the MDDL equivalent

MT564 fields	MDDL element (N/A – Not Applicable)	MDDL (MT564, if different) value	Description of contents
:16R:GENL	N/A	N/A	Start of common data block
:20C::SEME//	<header> <sequence>	2007189-012	Sender's reference
:20C::CORP//	<snap> <caeDomain> <corporateActionsClass> <other> <sequence>	SDIVCW001	Corporate action reference

Table 10.1

MT564 fields	**MDDL element (N/A – Not Applicable)**	**MDDL (MT564, if different) value**	**Description of contents**
:23G:NEWM	<snapType>	New (NEWM)	New message
:22F::CAEV//	<caeType> Also 'dividends' denotes the use of <distributionSubclass> within <caeDomain> <corporateActionsClass>	specialDivident (DVSE)	Corporate action event type
:22F::CAMV//	<ext:mandatoryVoluntaryType>	CHOS	Choice indicator
:25D::PROC// COMP	N/A	(COMP)	Details are complete
:16S:GENL	N/A		End of common data block
:16R:USECU	<instrumentIdentifier>		Start of underlying security block
:35B:ISIN	<code scheme='http://www.mddl.org/ext/scheme/iso6166'>	GB0001625572	ISIN
/PLIS/	<marketIdentifier> <marketCenter> <code scheme="http://www.mddl.org/ext/scheme/iso10383.xml">	XLON	Market identifier code (MIC)
[name]	<name>	CABLE AND WIRELESS ORD 25P	Security name
:16S:USECU	</instrumentIdentifier>		Start of underlying security block

(Continued/)

Table 10.1 *(/Continued)*

MT564 fields	MDDL element (N/A – Not Applicable)	MDDL (MT564, if different) value	Description of contents
:16R:CADETL	<ext:corporateAction Details>		start of corporate action details block
:98A::XDTE//	<ext:ex-divDate>	2002-01-30 (20020130)	Ex-div date
:98A::RDTE//	<ext:recordDate>	2002-02-01 (20020201)	Record date
:98A::MKDT//	<ext:marketDate>	2002-01-23 (20020123)	Market date
:22F::DIVI//	<ext:dividendType>	SPEC	Dividend type (special one-time)
:16S:CADETL	</ext:corporateAction Details>		End of corporate action details block
:13A::CAON//	<corporateAction> <sequence>	001	CA option number
:22F::CAOP//	N/A	CASH	Cash option
:17B::DFLT//	<ext:corporateAction Default>	true/false (Y/N)	Default corporate action indicator if more than one option available
:98A::PAYD//	<ext:paymentDate>	2002-03-01 (20020301)	Payment date
:92F::GRSS//	<currency>c</currency> <dividend>d</dividend>	c=GBP, d=0.33 (GBP0, 33000)	Gross per share in pence

Security definitions

Instruments are usually defined once, at the time of their inception (or set-up), and thereafter rarely change. Certain pieces of information may change over time – for example agency ratings, amount in issue or income may change where the product is linked to economic indicators and the amount of debt outstanding.

The examples that follow cover a comprehensive set of instruments, and from these it should be possible to construct other products.

INSTRUMENT CODE LIST

One of the key considerations when disseminating a financial instrument definition is the need to understand how to represent industry standard codes, propriety symbologies and ratings. Throughout this book the sample XML documents have shown how to represent codes like ISINs and BICs using the scheme attribute within the code element. Understanding this concept for disseminating security dissemination is essential. Table 10.2 lists all the key schemes that the reader

Table 10.2 Key schemes for instrument codes

Code	Scheme
AP – Associated Press	http://www.mddl.org/ext/scheme/symbol?SRC=AP
APID – Associated Press Identification Code	http://www.mddl.org/ext/scheme/symbol?SRC=APID
BBC Bloomberg Code	http://www.mddl.org/ext/scheme/symbol?SRC=BBC
CINS	http://www.mddl.org/ext/scheme/symbol?SRC=CINS
Classification of Instrument (CFI – ISO 10962)	http://www.mddl.org/ext/scheme/iso10962.xml (used as an attribute to instrumentType RE: <instrument Type scheme=...>)
COMSTOCK	http://www.mddl.org/ext/scheme/symbol?SRC= COMSTOCK
CUSIP	http://www.mddl.org/ext/scheme/symbol?SRC=CUSIP

(Continued/)

Table 10.2 (*/Continued*)

Code	Scheme
CUSIP – Committee on Uniform Securities Identification Procedures	http://www.mddl.org/ext/scheme/symbol?SRC=CUSIP
DTCC	http://www.mddl.org/ext/scheme/symbol?SRC=DTCC
ECCC – Euroclear/ Clearstream Common Code	http://www.mddl.org/ext/scheme/symbol?SRC=ECCC
FITCH – Fitch's Rating	http://www.mddl.org/ext/scheme/symbol?SRC=FITCH
FNMA – Fannie Mae Federal National Mortgage Association	http://www.mddl.org/ext/scheme/symbol?SRC=FNMA
Freddie Mac Federal Home Loan Mortgage Corporation	http://www.mddl.org/ext/scheme/symbol?SRC= FHLMC
FTID – FT Interactive Data	http://www.mddl.org/ext/scheme/symbol?SRC=FTID
GICS – Global Industry Classification System (aka Standard and Poors/Morgan Stanley)	http://www.mddl.org/ext/scheme/symbol?SRC=GICS
GNMA – Ginnie Mae Government National Mortgage Association	http://www.mddl.org/ext/scheme/symbol?SRC= GNMA

Table 10.2

Code	Scheme
ISIN (ISO 6166)	http://www.mddl.org/ext/scheme/iso6166.xml
MIC (ISO 10383)	http://www.mddl.org/ext/scheme/iso10383.xml
MOODYS – Moody's Rating	http://www.mddl.org/ext/scheme/symbol?SRC=MOODYS
NAICS – National American Industry Classification System(ala US Census Bureau)	http://www.mddl.org/ext/scheme/symbol?SRC=NAICS
QUIK	http://www.mddl.org/ext/scheme/symbol?SRC=QUIK
RIC – Reuters Identification Code	http://www.mddl.org/ext/scheme/symbol?SRC=RIC
SANDP – Standard & Poor's Rating	http://www.mddl.org/ext/scheme/symbol?SRC=SANDP
SBA – Small Business Association	http://www.mddl.org/ext/scheme/symbol?SRC=SBA
SEDOL – Stock Exchange Daily Official List	http://www.mddl.org/ext/scheme/symbol?SRC=SEDOL
SIC – Standard Industrial Classification System	http://www.mddl.org/ext/scheme/symbol?SRC=SIC
SICOVAM	http://www.mddl.org/ext/scheme/symbol?SRC=SICOVAM
SVM	http://www.mddl.org/ext/scheme/symbol?SRC=SVM
VALOREN	http://www.mddl.org/ext/scheme/symbol?SRC=VALOREN
WKN –WertpapierKen Nummer	http://www.mddl.org/ext/scheme/symbol?SRC=WKN

should require, with a brief description of content. A list of third-party codings can be found at http://www.mddl.org/ext/scheme/thirdparty.xml. Use of these third party coding is on the hole use the SRC parameter in conjunction with the scheme http://www.mddl.org/ext/scheme/symbol (Figure 10.5).

```
<code
scheme="http://www.mddl.org/ext/scheme/SYMBOL?SRC=
CUSIP">
            <mdString>912795XW6</mdString>
</code>
```

Figure 10.5 Instrument identification (CUSIP)

Security details

What follows is a selection of financial instruments represented in MDDL; on the whole this information is defined at the time of issuance. The exceptions to this include data that relates to the grey market or to auction/tender processes, when certain information is of a temporary nature or refers to a specific event but not to the instrument itself. For example, government bonds may be issued with temporary instrument identification codes; similarly, the dates, such as auction and announcement dates, relate to a release.

Cash equity

Common stock or ordinary shares (in the UK) are the backbone of the world's financial markets. From the perspective of market data, these are normally instruments that are exchange-traded and the holders share ownership of an enterprise, providing them with the right to participate in dividends and voting rights on key issues. Throughout the lifecycle of such instruments identifiers are allocated by various organizations that participate in the trade lifecycle (from trade inception through to completion), as well as by IT applications themselves with the aim of ensuring the unique identification of an instrument – hence the importance of the instrumentIdentifier container (Figure 10.6). The use of the *code* element in conjunction with the scheme *attribute* to provide meaning to the identifier supplied.

```
<snap>
  <instrumentDomain>
    <!-- The data has been taken from the Marvin Newsletter 24,
      Dated 05 September 2001 -->
    <instrumentIdentifier>
      <instrumentData>
      <instrumentType scheme="../../../schemes/instrumentType.xml">
        equityCommonStock</instrumentType>
      <!-- CFI Code for RTR -->
      <instrumentType scheme="http://www.mddl.org/ext/scheme/
       iso10962.xml">ESVUFR</instrumentType>
      </instrumentData>
      <name>REUTERS GROUP PLC</name>
      <scopeType>country</scopeType>
      <code
          scheme="http://www.mddl.org/ext/scheme/symbol?SRC=
          CUSIP">
        <mdString>G7540P109</mdString>
      </code>
      <scopeType>International</scopeType>
      <code
          scheme="http://www.mddl.org/ext/scheme/iso6166.xml"
          >
        <mdString>GB0002369139</mdString>
      </code>
      <code
          scheme="http://www.mddl.org/ext/scheme/symbol?SRC=
          RIC">
        <mdString>RTR.L</mdString>
      </code>
      <scopeType>listing</scopeType>
      <code
          scheme="http://www.mddl.org/ext/scheme/symbol?SRC=
          SEDOL">
        <mdString>0065805</mdString>
      </code>
      <scopeType>market</scopeType>
      <code
          scheme="http://www.mddl.org/ext/scheme/symbol?SRC=
          TIDM">
        <mdString>RTR</mdString>
      </code>
      <scopeType>country</scopeType>
      <code
          scheme="http://www.mddl.org/ext/scheme/symbol?SRC=
          VALOREN">
        <mdString>832614</mdString>
      </code>
      <scopeType>country</scopeType>
```

Figure 10.6 Common stock instrument identification (Continued/)

```
      <code
        scheme="http://www.mddl.org/ext/scheme/symbol?SRC=
        WKN">
       <mdString>911958</mdString>
      </code>
    </instrumentIdentifier>
    <issueData>
      <!-- Country of Register -->
      <location>
        <country>GB</country>
        <locationType>register</locationType>
      </location>
      <!-- OPOL based on Market Identifier Code (MIC) -->
      <placeOfListing>
        <code
          scheme="http://www.mddl.org/ext/scheme/iso10383.x
          ml">
         <mdString>XLON</mdString>
        </code>
      </placeOfListing>
      <placeOfTrade>
        <code
          scheme="http://www.mddl.org/ext/scheme/iso10383.x
          ml">
         <mdString>XLON</mdString>
        </code>
      </placeOfTrade>
    </issueData>
  </instrumentDomain>
</snap>
```

Figure 10.6 (/Continued)

Covered warrant

Covered warrants are growing in popularity, especially in Europe. A covered warrant differs from a traditional warrant in that it is issued by a third party (a market-maker) and not by the business owner. Covered warrants are more akin to equity options; however, they are *bona fide* instruments that go through clearing as a common stock equity would. Although similar to equity options, there is no physical delivery of the underlying instrument and there is a limited selection of strike prices on which to exercise. Some, like the example shown in Figure 10.7, provide the investor with the opportunity to spread risk across a number of underlying instruments.

```
<snap>
 <instrumentDomain>
  <instrumentData>
  <instrumentType scheme="../../../schemes/instrumentType.xml">
  <mdString>coveredWarrant</mdString>
  </instrumentType>
  </instrumentData>
    <!-- Currency of the Instrument -->
    <currency>GBP</currency>
    <instrumentIdentifier>
      <name>Football 2006 Warrant</name>
      <code
          scheme="http://www.mddl.org/ext/scheme/i
          so6166">
        <mdString>ANN812692146</mdString>
      </code>
      <code
          scheme="http://www.mddl.org/ext/scheme/s
          ymbol?SRC=SEDOL">
        <mdString>B0XM035</mdString>
      </code>
    <!-- LSE's Local Market Code -->
    <code
       scheme="http://www.mddl.org/ext/scheme/s
       ymbol? SRC=TIDM"">
     <mdString>SGWC</mdString>
    </code>
  </instrumentIdentifier>
  <instrumentData>
    <instrumentType>Securitised
       Derivative</instrumentType>
  </instrumentData>
  <issueData>
    <announcementDate>2006-01-
       23</announcementDate>
    <issueDate>2006-02-02</issueDate>
    <settlementDate>2006-09-09</settlementDate>
    <issuePrice>
      <mdDecimal>1020</mdDecimal>
    </issuePrice>
    <issueAmount>5000</issueAmount>
    </partiesInvolved>
      <agent>
        <name>Computershare</name>
        <agentType>paying</agentType>
      </agent>
```

Figure 10.7 Covered warrant based on a Societé Generale terms sheet (http://uk.warrants.com/) (Continued/)

```
      <agent>
        <name>SG</name>
        <agentType>calculation</agentType>
      </agent>
    </partiesInvolved>
      <clearingSettlement>
        <clearingHouse>CREST</clearingHouse>
      </clearingSettlement>
      <governingLaw>UK</governingLaw>
    <placeOfListing>
      <code
         scheme="http://www.mddl.org/ext/scheme
         /iso10383.xml">XLON</code>
      <name>London Stock Exchange</name>
    </placeOfListing>
    <issuerRef>http://uk.warrants.com/</issuerRef>
  </issueData>
  <underlying>
    <instrumentIdentifier>
      <name>Accor</name>
      <code scheme="http://uk.warrants.com/">
        <mdString>ACCP.PA</mdString>
      </code>
    </instrumentIdentifier>
    <instrumentIdentifier>
      <name>Continental</name>
      <code scheme="http://uk.warrants.com/">
        <mdString>CONG.DE</mdString>
      </code>
    </instrumentIdentifier>
    <!-- Currency of the uderlyings in EUR, apart from
      Nestle which is CHF -->
    <instrumentIdentifier>
      <name>Nestle</name>
      <code scheme="http://uk.warrants.com/">
        <mdString>NESN.VX</mdString>
      </code>
    </instrumentIdentifier>
    <instrumentIdentifier>
      <name>Adidas-Salomon</name>
      <code scheme="http://uk.warrants.com/">
        <mdString>ADSG.DE</mdString>
      </code>
    </instrumentIdentifier>
    <instrumentIdentifier>
      <name>Danone</name>
      <code scheme="http://uk.warrants.com/">
        <mdString>DANO.PA</mdString>
      </code>
    </instrumentIdentifier>
```

Figure 10.7 (/Continued)

```
    <instrumentIdentifier>
      <name>Beiersdorf</name>
      <code scheme="http://uk.warrants.com/">
        <mdString>BEIG.DE</mdString>
      </code>
    </instrumentIdentifier>
    <instrumentIdentifier>
      <name>Heineken</name>
      <code scheme="http://uk.warrants.com/">
        <mdString>HEIN.AS</mdString>
      </code>
    </instrumentIdentifier>
    <instrumentIdentifier>
      <name>PPR</name>
      <code scheme="http://uk.warrants.com/">
        <mdString>PRTP.PA</mdString>
      </code>
    </instrumentIdentifier>
    <instrumentIdentifier>
      <name>Puma</name>
      <code scheme="http://uk.warrants.com/">
        <mdString>PUMG.DE</mdString>
      </code>
    </instrumentIdentifier>
  </underlying>
 /instrumentDomain>
</snap>
```


Figure 10.7 (/Continued)

Debt (bond) instruments

Earlier in this book the issuance process was examined by showing a fixed-rate instrument. To complete the set of debt instruments, examples of a floating rate note, an index-linked and a discounted (zero) coupon interest bonds have been provided.

IT systems that undertake any form of analytics will need to know the accrual basis used for a given debt instrument to be able to calculate the interest accrued and the instrument's current valuation (dirty price), taking into consideration the accumulation of interest within the price over time. The accrual container with *debtIssueData* is used to define the accrual basis that applies. In Figure 10.8, the fixed-interest bond pays an annual yield of 6.5% as defined by the *rate* property.

Index-linked bond

To define the income associated with an index-linked instrument, the *linked* property should be used within the *interestRate* container, within *debtIssueData*. The rate

```
<snap>
  <instrumentDomain>
   <instrumentData>
   <instrumentType scheme="../../../schemes/instrumentType.xml">
   <mdString>fixedInterestBond</mdString>
   </instrumentType>
   </instrumentData>
   <debtIssueData>
     <interestRate>
       <rate>6.5</rate>
       <accrual>
         <period>
           <dayRuleType>actual</dayRuleType>
           <duration>semi-annual</duration>
         </period>
         <accrualBasis>

           <accrualBasisType>actual/365</accrualBasisType>
         </accrualBasis>
       </accrual>
     </interestRate>
   </debtIssueData>
  </instrumentDomain>
</snap>
```

Figure 10.8 Fixed-rate income accrual basis definition

property is then used to indicate the offset from the index itself. For example, to represent a return of 2.5% above the United Kingdom General Index of Retail Prices (RPI+2.5%) in MDDL, the code given in Figure 10.9 would be used.

Floating rate note

An FRN is similar to an index-linked in that both pay interests at a variable. In both cases there may be a need to specify the return on investment in a descriptive form, this is where the formula term can be used. (see Figure 10.10).

Discounted (zero coupon) bond

Discounted bonds are different from others in that the income is 'discounted' in the principal amount invested.

Normally, the issue price of a bond is to par value (or the nominal value represented in terms of a percentage, i.e. 100); with a discounted bond the issue price is reduced by the interest, and on maturity the investor gets in return par (this is equivalent to the original amount invested + interest).

```xml
<snap>
  <instrumentDomain>
    <instrumentData>
    <instrumentType scheme="../../../schemes/instrumentType.xml">
    <mdString>indexLinkedBond</mdString>
    </instrumentType>
    </instrumentData>
    <debtIssueData>
      <interestRate>
          <rate>2.5</rate>
        <linked>
          <mdBoolean>true</mdBoolean>
          <instrumentIdentifier>
            <code
                scheme="http://www.statistics.gov.uk">
              <mdString>RPI</mdString>
            </code>
            <name>United Kingdom
                General Index of Retail
                Prices</name>
          </instrumentIdentifier>
        </linked>
        ...
        </debtIssueData>
        ...
  </instrumentDomain>
<snap>
```

Figure 10.9 Index-linked income terms

```xml
<interestRate>
  <instrumentIdentifier>
    <name>USD-LIBOR</name>
  </instrumentIdentifier>
  <rate>0.6</rate>
  <nonFixedRate>
    <mdBoolean>true</mdBoolean>
    <nonFixedRateType>
      <mdString>floating</mdString>
    </nonFixedRateType>
    <formula>
      <mdString>USD 3M LIBOR+60BP</mdString>
    </formula>
  </nonFixedRate>
</interestRate>
```

Figure 10.10 FRN (variable interest) reference rate and reference margin

Issuer	Security	Issue date	Maturity date	Discount rate (%)	Investment rate (%)	Price per $100
US Treasury	13-WEEK BILL	09-28-2006	12-28-2006	4.770	4.895	98.794250

A US Treasury (discounted) bill can be represented in MDDL using the terms shown in Figure 10.11.

Other flavours of debt instruments exist, and terms exist in MDDL to support mortgage asset backed, instruments, step-ups, pooled, and so on. The market is now moving towards more complex instruments like structured products, which are instruments that take on properties from one of more instrument asset class. An index tracker bond that protects the investor's original investment and the issuer's exposure to a maximum return on investment is a good example.

```
<instrumentDomain>
  <instrumentData>
  <instrumentType scheme="../../../schemes/instrumentType.xml">
  <mdString>zeroCouponBond</mdString>
  </instrumentType>
  </instrumentData>
  <debtIssueData>
    <interestRate>
      <rate>4.895</rate>
    </interestRate>
    <maturity>
      <maturityDate>2006-12-
          28</maturityDate>
    </maturity>
  </debtIssueData>
  <issueData>
    <issuePrice>
      <mdDecimal>98.794250</mdDecimal>
      <yield>
        <mdDecimal>4.770</mdDecimal>
        <yieldType>discount</yieldType>
      </yield>
    </issuePrice>
    <issueDate>2006-09-28</issueDate>
  </issueData>
</instrumentDomain>
```

Figure 10.11 Discount (zero) coupon income terms

Bond analytics

Historically speaking, debt analytics has not been comprehensively covered by the majority of vendor data feeds. However, Bloomberg has stood out as the frontrunner for supplying debt instrument data. Analytical information includes accrued interest, yields calculations and sensitivity analysis, etc. This information changes over the life of an instrument, normally on a day-by-day basis. In version 2 of MDDL, the container *analytic* was created for the purpose of supporting the such requirements.

The MDDL example in Figure 10.12 shows a typical selection of information that might be expected to show on a yield analysis screen. The major headings are accrued analysis, yield calculations, and sensitivity analysis.

```
<snap>
 <instrumentDomain>
  <analytics>
   <other>
    <ext:accrued>
     <ext:daysAccrued>134</ext:daysAccrued>
     <ext:accruedInterest>3.989</ext:accruedInterest>
    </ext:accrued>
    <ext:yieldCalculations>
     <yield>
      <mdDecimal>3.989</mdDecimal>
      <yieldType>streetConvention</yieldType>
     </yield>
     <yield>
      <mdDecimal>3.988</mdDecimal>
      <yieldType>treasuryConvention</yieldType>
     </yield>
     <yield>
      <mdDecimal>3.987</mdDecimal>
      <yieldType>trueYield</yieldType>
     </yield>
     <yield>
      <mdDecimal>4.029</mdDecimal>
      <yieldType>oneYearConpound</yieldType>
     </yield>
     <yield>
      <mdDecimal>3.797</mdDecimal>
      <yieldType>japaneseYield</yieldType>
     </yield>
     <yield>
      <mdDecimal>3.99</mdDecimal>
      <yieldType>toMaturity</yieldType>
     </yield>
    </ext:yieldCalculations>
    <ext:sensitivity>
     <conventionalDuration>4.762</conventionalDuration>
     <modifiedDuration>4.668</modifiedDuration>
     <risk>5.366</risk>
     <convexity>0.266</convexity>
    </ext:sensitivity>
   </other>
  </analytics>
 </instrumentDomain>
</snap>
```

Figure 10.12 Bond analytics in MDDL

STRUCTURED PRODUCTS

Any feed designer will find it difficult to understand how to represent any product apart from plain vanilla instruments in MDDL. Sufficient terms are in place to support the business contexts of quoting and reporting requirements; however, for security definitions, particularly in the areas of pre-release and immediate post-issue, there is the need to take advantage of the *other* facility. Don't be afraid to do so; that's what it's there for. So take a stab at using it and/or contact an expert for some pointers. With the advent of MDDL version 3, the consolidation of the instrument domains (equity, debt, civ and so on) into a single domain (*instrumentDomain*) will hopefully make this excercise easier.

Index tracker bond

A dummy instrument has been created to provide an example of a structured product and thus evidence that MDDL can be used to represent any flavour of financial product – with the exception of OTCs, of course.

The summary of an index tracker bond instrument is outlined below. Investors are invited to purchase a bond which will track the S&P 500 index for a period of 5 years. They will be guaranteed their original investment upon maturity plus any increase in the index up to 100% in value. At regular intervals, at each anniversary, the issuer will call the instrument early if the return on investment reaches the 100% threshold; these dates are referred to as 'kick-out dates'. If this figure is reached prior to a kick-out date or maturity, the return on investment (income) will be limited to 100% of the principle amount invested. The launch date is different from the date at which the reading of the index is taken (the strike date), thus ensuring that the issuer has all the funds available at the time the index reading is taken.

The table below is a visual representation of the MDDL document; it can be used to advertise to clients the opportunity to participate in the bond, as well as for client reporting purposes, as it's updated throughout its life.

Name	Launch date	Strike date	Maturity date	Minimum balance
5-year S&P 500 growth tracker	31.1.05	31.3.05	31.3.11	3,000

% Potential max. return	Indices at strike date	1st reading	Equivalent yield	2nd	3rd	4th	Indices at maturity
100	1152.78	1215.00	5.4%	–	–	–	–

The MDDL document shown in Figure 10.13 can be used to populate trading applications with security definitions.

```
<snap>
  <instrumentDomain>
    <instrumentData>
    <instrumentType scheme="../../../schemes/instrumentType.xml">
    structuredProduct
    </instrumentType>
    </instrumentData>
    <instrumentIdentifier>
      <name>5 Year S&P 500 Growth Tracker</name>
    </instrumentIdentifier>
    <debtIssueData>
      <maturity>
        <maturityDate>2010-04-18</maturityDate>
      </maturity>
      <callable>
        <mdBoolean>true</mdBoolean>
        <callConditionType>maxExcericeValueReached</callConditionType>
        <callableType>discrete</callableType>
        <other>
          <!-- 100% increase in the value of the index -->
          <ext:maxReturnRate>100</ext:maxReturnRate>
        </other>
        </callable>
        <denomination>
          <mdDecimal>1000</mdDecimal>
          <minVal>3000</minVal>
          <increment>1000</increment>
        </denomination>
        <redemption>
          <principalProtection>
            <mdDecimal>100</mdDecimal>
            <other>
              <ext:originalInvestment>true</ext:originalInvestment>
            </other>
          </principalProtection>
        </redemption>
        <other>
          <ext:strikeDate>2005-04-18</ext:strikeDate>
          <ext:strikeValue>1152.78</ext:strikeValue>
        </other>
      </debtIssueData>
      <issueData>
        <issueDate>2005-01-05</issueDate>
         <issuerRef>
           <mdUri>http://www.bankofamerica.com</mdUri>
           <name>Bank of America</name>
         </issuerRef>
       </issueData>
       <other>
         <ext:readings>
```


Figure 10.13 Structured product – 5-year index tracker with protected principle (Continued/)

```
        <ext:reading>
          <dateTime>2006-04-18</dateTime>
          <ext:readingValue>1215</ext:readingValue>
          <interestRate>
            <rate>5.4</rate>
          </interestRate>
        </ext:reading>
        <ext:reading>
          <dateTime>2007-04-18</dateTime>
          <ext:readingValue />
        </ext:reading>
        <ext:reading>
          <dateTime>2008-04-18</dateTime>
          <ext:readingValue />
        </ext:reading>
        <ext:reading>
          <dateTime>2009-04-18</dateTime>
          <ext:readingValue />
        </ext:reading>
      </ext:readings>
    </other>
  </instrumentDomain>
</snap>
```

Figure 10.13 (/Continued)

Derivative products

Derivative products raise an interesting point when it comes to market data, and in particular in describing the properties of such instruments. There is no associated issuance process *per se*; however, there is the requirement for the exchange to define the market conventions and the symbology (acronyms or abbreviations) to identify the instrument. These are normally identified by a short code, the exercise (strike) price and expiry month, and, in the case of options, an indicator to identify whether it's a call or put. In addition, there are other properties of interest to the investor, including identifying the underlyer (which can be a security, bond, indicator, rate or indices), the exercise style and the strike price interval, which may be based on a number of aspects – the most obvious being the option price itself.

Options

To help convey the instrument definition capabilities of MDDL relating to derivative products, the following example has been provided based on the Daimler Chrysler AG

(DCX) Jan 2007 20.0000 call, supplemented with the current underlying mid-price; this information can also be represented in MDDL.

The strike price for an option is initially set at a price which is reasonably close to the current share price of the underlying security – in this case, this is $50. Additional or subsequent strike prices are set at the following intervals: 2.5 points when the strike price to be set is $25 or less; 5 points when the strike price to be set is between $25 and $200; and 10 points when the strike price to be set is over $200. New strike prices are introduced when the price of the underlying security rises to the highest, or falls to the lowest, strike price currently available. In this example (Figure 10.14), the trading summary comprises a spread of strike prices from $30 up to $70.

From a semantic perspective, it can be argued that the definitions of derivatives should be represented in FpML; however, in this instance and others where the product is exchanged traded, MDDL does hit the spot. It is recommended, though, that each organization's data architect has the final say on what is the appropriate route to take.

```
<snap>
  <instrumentDomain>
    <instrumentData>
      <instrumentType
         scheme="../../../schemes/instrumentType.xml">equityOption</instrumentType>
    </instrumentData>
    <callable>true</callable>
    <currency>USD</currency>
    <instrumentIdentifier>
      <code scheme="www.phlx.com">
            <!--
             The 't' in <code> is substituted with either an A to represent a call, whilst
            a M donates a put. The next character that immediately follows ('s') is used
            to represent the strike price (D stands for $20.00, F for 30...).
            Thus the symbol, DCXAD.X is the symbol for Daimler Chrysler AG (DCX)
            Jan 2007 20.0000 call.
         -->
        <mdString>DCXxx.X</mdString>
      </code>
    <marketIdentifier>
      <marketCenter>
        <code
            scheme="http://www.mddl.org/ext/scheme/iso10383.xml">XPHL</code>
      </marketCenter>
    </marketIdentifier>
  </instrumentIdentifier>
  <underlying>
  <instrumentIdentifier>
```

Figure 10.14 Equity option definition (Continued/)

```
        <name>Daimler Chrysler AG</name>
        <code scheme="http://www.mddl.org/ext/scheme/iso6166.xml">
           <mdString>DE0007100000</mdString>
        </code>
        <code scheme="http://www.mddl.org/ext/scheme/symbol?SRC=CUSIP">
          <mdString>D1668R123</mdString>
        </code>
      </instrumentIdentifier>
    </underlying>
    <issueData>
      <maturity>
        <!-- Jan 07 Expiry (close Sat, Jan 20, 2007) -->
        <maturityDate>20070120</maturityDate>
      </maturity>
    </issueData>
    <!-- Current share price of the underlying security. -->
    <mid>
      <last>49.18</last>
    </mid>
    <other>
      <ext:exercisePriceIntervals>
        <ext:interval>
          <sequence>1</sequence>
          <when>
            <otherFunction>
              <exercisePrice />
            </otherFunction>
            <lessThan />
            <mdDecimal>20</mdDecimal>
          </when>
          <size>2.50</size>
        </ext:interval>
        <ext:interval>
          <sequence>2</sequence>
          <when>
            <otherFunction>
              <exercisePrice />
            </otherFunction>
            <lessThan />
            <mdDecimal>200</mdDecimal>
          </when>
          <size>5.00</size>
        </ext:interval>
        <ext:interval>
          <sequence>3</sequence>
          <when>
            <otherFunction>
              <exercisePrice />
            </otherFunction>
            <greaterOrEqualTo />
            <mdDecimal>200</mdDecimal>
          </when>
          <size>10.00</size>
        </ext:interval>
      </ext:exercisePriceIntervals>
    </other>
  </instrumentDomain>
</snap>
```

Figure 10.14 (/Continued)

Alternative solutions to securities definitions

So, what are the alternatives to the hierarchical message design approach as deployed by earlier versions of MDDL? Version 3 removes the instrument hierarchy (domains, classes and subclasses) and replace it with a single instrument domain. This results in all instrument specific terms and thier existing relationships being grouped under the *InstrumentDomain*

Another solution is to use the building block approach to designing your own securities definitions message model. This technique involves creating instruments from a small set of components (including the likes of instrument identification, issuance, payment details and so on). This does mean that all components and the majority of their properties being optional, making it difficult to enforce schema validation. However it has the advantage of being able to support instruments that bridge multiple asset classes. Figure 10.15 shows how an Index-linked bond could be represented using the building block approach.

```
<instrument>
  <!-- Instrument Identification -->
  <identification>
    <name>MCS Bank Standard and Poor's 500 Equity Linked Bonds</name>
    <code codeType="isin">US12345UED28</code>
    <code codeType="cusip">12345UED2</code>
    <code codeType="commonCode">012345678</code>
  </identification>
  <!-- Issuance Terms normally found in the Term Sheet or Prospectus -->
  <issuance>
    <maturityDate maturityType="fixed">2011-11-26</maturityDate>
    <denomination>1000</denomination>
    <issuePrice>100</issuePrice>
    <issueDate>2004-11-26</issueDate>
    <issueAmount>10000000</issueAmount>
    <governingLaw>New York</governingLaw>
    <clearing>
      <clearingHouse>DTC</clearingHouse>
    </clearing>
    <payments>
      <payment>
        <rate>
          <percentage>1.5</percentage>
        </rate>
        <dates>
          <date>11-26</date>
```

Figure 10.15 A Index-linked bond based on a building block message design approach (Continued/)

```
        </dates>
        <!-- Payment Annually (1*Year) -->
        <period>
          <multiplier>Y</multiplier>
          <multiplierValue>1</multiplierValue>
        </period>
        <accrual>
          <dayRuleType>act/act</dayRuleType>
          <accrualBasis>30/365</accrualBasis>
        </accrual>
      </payment>
      <payment>
        <variable>
          <referenceRate>
            <code
                codeType="http://www.standardandpoors.com">SandP500</code>
            <name>Standard and Poor's 500</name>
          </referenceRate>
        </variable>
      </payment>
    </payments>
  </issuance>
  </instrument>
```

Figure 10.15 (/Continued)

Change mechanism

Mergers and acquisitions provide an obvious example where a change in both the instruments' definitions and the naming and relationship of business entities might be expected. In such a scenario the mechanism to manage the change is important, and the simpler that this is, the better.

Data can be and is normally supplied by multiple vendors, and upon entering the organization this will need to be managed. To achieve this, a number of organizations have or are considering creating a central repository which absorbs the data from the various sources, in some cases cleanses it, and then broadcasts this throughout the organization.

The minimum amount of information needed, based on a centralized broadcast model, is the *sequence* identifier plus a version identifier that defines the format that the message complies to.

The message version identification can be handled by the use of the namespace definition within the XML document itself. The receiving application can be configured to process only the messages which it has been designed to receive. For example, one application may be designed to process MDDL version 2.1 draft only, whilst another 2.5 beta. This does mean that the sending application will be required to disseminate in multiple formats until all applications are put on the same version; however, there is the advantage that applications can be updated and rolled out without the risk of rebuilding and testing all the applications across the enterprise.

This transport model will require a fall-back recovery scenario to cover situations where an application becomes out of sync. – where, for example, a message is missed. In such a situation a re-request mechanism, preferably using an independent circuit, should be considered. The receiving application can then request that it is re-sent missing transactions, or all transactions from the point at which it became out of sync. (Figure 10.16). This centralized broadcast mechanism is based on the successful London Stock Exchange's Infolect/LMIL network, and as such is tried and tested approach.

The re-request message sent by the receiving application can be as simple as an MDDL message comprising the sequence number (Figure 10.17). The re-request sending application can then initiate sending the missing material to the receiving

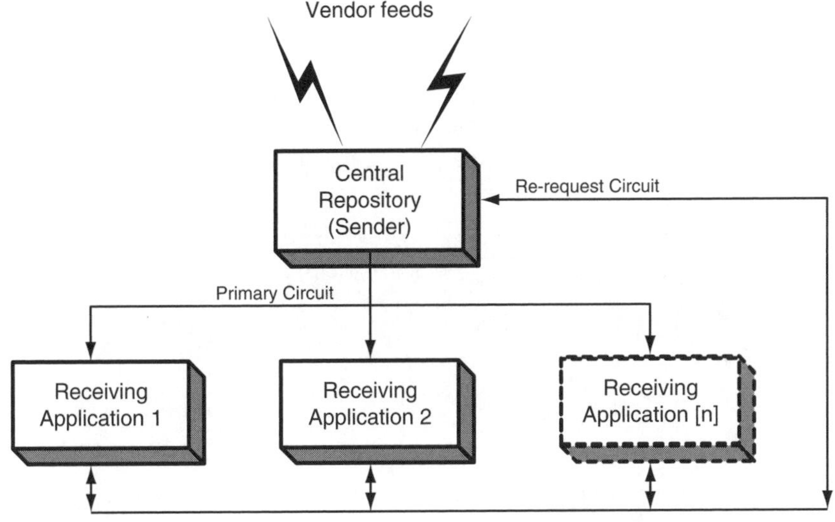

Figure 10.16 Dual circuit recovery mechanism

```
<header>
  <dateTime>2006-09-12</dateTime>
  <sequence>67+</sequence>
</header>
```

Figure 10.17 Re-request transmission

application across the re-request circuit; the main circuit will remain unaffected whilst the application out of sync. catches up.

The decision needs to be made as to how to use the *sequence* element. For example, a number by itself could mean, please send just that transaction, while a transaction number followed by a plus (+) sign could be interpreted as 'send me everything from that transaction number onward' – in Figure 10.17, every transaction from and including 67.

Mechanism for updating reference data

Even if an organization follows the market recommendations regarding how to uniquely identify an instrument, there will always be a need to maintain a unique reference internally. This can be achieved by the using of *code scheme* and in the case of the example that follows, the scheme is defined as "www.yourcompany.com/instrumentld" and the unique identifier is "00007". Why is this so important?

Consider the scenario where an external identifier changes – for example, the ISIN for a product was originally entered as US652482AH31, and it has now been updated to US652482AH30. When updating this information, if a system uses the ISIN and the unique identifier, then the relationship could potentially be lost.

```
<header>
<dateTime>2006-9-12</dateTime>
<sequence>67</sequence>
</header>
<snap>
  <snapType>new</snapType>
  <instrumentDomain>
    <instrumentIdentifier>
      <code
          scheme="www.yourcompany.com/instrumentId"
          >00007</code>
      <code
          scheme="http://www.mddl.org/ext/scheme/iso
          6166.xml">UK652482AH31</code>
      <name>NEWS AMER INC
          7.300%,04/30/2028</name>
   <sequence>1</sequence>
   </instrumentIdentifier>
   </instrumentDomain>
</snap>
```

Figure 10.18 Original security definition

```
<header>
<dateTime>2006-9-12</dateTime>
<sequence>1001</sequence>
</header>
<snap>
  <snapType>update</snapType>
  <instrumentDomain>
    <instrumentIdentifier>
      <code
          scheme="www.yourcompany.com/instrumentId">
          00007</code>
      <code
          scheme="http://www.mddl.org/ext/scheme/iso6
          166.xml">US652482AH30</code>
      <name>NEWS AMER INC
          7.300%,04/30/2028</name>
  <sequence>2 </sequence>
  </instrumentIdentifier>
  </instrumentDomain>
</snap>
```

Figure 10.19 The update to the security definition

An update to the securities definition for the instrument in question could be represented in MDDL – see Figures 10.18 and 10.19. Sequence numbering can be supported at various levels within MDDL, in addition to the message level it can also be applied at instrument level or entity level. The two samples (Figure 10.18 and 10.19) show the use of the *sequence* number within the instrumentIdentifier container to indicate the order that applies to the instrument updates.

As a final point it is also worth pointing out that MDDL will support updates of only the terms that have changed (this is sometimes referred to as deltas), therefore the user is not forced to include unnecessary terms.

Chapter 11

Industry standards – mix and match

"Market Data manifests itself in various forms within other industry standards, therefore it only appropriate to examine its use and the relationship of these standards with MDDL."

MDDL to FIX, FIX to MDDL

Market data terms are used in FIX to support bilateral communications. Introduced in FIX 4.4, market data messages are becoming more popular as FIX has migrated from its traditional buy-side/sell-side stronghold into providing capabilities for supporting exchange connectivity and book management. Within the pre-trade/trade environment, the effective warehousing of market data for instrument identification, bids/offers and order books in a timely manner is essential. The user will need to decide what standard (MDDL or FIX) is appropriate within a business context; both are valid.

Given that there may be occasions where it may be necessary to transform from MDDL to FIX or *vice versa*, Table 11.1 provides cross-references. A few samples have also been provided so that developers can get a feel for the transformation considerations between the two formats (MDDL and FIX) – see Figures 11.1–11.4 (pages 162–5).

Table 11.1 MDDL/FIX terms cross-reference matrix

MDDL terms	FIX tag number	FIX tag name (FIXML Attribute)	Explanation
<code scheme="..."> within instrument-Identifier	22	SecurityIDSource (Src)	This FIX tag is an enumerated list that identifies the source of the code. MDDL is NOT limited to such code list. Possible values of this tag are: 1 : CUSIP 2 : SEDOL 3 : QUIK 4 : ISIN number 5 : RIC code
<code> within instrument-Identifier	48	SecurityID (ID)	Instrument identifier published by the source – for example, ISIN: US3453708600
<code> within instrument-Identifier	55	Symbol (Sym)	Ticker symbol or local market identifier.
<name> within instrument-Identifier	107	SecurityDesc (Desc)	A description of the instrument – for example: 'Ford Motor Company'

Table 11.1

MDDL terms	FIX tag number	FIX tag name (FIXML Attribute)	Explanation
N/A in MDDL	268	NoMDEntries	The number of market data records
<bid>, <ask> or <trade>	269	MDEntryType	An enumerated list, in FIX, a subset of the full list can be used for book management – for example: 0 : Bid (bid) 1 : Offer (ask) 2 : Trade
<mdDecimal> within <last>	270	MDEntryPx	Price
<size>	271	MDEntrySize	Quantity
<last> <dateTIme>	272	MDEntryDate	Fix date (YYYYMMDD); in MDDL date and time are combined, complying to ISO 8601
N/A	273	MDEntryTime	Fix time (hh:mm:ss.s); see tag 272
<changeDirection>	274	TickDirection	Tick direction 0 : Positive 1 : Even 2 : Negative
<marketIdentifier> <marketCenter> <code>	275	MDMkt	Principally the ISO MIC or exchange code, some non-MICs exist within the FIX enumerated list. Some example values are: XBUL : FIRST BULGARIAN STOCK EXCHANGE XLON : LONDON STOCK EXCHANGE EURO

(Continued/)

Table 11.1 *(/Continued)*

MDDL terms	FIX tag number	FIX tag name (FIXML Attribute)	Explanation
			XNAS : NASDAQ SMALL CAP XNAY : NANCY STOCK EXCHANGE XNYM : NEW YORK MERCANTILE EXCHANGE Y : INTERNATIONAL SECURITIES EXCHANGE (IZE)
MDDL handles these via the use of various XML elements and attributes.	276	QuoteCondition	Quote condition. Values are: A : Open/Active B : Closed/Inactive C : Exchange best D : Consolidated best E : Locked F : Crossed G : Depth H : Fast trading I : Non-firm
MDDL does not support this granularity of information that is required for transactions between two counterparties, not considered market data.	277	TradeCondition	A : Cash (only) market B : Average price trade C : Cash trade (same day clearing) D : Next day (only) market E : Opening/reopening trade detail F : Intraday trade detail

(Continued/)

Table 11.1 *(/Continued)*

MDDL terms	FIX tag number	FIX tag name (FIXML Attribute)	Explanation
<sequence>	278	MDEntryID	Unique market data entry identifier
<snapType>	279	MDUpdateAction	Values are: 0 : New 1 : Change (update) 2 : Delete
Required as part of a message sequence flow between two or more parties.	320	Security ReqID (ReqID)	Unique ID of a security definition request
<sequence>	322	Security ResponseID (RspID)	Unique ID of a security definition message
Not applicable to MDDL required as part of a message sequence flow between two or more parties.	323	Security ResponseType (RspTyp)	Type of security definition message response: 1 : Accept security proposal as is 2 : Accept security proposal with revisions as indicated in the message 3 : List of security types returned per request 4 : List of securities returned per request 5 : Reject security proposal 6 : Cannot match selection criteria
N/A	454	NoSecurityAltID	Number of alternate security identifiers

(Continued/)

Table 11.1 *(/Continued)*

MDDL terms	FIX tag number	FIX tag name (FIXML Attribute)	Explanation
<code> within instrumentIdentifier	455	SecurityAltID	Multiple instrumentidentifiers (see tag 48)
<code scheme="..."> within instrumentIdentifier	456	SecurityAlt IDSource	Source of alternative identifiers (see tag 22)
<instrumentType scheme="http://www.mddl.org/ext/scheme/iso10962.xml">...	461	CFICode (CFI)	ISO 10962 standard, Classification of Financial Instruments
<rank>	1021	MDBookType	Values are: 1 : Top of book 2 : Price depth 3 : Order depth MDDL uses the term *rank* to identify the position within a book – 1 = top of book

MDDL TOP-OF-BOOK SAMPLE

```
<snap>
  <!-- 279=0^ (MDUpdateAction = New) -->
  <snapType>new</snapType>
  <instrumentDomain>
    <instrumentIdentifier>
      <!-- 107=Ford Motor Company^ (SecurityDesc) -->
      <name>Ford Motor Company</name>
      <!-- 22=4^ (SecurityIDSource = ISIN Number) -->
```

Figure 11.1 Top of book in MDDL

```
      <code
          scheme="http://www.mddl.org/ext/scheme/iso616
          6">
        <!-- 48=US3453708600^ (SecurityID) -->
        <mdString>US3453708600</mdString>
      </code>
    </instrumentIdentifier>
    <orderbook>
      <!-- 269=0^ (MDEntryType = Bid) -->
      <bid>
        <last>
          <!-- 270=781^ (MDEntryPrice) -->
          <mdDecimal>781</mdDecimal>
          <!-- 272=200818^ & 272=16:20:59.000^
            (MDEntryDate & MDEntryTime) -->
          <dateTime>2006-08-18T16:20:59Z</dateTime>
        </last>
        <!-- 271=1250^ (MDEntrySize) -->
        <size>1250</size>
        <!-- 1021=1 (MDBookType = Top-Of-Book) -->
        <rank>1</rank>
        <marketIdentifier>
          <marketCenter>
            <!-- 275=NYSE^ (MDMkt) -->
            <code
                scheme="http://www.mddl.org/ext/scheme/i
                so10383.xml">NYSE</code>
          </marketCenter>
        </marketIdentifier>
      </bid>
    </orderbook>
  </instrumentDomain>
</snap>
```

Figure 11.1 (/Continued)

FIX TOP-OF-BOOK SAMPLE

```
1021=1^279=0^269=0^271=1250^270=781^272=200818^2
73=16:20:59.000^107=Ford Motor
Company^22=4^48=US3453708600^
275=NYSE^
```

Figure 11.2 Top of book in FIX

MDDL LAST TRADE SAMPLE

```
<snap>
  <!-- 279=0^ (MDUpdateAction = New) -->
  <snapType>new</snapType>
  <instrumentDomain>
      <instrumentIdentifier>
        <!-- 107=Ford Motor Company^ (SecurityDesc) -->
        <name>Ford Motor Company</name>
        <!-- 22=4^ (SecurityIDSource = ISIN Number) -->
        <code
            scheme="http://www.mddl.org/ext/scheme/iso616
            6">
          <!-- 48=US3453708600^ (SecurityID) -->
            <mdString>US3453708600</mdString>
        </code>
      </instrumentIdentifier>
      <!-- 269=2^ (MDEntryType = Trade) -->
      <trade>
        <last>
          <!-- 270=782^ (MDEntryPrice) -->
          <mdDecimal>782</mdDecimal>
          <!-- 272=200818^ & 272=16:10:06.000^
            (MDEntryDate & MDEntryTime) -->
          <dateTime>2006-08-18T16:10:06.050Z</dateTime>
        </last>
        <!-- 271=1250^ (MDEntrySize)-->
        <size>500</size>
        <marketIdentifier>
          <marketCenter>
            <!-- 275=NYSE^ (MDMkt)-->
            <code
                scheme="http://www.mddl.org/ext/scheme/iso
                10383.xml">NYSE</code>
          </marketCenter>
        </marketIdentifier>
        <!-- 274=2^ (TickDirection=Minus Tick) -->
        <changeDirection>negative</changeDirection>
        <!-- No FIX term identified to support the amount of
          change. -->
        <change>
          <mdDecimal>0.17</mdDecimal>
        </change>
      </trade>
  </instrumentDomain>
</snap>
```

Figure 11.3 Last trade in MDDL

FIX LAST TRADE SAMPLE

```
279=0^269=2^271=500^270=782^272=200818^273=16:10:
06.050^107=Ford Motor Company^22=4^48=US3453708600^
275=NYSE^277=A^
```

Figure 11.4 Top of book equivalent in FIX

The headers for both the MDDL and FIX examples are not included, as it's only the message content that is of importance regarding the transformation between the standards. The samples are based on the equity 'Ford Motor Company', which is listed on the New York Stock Exchange and includes a top-of-book and a trade report. The later could be extended to support the transaction reporting requirements associated with MiFID. (Refer to Chapter 9 and Appendix B – MiFID terms).

MDDL and FIXml

There are a small number of market data messages defined within the standard (FIX), and it's important that the reader is made aware of them so as to make a judgement as to how appropriate they are to a particular organization's environment. These messages form part of a request response message flow, and do not cleanly fit within a broadcast or notification style of message flow. This is emphasized in the FIXml security definition (*SecDef*) message, which requires the SecurityReqID (*ReqID*), SecurityResponseID (*RspID*) and the SecurityResponseType (*RspTyp*) to be populated (see Table 11.1).

As can immediately be seen, MDDL is human-readable when compared to the FIXml equivalent. Is this an important factor? FIX has always been concerned about bandwidth, and, given the volumes of transaction, it is possible to understand

```
?xml version="1.0" encoding="UTF-8" ?>
<mddl xmlns:xsi="http://www.w3.org/2001/XMLSchema-instance"
    xmlns:xlink="http://www.w3.org/1999/xlink"
    xmlns:mdref="http://www.mddl.org/mddl/3.0-beta/ref"
    xmlns="http://www.mddl.org/mddl/3.0-beta"
    xmlns:xsd="http://www.w3.org/2001/XMLSchema"
    xmlns:mddl="http://www.mddl.org/mddl/3.0-beta"
    xsi:schemaLocation="http://www.mddl.org/mddl/3.0-beta
    D:\mddl\3.0-beta\mddl-3.0-beta-full.xsd">
```

Figure 11.5 Security definition represented in MDDL (Continued/)

```
<snap>
  <instrumentDomain>
      <instrumentIdentifier>
        <name>Ford Motor Company</name>
        <code
            scheme="http://www.mddl.org/ext/scheme/iso6166.
            xml">US3453708600</code>
        <code scheme="http://www.nyse.com">F</code>
        <instrumentData>
          <instrumentType
              scheme="http://www.mddl.org/ext/scheme/iso109
              62.xml">ESVUFR</instrumentType>
        </instrumentData>
      </instrumentIdentifier>
      <issueData>
        <placeOfListing>
          <code
              scheme="http://www.mddl.org/ext/scheme/iso103
              83.xml">NYSE</code>
        </placeOfListing>
      </issueData>
  </instrumentDomain>
 </snap>
</mddl>
```

Figure 11.5 (/Continued)

the thinking behind using abbreviated definitions and attributes within elements. However, with the various data compression initiatives and techniques, is this still really an issue, with information being wrapped in verbose human-readable XML structures? In the days of 65K lines maybe.

```
<?xml version="1.0" encoding="UTF-8" ?>
<FIXML xmlns="http://www.fixprotocol.org/FIXML-4-4"
    xmlns:xsi="http://www.w3.org/2001/XMLSchema-instance"
    xsi:schemaLocation="http://www.fixprotocol.org/FIXML-4-4
    C:\FIX4-4\fixml-securitystatus-base-4-4.xsd">
  <SecDef ReqID="1002" RspID="204" RspTyp="1">
    <Instrmt Sym="F" Desc="Ford Motor Company"
        ID="US3453708600" Src="4" CFI="ESVUFR" Exch="NYSE"
        />
  </SecDef>
</FIXML>
```

Figure 11.6 Security definition represented in FIXml

MDDL and ISO 20022

ISO 20022 market data messages are hypothetical, given that there has been no submission for this business context so far. However, there is nothing to stop an organization creating messages that adhere to the standard and, if feeling brave, submitting them through the ISO 20022 approval into the repository. How about basing a submission on ISO 19312.

By taking the top-of-book example shown in Figure 11.1, it is possible to create a market data message that looks and feels like ISO 20022 (see Figure 11.7 on page 167).

This standard is a book in its own right or possibly a novel, given the goings-on behind the scenes regarding the interpretation of the standard and the approval process associated with submissions.

```
<?xml version="1.0" encoding="UTF-8" ?>
<Document xmlns:xsi="http://www.w3.org/2001/XMLSchema-instance"
   xsi:noNamespaceSchemaLocation="C:\iso20022\mdsd001.001.01.x
   sd">
<!--
     The Message Identifier is normally defined by the ISO 20022 Registration
     Authority. The Message Identifier ("xxxx.nnn.aaa.bb") is broken down as
     follows: where
     - xxxx is an abbreviation of the Business Process;
     - nnn is an alphanumeric code identifying the Message Function;
     - aaa is a numeric code identifying a particular flavor of Message Functionality;
     - bb is a numeric code identifying the version of the message.
 -->
 <!-- mdsd - Business Process "Market Data Securities Definition
   Dissemination" -->
 <mdsd.001.001.01>
   <FinInstrmDtls>
     <!-- Full Descriptive name of the instrument -->
     <FinInstrmNm>Ford Motor Company</FinInstrmNm>
     <!-- Instrument Identifiers (ISIN and the Local Market Identifier) -
       ->
     <Id>
       <ISIN>US3453708600</ISIN>
     </Id>
     <Id>
        <TckrSymb>F</TckrSymb>
     </Id>
     <!-- Primary Place of Listing - ISO 10383 Exchange codes -
       Market Identification Code (MIC) -->
     <PmryPlcOfListg>NYSE</PmryPlcOfListg>
     <!-- Classification of Financial Instruments - ISO 10962 - CFI -->
     <ClssfctnTp>ESVUFR</ClssfctnTp>
   </FinInstrmDtls>
 </mdsd.001.001.01>
</Document>
```

Figure 11.7 Security definition represented in ISO 20022 equivalent

FpML

FpML has been developed by the International Swaps & Derivatives Association (ISDA), and is the industry standard designed to support Off-The-Counter (OTC) agreements between two or more parties. Each agreement is tailored to the unique requirements of the parties and is binding.

So what is an OTC? A simple currency swap example will help explain. A Chinese firm intends to sell goods to the US, and wishes to obtain financing denominated in US dollars. However, the Chinese company may not be able to obtain a competitively priced loan from a US bank. Similarly, a US company wishes to enter the Chinese market. Both firms are at a disadvantage in their new respective markets, given their poor or non-existent credit rating. However, within their own market they have a competitive advantage in obtaining credit, and cooperation between the two parties makes commercial sense. Solution: each party takes out a loan in their respective home markets and they 'swap' the loans (principle amounts) and interest payments (income streams); in this way they can take advantage of each other's strengths and leverage (see Figure 11.8).

As can be seen, OTC financial transactions are in fact contracts and cannot be represented in terms of market data feed; however, mark-to-market valuations of contracts and position may be disseminated in MDDL. Likewise, the user may consider using FpML; the later versions (4.2 onward) support valuation and position reporting.

MDDL can be used to disseminate benchmark rates – for example ISDAFIX®, which is the leading benchmark for fixed rates on interest rate swaps world-wide.

This ISDAFIX® service provides historical data, maintained in Excel file format, which is average mid-market swap rates for six major currencies at selected maturities

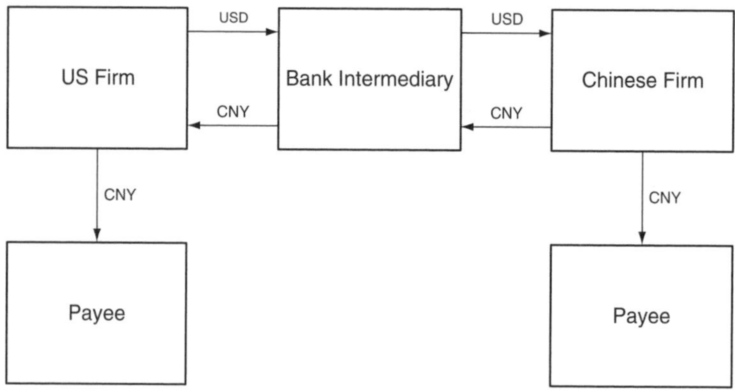

Figure 11.8 Simple currency swap

on a daily basis. ISDAFIX® rates are based on a mid-day and, in some markets, end-of-day polling of mid-market rates:

Date	**Y1**	Y2	Y3	Y4	Y5	Y6	Y7	Y8	Y9	**Y10**	Y12	Y15	**Y20**	Y25	Y30
20/09/06	**3.63**	3.76	3.82	3.87	3.92	3.97	4.02	4.06	4.11	**4.15**	4.22	4.3	**4.39**	4.42	4.42
21/09/06	3.66	3.82	3.89	3.94	3.99	4.04	4.08	4.12	4.16	4.2	4.27	4.35	4.43	4.46	4.46

The EUR-Euribor benchmark table shown here can be represented in MDDL as in Figure 11.9, where Y refers to the time in the future (the maturity as an offset).

```
<header>
  <dateTime>2006-09-20</dateTime>
  <source>ISDAFIX</source>
</header>
<snap>
  <indicatorDomain>
    <interestRateClass>
      <instrumentIdentifier>
        <name>EUR-Euribor Y1</name>
      </instrumentIdentifier>
    </interestRateClass>
    <interestRate>
      <rate>
        <mdDecimal>3.63</mdDecimal>
      </rate>
    </interestRate>
  </indicatorsDomain>
  <indicatorsDomain>
    <interestRateClass>
      <instrumentIdentifier>
        <name>EUR-Euribor Y10</name>
      </instrumentIdentifier>
    </interestRateClass>
    <interestRate>
      <rate>
        <mdDecimal>4.15</mdDecimal>
      </rate>
    </interestRate>
  </indicatorsDomain>
  <indicatorsDomain>
    <interestRateClass>
      <instrumentIdentifier>
        <name>EUR-Euribor Y20</name>
      </instrumentIdentifier>
    </interestRateClass>
    <interestRate>
      <rate>
        <mdDecimal>4.39</mdDecimal>
      </rate>
    </interestRate>
  </indicatorDomain>
</snap>
```

Figure 11.9 ISDAFIX® rates sample

Y1 is 1-year EUR-Euribor, Y2 is 2-year EUR-Euribor etc. Y1, Y10 and Y20 are shown.

RIXML

RIXML is an XML standard that is designed to support the requirements for publishing research information to assist consumers in making investment decisions. It contains elements of market data; however, these are not as granular as can be supported by MDDL. RIXML supports issuer identification, securities details, agency rating and sector/industry classifications. These elements of market data are used as metadata, providing context to research publications including Company Reports, 'Industry Comments' and 'Morning Call Summaries'.

Security identification and agency credit rating are represented in RIXML as shown in Figure 11.10.

The equivalent in MDDL would be represented as shown in Figure 11.11.

```
<IssuerDetails>
  <Issuer issuerType="Corporate" primaryIndicator="Yes"
     sequence="1" ratingAction="Upgrade">
    <SecurityDetails>
      <Security primaryIndicator="Yes" sequence="1">
        <SecurityID idType="CUSIP" idValue="61745ETZ4" />
        <SecurityName>Morgan Stanley SENIOR NOTES-
          F</SecurityName>
        <SecurityShortName>TP415</SecurityShortName>
        <AssetClass assetClass="FixedIncome" />
        <AssetType assetType="SupranationalCredit" />
        <Rating rating="TopRating">
          <RatingEntity ratingEntity="Moodys" />
        </Rating>
      </Security>
    </SecurityDetails>
    <IssuerName nameType="Display">
      <NameValue>Morgan Stanley</NameValue>
    </IssuerName>
  </Issuer>
</IssuerDetails>
```

Figure 11.10 Security identification and agency credit rating (RIXML)

```
<snap>
  <instrumentDomain>
    <instrumentIdentifier>
      <name>Morgan Stanley SENIOR NOTES-F
         9/1/2006</name>
      <code
         scheme="http://www.mddl.org/ext/scheme/iso6166.x
         ml">
        <mdString>US0373891037</mdString>
      </code>
      <code
         scheme="http://www.morganstanleyindividual.com/ma
         rkets/ipocenter/debtsyn/">
        <mdString>TP415</mdString>
      </code>
    </instrumentIdentifier>
    <agencyRatings>
      <rating>
        <code scheme=
           "http://www.mddl.org/ext/scheme/symbol?SRC=MOO
           DYS">
          <mdString>Aa3</mdString>
        </code>
      - <!-- Credit Risk -->
        <ratingType>risk</ratingType>
      </rating>
    </agencyRatings>
  </instrumentDomain>
</snap>
```

Figure 11.11 Security identification and agency credit rating (MDDL)

XBRL

XBRL is the accepted XML standard for all business and financial reporting. It is the *de facto* standard in the area of all aspects of company accounts reporting, including the general ledger, internal reporting, end-of-year reporting and statutory reports. XBRL supports the creation of separate taxonomies for different requirements and reporting regimes. Taxonomies exist for internal and regulatory reporting, and new ones are currently under development to support broker–dealer and investment management organizations. It supports terms such as portfolio valuations, which are derived from market data; however, it does not support market data *per se*. It is possible to create an XBRL taxomony that could support market data terms, although this would be outside the remit of the standard.

From a market data perspective, corporate announcements fall within the remit of XBRL. These announcements may result in the creation of one or many corporate action events that may have an impact on the issuer and/or an issue, which is within the scope of MDDL. Some may argue that the corporate action events themselves should also be managed by an XBRL taxonomy; however, these are currently outside the scope of the standard. An XBRL adherent sample of a dividend announcement has been provided in Figure 11.12 to show how a corporate announcement could be represented. Corporate action events in MDDL are discussed in Chapter 10.

```
<CorporateActionAnnouncement>
  <AnnouncementDetails>
    <IssuerName>HSBC Holdings plc</IssuerName>
    <IssuerTIDM>HSBA</IssuerTIDM>
    <Headline>Interim Dividend
      Announcement</Headline>
    <Released>07/09/2006 12:14:00</Released>

      <AnnouncementNumber>12345</AnnouncementN
      umber>
  </AnnouncementDetails>
  <Announcement>
    <Title seq="1">Fourth interim dividend for
      2006</Title>
    <Title seq="2">As published on the HSBC website:
      www.hsbc.com/hsbc/investor_centre/dividends</Ti
      tle>
    <Paragraph seq="1">05 Mar 07
      Announcement</Paragraph>
    <Paragraph seq="2">21 Mar 07 ADSs quoted ex-
      dividend in New York.</Paragraph>
    <Paragraph seq="3">21 Mar 07 Shares quoted ex-
      dividend in London, Hong Kong and
      Bermuda.</Paragraph>
    <Paragraph seq="4">23 Mar 07 Record
      date.</Paragraph>
    <Paragraph seq="5">23 Mar 07 Closure of Hong Kong
      Overseas Branch Register of shareholders for one
      day.</Paragraph>
    <Paragraph seq="6">26 Mar 07 Shares quoted ex-
      dividend in Paris.</Paragraph>
    <Paragraph seq="7">10 May 07 Payment
      date.</Paragraph>
  </Announcement>
</CorporateActionAnnouncement>
```

Figure 11.12 A snippet of an XBRL corporate announcement

SDMX

SDMX is an initiative to promote standardization for the exchange of statistical information. It has the backing of the Bank for International Settlements (BIS), the European Central Bank (ECB), the European Commission's Statistical Arm (Eurostat), the International Monetary Fund (IMF), the Organization for Economic Co-operation and Development (OECD), the United Nations (UN) and the World Bank. It has been approved as an ISO standard as a technical specification, ISO/TS 17369:2005 SDMX.

Statistical information within the standard is broken down into structural metadata and observational data. Data typically consists of a set of numeric observations at specific points in time, organized into 'data sets'.

The mechanism exists for updating the terms in the registry – in particular, its ability to take on terms of other taxonomies such as XBRL (corporate reporting) and RIXML (financial research information) makes it the front runner for the dissemination of data extracted from the statistical analytics process (see Figure 11.13).

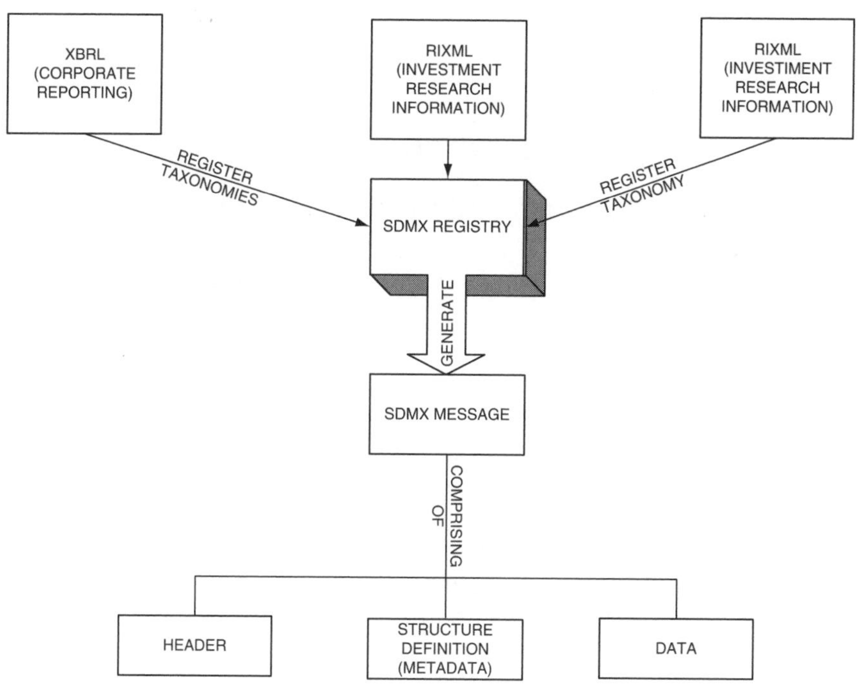

Figure 11.13 Registration and message generation

ISO standards in the financial sector

Since its creation over 60 years ago, ISO, and in particular Technical Committee 68 (TC68), has played an important role in directing the financial industry.

Some of the success stories include the creation of ISO 15022 (Post-Trade and Settlement Messages) and ISO 16372 (International Business Entity Identification) (see Figure 11.14). ISO 15022 is a non-XML standard that provides a set of messages to support the settlement process. These messages, in general, are transported over the SWIFT network, which provides a reliable backbone for the interaction of industry participants. It incorporates and is upwardly compatible with the previous securities message standards, ISO 7775 and ISO 11521. Working Group 8 designed the mechanism for the International Business Entity Identification (IBEI).

With the continued take-up of Unified Modeling Language (UML) by the financial industry, many companies have been examining the work being undertaken by the ISO standards 19312 (Securities Data Model) and 20022 (Universal Financial Industry Message Scheme), both of which are based on UML.

These standards effectively cover the two distinct dimensional aspects of financial data. ISO 20022 defines the terms and messages required by the processes within the

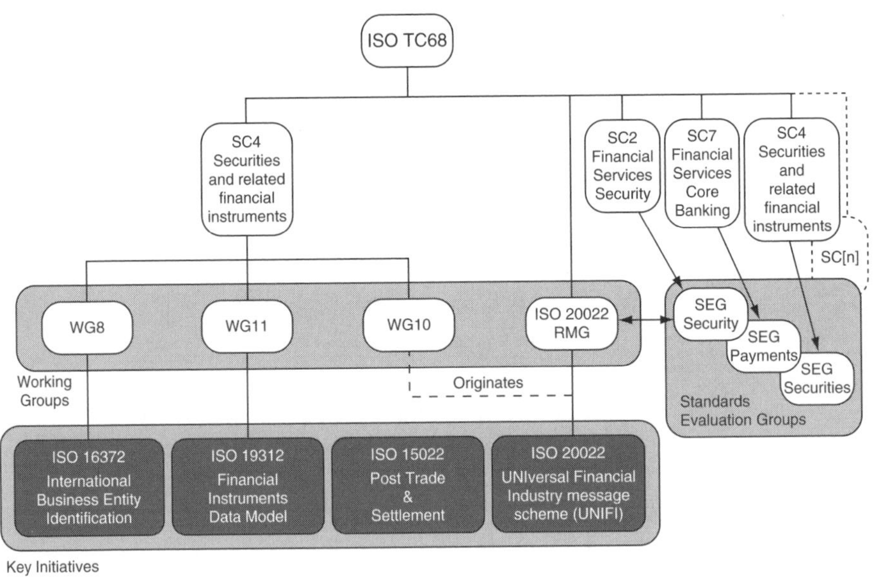

Figure 11.14 ISO initiatives in the financial sector

trade lifecycle, which are on the whole bilateral in nature, and ISO 19312 defines the reference data terms that are needed to support trade automation.

ISO 19312 and MDDL

ISO 19312 (the Securities Data Model) under development by ISO Working Group II (WGII) defines the terms, definitions and relationships between those terms for an instrument at the time of set-up, pricing and corporate actions.

MDDL's scope overlaps ISO 19312 in these areas; however, MDDL extends this scope to cover economic indicators, book management and reporting. ISO TC68/SC4/WG11's mission statement is as follows:

> *WG11 will produce a data model and an ISO Technical Specification that provides a single standard for describing a financial instrument throughout its lifecycle comprised of completely defined data elements and the relationship among these data elements.*

Any potential user may wish to consider using the ISO 19312 data model to generate XML messages.

The following scenario has been created to show how MDDL and an alternative 'security identification' structure (similar to ISO 19312 terms and terms relationship) can be used to identify the security in the context of regulatory reporting.

It's important to recognize that at the time of reporting there is no guarantee that all IT systems will have the international (global) identifier available. Some Front Office systems may only have the venue symbol (or ticker) to hand, and some securities may not have one at all. Many exchange-traded derivatives, such as options, will only have venue symbols allocated.

Uniqueness can be achieved by combining a small number of terms. For international identifiers these include:

- the market identifier based on the ISO 10383 MIC – the assumption is that the MIC will be extended to include systematic internalizers (or internal order books)
- the international identifier (ISO 6166 ISIN fills this requirement).

Where an ISIN is not available or if different instruments share the same ISIN, it is recommended that the national code be used. The terms required to support the national code are listed below (note the inclusion of the country code):

- market identifier
- national code
- country of share registration (ISO 3166 – two-alpha character code).

Figure 11.15 provides an example of a national code.

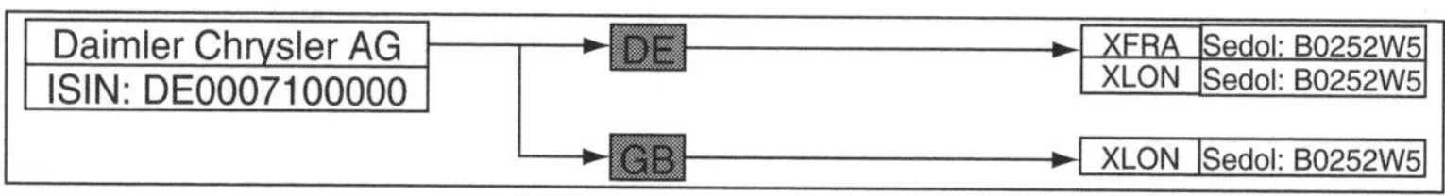

Figure 11.15 A national code example, highlighting the need for country code term

When the national or international identifiers are not known or do not exist, then the venue instrument identifier should be used:

- market identifier
- venue (or proprietary ticker) symbol.

It is important that the identification structure has the ability to support one or more security identifiers (international, national and multiple symbols), as defined in the model diagram. The *securityIdentificationScheme* is used to identify the source of the identifier (ISIN, SEDOL, RIC, etc.).

The security identification model, as defined, provides the user with the ability to support multiple identifiers (international, national and ticker symbol). The *securityIdentificationScheme* is used to identify the source of the identifier (ISIN, SEDOL, RIC, etc.).

It cannot be assumed that the reporting party always has the security identifiers available, and therefore the ability to supply the security name, short name and the language that applies should also be considered as part of the reporting message. Figure 11.16 shows an appropriate structure for supporting security names. To support this textual information (security names) there is a need to specify the associated language. ISO 639 – the two-alpha character version – would be able to meet this requirement (see Table 11.2, Figure 11.17, see page 178).

A message schema based on ISO 19312 or an alternative (as above) could easily be created; however, given that the business context of 'issuance' is supported by MDDL, it is more appropriate to use the MDDL equivalent (Figure 11.18, see page 179).

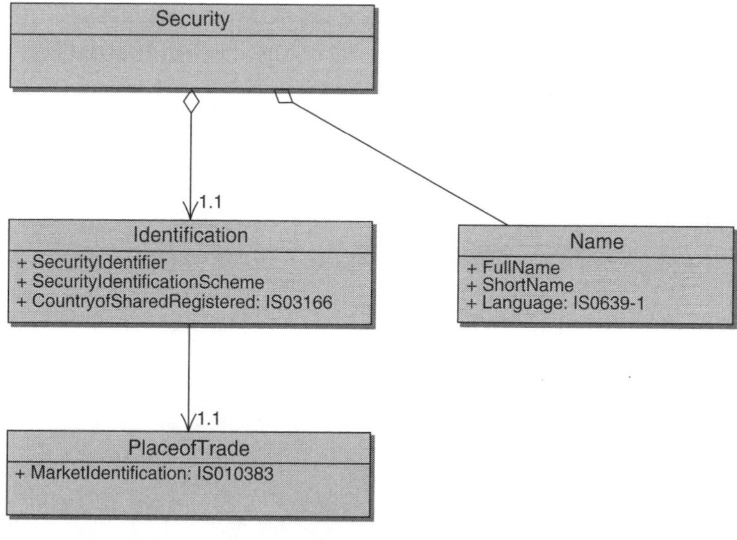

Figure 11.16 An alternative security identification structure (to MDDL)

Table 11.2 Language codes associated with EU countries

ISO code	Native language	English translation
ES	Español	Spanish
DA	Dansk	Danish
DE	Deutsch	German
EL	Elinika	Greek
EN	English	English
FR	Français	French
IT	Italiano	Italian
NL	Nederlands	Dutch
PT	Português	Portuguese
FI	Suomi	Finnish
SV	Svenska	Swedish
CS	Čeština	Czech
ET	Eesti	Estonian
LV	Latviesu valoda	Latvian

(Continued/)

Table 11.2 (/Continued)

ISO code	Native language	English translation
LT	Lietuviu kalba	Lithuanian
HU	Magyar	Hungarian
MT	Malti	Maltese
PL	Polski	Polish
SK	Slovenčina	Slovak
SL	Slovenščina	Slovene
GA	Irish	Gaeilge
BG	български език	Bulgarian
RO	română	Romanian

```
<Security>
  <!--  Security Name -->
  <Name>
    <FullName>Daimler Chrysler AG</FullName>
    <Language>EN</Language>
  </Name>
  <!-- International (Global) Identifier -->
  <Identification>
    <SecurityIdentifier>DE0007100000</SecurityIdentifier>
    <SecurityIdentificationScheme>ISIN</SecurityIdentificationScheme>
    <PlaceOfTrade>
      <MarketIdentifier>XLON</MarketIdentifier>
    </PlaceOfTrade>
  </Identification>
  <!--  National Identifier -->
  <Identification>
    <SecurityIdentifier>B0252W5</SecurityIdentifier>
    <SecurityIdentificationScheme>SEDOL</SecurityIdentificationScheme>
    <CountryOfShareRegistration>GB</CountryOfShareRegistration>
    <PlaceOfTrade>
      <MarketIdentifier>XLON</MarketIdentifier>
    </PlaceOfTrade>
    <!-- Venue Symbol -->
  </Identification>
  <Identification>
    <SecurityIdentifier>DCX</SecurityIdentifier>
    <PlaceOfTrade>
      <MarketIdentifier>XLON</MarketIdentifier>
    </PlaceOfTrade>
  </Identification>
</Security>
```

Figure 11.17 An alternative XML representation of a security

```
<snap>
  <instrumentDomain>
    <instrumentIdentifier>
      <name xml:lang="EN">Daimler Chrysler AG</name>
      <scopeType>international</scopeType>
      <code scheme="http://www.mddl.org/ext/scheme/iso6166.xml">
        <mdString>DE0007100000</mdString>
      </code>
      <code scheme="http://www.mddl.org/ext/scheme/symbol?SRC=SEDOL">
        <mdString>B0252W5</mdString>
      </code>
      <code scheme="http://www.mddl.org/ext/scheme/symbol?SRC=TIDM">
        <mdString>DCX</mdString>
      </code>
    </instrumentIdentifier>
    <trade>
      <last>
        <mdDecimal>100</mdDecimal>
        <marketCenter>
          <code scheme="http://www.mddl.org/ext/scheme/iso10383.xml">
            <mdString>XLON</mdString>
          </code>
        </marketCenter>
      </last>
    </trade>
  </instrumentDomain>
</snap>
```

Figure 11.18 MDDL security identification

ISO 20022 and MDDL

ISO 20022, or the UNIversal Financial Industry message scheme (UNFI), is a standard designed to further the development of a set of standard messages to support the needs of the financial industry. It comprises two main parts; the first is a repository of messages organized by business functions, and the second is a process by which these messages are developed for inclusion within the repository. When this process is properly followed, this top-down approach to message development allows for the creation of messages specifically to support the needs of the business. Standards in the past have been generally conceived, by making popular 'bilateral' data-feeds the industry standard.

Early versions of MDDL were loosely based on a small set of business requirements (for example, the Bond Markets Association's Issuance process); however, it became apparent that for the future adoption of the standard a more formal approach to managing requirements was important. There is nothing to stop organizations from following the ISO 20022 process for developing messages to meet their own requirements, or for doing so and then submitting them to be placed into the 20022 repository later. In 2005, London Market Systems developed a method based around the ISO 20022 for the creation of XML messages that were generated from Unified Modeling Language (UML). This technique was successfully deployed at the International Capital Market Association (ICMA) to create a new suite of messages to support the needs of TRAX (the trade matching and regulatory reporting system) and the CSDB (Central Securities DataBase).

Like ISO 20022, MDDL version 3, starts life as a UML model which is transformed into XML via some innovative scripts. So why spend the time mapping XML schemas into UML in the first place? Why not just manually edit the schema itself? Not going into technobabble to answer this question could be a little difficult; however, let's try. UML provides clear, graphical representations of message models, allowing business analysts to bind them to abstract business processes and create XML messages that meet the requirements of a business. It is also the standard notation for enterprise-wide software development, with a number of generally available tools specifically designed to enable rapid applications development.

Concepts of the ISO 20022 process

A top-down approach to the development of messages has been conceived by the process, which is fundamentally based around UML and, more specifically, a modified version of IBM's Rational Rose Data Modeler package.

The ISO 20022 process mandates the creation of models, these being:

- a business model
- a requirements model
- a logical model (of business transactions)
- a message model.

The business model itself comprises of a set of discrete Use Case diagrams that define the overall business process, the business activities covered, the roles undertaken by participants within the process and, finally, the business component(s) that define the terms required.

The aim of the requirements model is analysis to discover the communication requirements and identify the goals in the form of business transactions and message sets. It comprises of a requirements diagram, a business component diagram, defining the roles. Both the business and requirements models are part of the business process catalogue.

The logical model comprises a business transactions diagram and a set of sequence/collaboration diagrams defining the message flows between the business actors and roles (known as the business concept).

The final aspect is the creation of a message model comprising message components and elements (the message concept), combined with the data types definitions used to generate the messages schemas.

A submission for inclusion in the repository will follow this process, and once complete it will be submitted, in the form of a business justification, to the Registration Management Group (RMG). If this committee approves the submission, then the job of the Standards Evaluation Group(s) is to scrutinize the submission in detail. If approved by the SEG(s), it is then incorporated into the ISO 20022 repository.

There were a number of issues identified with the ISO 20022:2004 process, which led to the creation of ISO Working Group 4 to assess how best to improve the standard.

Chapter 12

MDDL as payload

Routing information should always be separated from content. MDDL is the payload (the variable cargo) which can be transported by a number of forms of transport mechanisms. This chapter of the book is not intended to provide an in-depth tutorial into transportation mechanisms; it is merely being included to help the user to identify the appropriate mechanism for their particular environment and need. In theory, MDDL can be transmitted over any network; however, network providers tend to want certification prior to use. For example, the Swift network could be used for more than its own suite of messages, but prior to using it certification must be obtained to ensure that the network is being used appropriately. At time of going to press, a FIX certification for the Swift network had just been established. FIX session layer can take MDDL as a payload and, similarly, MDDL could use the FIXFast protocol too; this would be achieved by writing an API for Fast to enable the dissemination of MDDL messages.

One of the most talked about mechanisms for transporting XML messages is SOAP – the Simple Object Access Protocol.

MDDL and SOAP

SOAP is used for routing messages to the appropriate systems normally using the Hypertext Transfer Protocol (HTTP) (Figure 12.1). The use of the Secure Sockets Layer (SSL) can also be used for the delivery of messages, to enhance security of the transmission.

Figure 12.1 SOAP request response message flow

A SOAP message is an XML document in its own right, and comprises a number of discrete blocks of information – a header, a body and a fault container (Figure 12.2).

```
<?xml version="1.0"?>
<soap:Envelope xmlns:soap="http://www.w3.org/2001/12/soap-envelope"
soap:encodingStyle="http://www.w3.org/2001/12/soap-encoding">
   <soap:Header>...
   </soap:Header>
   <soap:Body>...
        <soap:Fault>...</soap:Fault>
   </soap:Body>
</soap:Envelope>
```

Figure 12.2 A SOAP record showing the full set of containers

The *header* is optional, and should contain all the routing information of the message. However, if proprietary middleware is deployed – such as IBM's MQSeries – then some (if not all) of this information is likely to be replicated within the middleware's header too. In instances like this, the user should seriously consider whether the use of SOAP is suitable.

The *body* is required, and should contain either the query that the SOAP server has to execute or the response to that query. The MDDL document resides within this component.

The other SOAP container is the *fault container*; this is used to provide information about errors that occurred while processing the message.

All these containers are declared in the default namespace for the SOAP envelope (http://www.w3.org/2001/12/soap-envelope).

The default namespace for SOAP data types and encoding can be found at http://www.w3.org/2001/12/soap-encoding.

SOAP/MDDL EXAMPLE

A request is sent by the client to the server for information about a given stock. The assumption with this example is that the server application, upon receipt of the request message, simply fills in the blank terms. I am aware that this may be considered an unorthodox way of using SOAP, and the envelope would normally contain nested structures of the name 'getQuote' or 'getQuoteResponse'. The aim here is to show how to represent MDDL within a SOAP message (see Figure 12.3, overleaf).

In this instance the server populates the missing values for bid and ask, or 1.10 and 1.12 respectively (Figure 12.4, see page 187).

MESSAGE VERSIONING

At this point in the proceedings it is relevant to bring up the question of message versioning. How should this be handled? Consider the scenario where a server may be able to response with a MDDL message in either MDDL version 2.5 or MDDL version 3.0 format thus adhesing to any client's request. Adding a version number in the SOAP header structure is one way of achieving this.

Alternatively, why not use XML namespaces? They provide an ideal mechanism for identifying versions of the components within the XML document. The server can disseminate a message in both MDDL 2.5 and 3.0 formats. The client SOAP application can simply check the namespace definition in the SOAP message and accept the message structure of interest and ignore the message that is not.

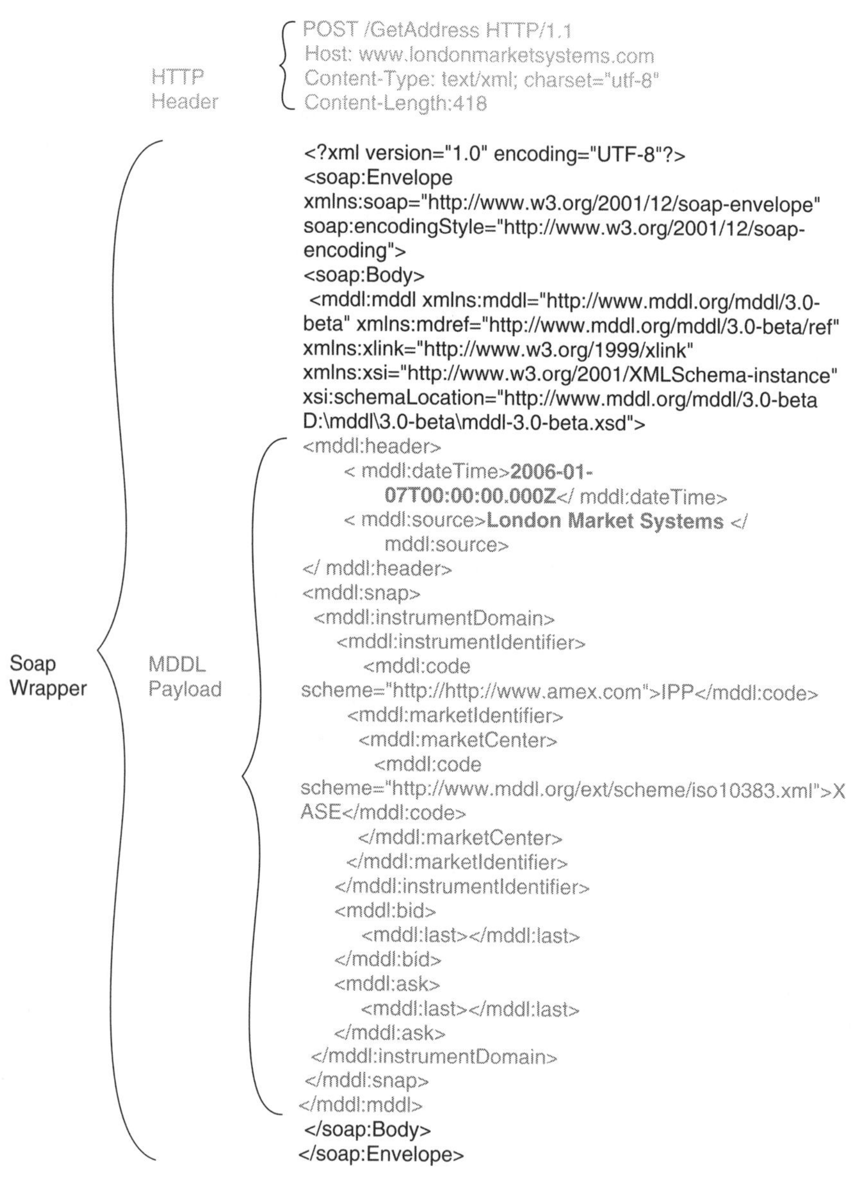
HTTP
Header
POST /GetAddress HTTP/1.1
Host: www.londonmarketsystems.com
Content-Type: text/xml; charset="utf-8"
Content-Length:418
Soap
Wrapper
MDDL
Payload
<?xml version="1.0" encoding="UTF-8"?>
<soap:Envelope
xmlns:soap="http://www.w3.org/2001/12/soap-envelope"
soap:encodingStyle="http://www.w3.org/2001/12/soap-encoding">
<soap:Body>
<mddl:mddl xmlns:mddl="http://www.mddl.org/mddl/3.0-beta" xmlns:mdref="http://www.mddl.org/mddl/3.0-beta/ref"
xmlns:xlink="http://www.w3.org/1999/xlink"
xmlns:xsi="http://www.w3.org/2001/XMLSchema-instance"
xsi:schemaLocation="http://www.mddl.org/mddl/3.0-beta
D:\mddl\3.0-beta\mddl-3.0-beta.xsd">
<mddl:header>
< mddl:dateTime>2006-01-07T00:00:00.000Z</ mddl:dateTime>
< mddl:source>London Market Systems </ mddl:source>
</ mddl:header>
<mddl:snap>
<mddl:instrumentDomain>
<mddl:instrumentIdentifier>
<mddl:code
scheme="http://http://www.amex.com">IPP</mddl:code>
<mddl:marketIdentifier>
<mddl:marketCenter>
<mddl:code
scheme="http://www.mddl.org/ext/scheme/iso10383.xml">XASE</mddl:code>
</mddl:marketCenter>
</mddl:marketIdentifier>
</mddl:instrumentIdentifier>
<mddl:bid>
<mddl:last></mddl:last>
</mddl:bid>
<mddl:ask>
<mddl:last></mddl:last>
</mddl:ask>
</mddl:instrumentDomain>
</mddl:snap>
</mddl:mddl>
</soap:Body>
</soap:Envelope>

Figure 12.3 The SOAP/MDDL request

```
<?xml version="1.0" encoding="UTF-8"?>
<soap:Envelope xmlns:soap="http://www.w3.org/2001/12/soap-envelope"
soap:encodingStyle="http://www.w3.org/2001/12/soap-encoding">
<soap:Body>
 <mddl:mddl xmlns:mddl="http://www.mddl.org/mddl/3.0-beta"
xmlns:mdref="http://www.mddl.org/mddl/3.0-beta/ref"
xmlns:xlink="http://www.w3.org/1999/xlink"
xmlns:xsi="http://www.w3.org/2001/XMLSchema-instance"
xsi:schemaLocation="http://www.mddl.org/mddl/3.0-beta D:\mddl\3.0-
beta\mddl-3.0-beta.xsd">
  <mddl:snap>
   <mddl:instrumentDomain>
      <mddl:instrumentIdentifier>
        <mddl:code scheme="http://http://www.amex.com">IPP</mddl:code>
      <mddl:marketIdentifier>
       <mddl:marketCenter>
         <mddl:code
scheme="http://www.mddl.org/ext/scheme/iso10383.xml">XASE</mddl:code>
       </mddl:marketCenter>
      </mddl:marketIdentifier>
      </mddl:instrumentIdentifier>
      <mddl:bid>
             <mddl:last>1.10</mddl:last>
      </mddl:bid>
      <mddl:ask>
             <mddl:last>1.12</mddl:last>
      </mddl:ask>
   </mddl:instrumentDomain>
  </mddl:snap>
 </mddl:mddl>
</soap:Body>
</soap:Envelope>
```

Figure 12.4 The SOAP/MDDL response

Web services wrapper

It's worth considering that a SOAP message is normally contained within a WSDL (Web Services Description Language) wrapper. This is a taxonomy that provides the applications with more control over the transmission. The information contained within specifies the location of the service and the operations (or methods), and may include the request–response mechanism (request–response, one-way and so on), as well as the port deployed.

This document is the wrapper for the SOAP message, and is used to identify the web pages displayed by web browsers, which normally use port 80. This is usually classified as the interface.

HTTP TRANSPORTATION LAYER

Hyper Text Transfer Protocol (HTTP) is a communications protocol that enables web-based applications to communicate. It is possible to bind the SOAP message either to the web service defined within the WSDL document, or to HTTP directly.

The relationship between SOAP, WSDL and HTTP is normally shown in the form of building blocks, and is known as the web services protocol stack; however, given the relationship between these components I prefer to show them as layers of an onion – and a square one at that (see Figure 12.5)!

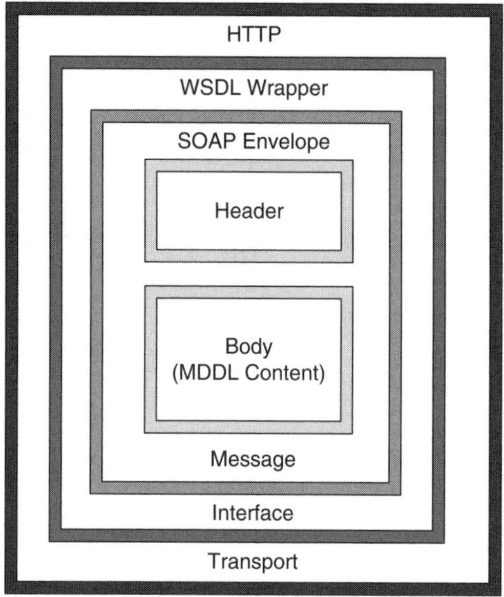

Figure 12.5 Web services protocol onion

The use of web services and SOAP could fill a couple of good books in their own right, so I am going to leave this to the experts in this field and direct the reader to 'References and futher reading' at the end of this book.

MDDL as a FIX payload

With the development of FIX version 4 came the creation of an XML variant (FIXml) of the FIX protocol. The creation of this new format required a mechanism for the encapsulation of this information within the transportation layer, known as the FIX session protocol. The method adopted was the creation of two new tags within the standard FIX message header which, when used in conjunction with the message type tag (35), could be used to ensure that the receiving FIX engine would be able to interpret the information disseminated. The two message header tags are 212, containing the length of the XML message, which is supplied in tag 213 (Figure 12.6).

```
8=FIX.4.4^9=1043^35=D^34=10^49=LMS^....
213=<FIXML xmlns="http://www.fixprotocol.org/FIXML-4-4" ... <Instrmt
Sym="IBM" ID=" US4592001014" Src="4"/>...</FIXML>
```

Figure 12.6 An example of a FIX message header

The disadvantages of using the XML transfer mechanism, where the message resides within the header, results in bypassing all the FIX session protocol behaviours and error checking. This also means that monitoring sequencing and the handshaking acknowledgement can be a bit problematic.

Of course, the real advantage of this technique is that any form of XML can be placed in tag 213, including MDDL.

In addition to populating tag 213 with the XML message, the user must set the message type, or tag 35, accordingly. With a FIXml message this would normally be set to an enumerated value to represent a specific FIX transaction, such as 'D' for an order or 'S' for a quote. In the case of an MDDL document it would be advisable to set the message type to U, which would normally be followed by a numeric value, to indicate that the message format is privately defined between the sender and receiver. Otherwise there is the risk of the receiving FIX engine attempting to validate the content assuming it's a FIXml document. It is also recommended that the MDDL document should contain the namespace definition so that the receiving application can interpret the contents correctly (Figure 12.7).

```
8=FIX.4.4^9=1043^35=D^34=10^49=LMS^....212=1025^213=<?xml
version="1.0" encoding="UTF-8" ?> <mddl
xmlns="http://www.mddl.org/mddl/2006/3.0-beta"
xmlns:ext="http://www.yourCompany.com/mddl/extensions"
xmlns:mdref="http://www.mddl.org/mddl/2006/3.0-beta/ref"
xmlns:xlink="http://www.w3.org/1999/xlink"
xmlns:xsi="http://www.w3.org/2001/XMLSchema-instance" ......
<instrumentIdentifier>
   <name>International Business Machines</name>
   <code
scheme="http://www.mddl.org/ext/scheme/iso6166.xml">US4592001014</code>
</instrumentIdentifier>
...</mddl>...
```

Figure 12.7 MDDL as FIX payload

MDDL as ebXML or OAGIS payload

> *ebXML (electronic business using eXtensible Markup Language) is a modular suite of specifications that enables enterprises of any size and in any geographical location to conduct business over the Internet. Using ebXML, companies now have a standard method to exchange business messages, conduct trading relationships, communicate data in common terms, and define and register business processes.*

(http://www.ebxml.org/geninfo.htm)

ebXML has also been registered as an ISO standard, ISO 15000, which has been broken down into modular suite of standards, these being:

- ISO 15000-1 – ebXML Collaborative Partner Profile Agreement
- ISO 15000-2 – ebXML Messaging Service Specification
- ISO 15000-3 – ebXML Registry Information Model
- ISO 15000-4 – ebXML Registry Services Specification.

OAG defines itself as follows:

> *The Open Applications Group, Inc. (OAGi) is a not-for-profit open standards group building process-based XML standards for both B2B and A2A integration. The Open Applications Group was formed in late 1994 as the first post-EDI organization focusing on improving the state of application integration.*
>
> *The OAGi's unique, technology neutral approach to building the OAGIS® standard ensures that both end-users and solution providers have the most robust XML standard in the world that can be deployed using ebXML, Web Services, or the Framework of their choice. The OAGIS® XML Standard is also completely Royalty-Free so you can be assured of easy and cost-effective use.*

(http://www.openapplications.org/global/intro.htm)

The creation of the 'OAGIS with Tibco' User Group is particularly interesting, given that one of Tibco's strengths was in the area of the timely dissemination of financial market data to trading floors via its TIB/Rendezvous product. In fact, I have fond memories of being on the management team that oversaw its roll-out to the Liffe Stock Exchange trading floor in London, supporting over 1000 positions – those were the days! This was shortly followed by the strategy change to migrate the London Financial Futures and Options market to a fully automated electronic system. That was an even more fascinating role – managing the closure of the trading floor, which indecently is now used as a common meeting area attached to an in-house coffee shop/restaurant.

Both OAGIS and ebXML can provide a useful insight into how MDDL can be applied to B2B (Business-to-Business) and A2A (Application-to-Application) message integration, especially when considering MDDL as a payload within this context.

An ebXML message is broken down into a number of key components. The header comprises definitions of an 'action' and a 'service', which refers to the message payload as well as details about the sender and the obligatory date timestamp information. This transport layer information is distinct from the payload or content itself. When put into the context of OAGIS, the ‘action’ and ‘service’ become the <VERB> and <NOUN> respectively. This information is contained within the OAGIS <CNTROLAREA> block.

Figure 12.8 shows the structure of an OAGIS document.

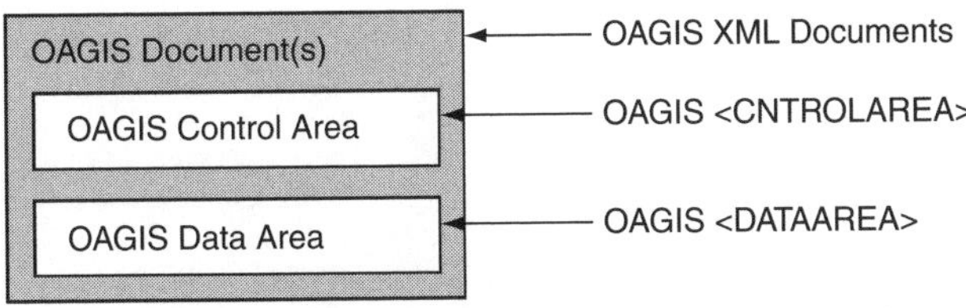

Figure 12.8 OAGIS document

Let’s assume that a business process scenario has been created to support market data. An appropriate business message, or Business Object Document (BOD) in OAGIS terminology, would be ‘SHOW LAST TRADE’.

The action or verb would be ‘SHOW’, and the service or noun would be ‘LAST-TRADE’. Sender and datetime information are also supported within ebXML and OAGIS; they have separate containers for each. There you have it! Now let’s construct the OAGIS and ebXML messages to support the MDDL payload (Figures 12.9 and 12.10, see overleaf).

```
<SHOW_LASTTRADE>
  <CNTROLAREA>
      <BSR>
            <VERB>SHOW</VERB>
            <NOUN>LASTTRADE</NOUN>
            <REVISION>001</REVISION>
      </BSR>
      <SENDER>
            <LOGICALID>12345678</LOGICALID>
            <COMPONENT>MD</COMPONENT>
            <TASK>LT</TASK>
            <REFERENCEID>100001</REFERENCEID>
            <CONFIRMATION>1</CONFIRMATION>
            <LANGUAGE>EN</LANGUAGE>
            <CODEPAGE/>
            <AUTHID>MSEXTON</AUTHID>
      </SENDER>
```

Figure 12.9 An OAGIS example with embedded MDDL document (Continued /)

```
        <DATETIME qualifier = "CREATION" >
                <YEAR>2000</YEAR>
                <MONTH>06</MONTH>
                <DAY>22</DAY>
                <HOUR>14</HOUR>
                <MINUTE>59</MINUTE>
                <SECOND>59</SECOND>
                <SUBSECOND>0000</SUBSECOND>
                /* British Summer Time */
                <TIMEZONE>-01:00</TIMEZONE>
        </DATETIME>
    </CNTROLAREA>
    <DATAAREA>
      <mddl ...>
        <mddl:header>
          <mddl:dateTime>2006-01-07T00:00:00.000Z</mddl:dateTime>
          <mddl:source>London Market Systems </mddl:source>
        </mddl:header>
        <mddl:snap>
        </mddl:snap>
      </mddl>
    </DATAAREA>
</SHOW_LASTTRADE>
```

Figure 12.9 (/Continued)

```
<MessageHeader id=... >
    <From>
        <PartyId>LMS</PartyId>
    </From>
    <To>BuySide</To>
    <ConversationId>12345678</ConversationId>
    <Service>LastTrade</Service>
    <Action>Show</Action>
    <MessageData>
        <MessageId>12345678</MessageId>
        <Timestamp>2006-01-07T00:00:00.000Z</Timestamp>
        <RefToMessageId>891012345</RefToMessageId>
    <mddl ...>
      <mddl:header>
        <mddl:dateTime>2006-01-07T00:00:00.000Z</mddl:dateTime>
        <mddl:source>London Market Systems </mddl:source>
      </mddl:header>
      <mddl:snap>
      </mddl:snap>
    </mddl>
    </MessageData>
</MessageHeader>
```

Figure 12.10 An ebXML example with embedded MDDL document

Unfortunately, some duplication of information may exist – for example, the <Timestamp> and <dateTime> in the ebXML message header and the MDDL <dateTime> elements. It can be hard to avoid if attempting to comply with multiple standards within a single message structure.

I hope this has provided you with food for thought. I've attempted to show how MDDL can be used not just within the exchange of messages using financial protocols. I believe it's important for the reader to have a more rounded picture to ensure that it is possible to make the decision regarding 'what's best for your business', rather than just following the market because 'I've heard that another company has taken the decision to go that route'.

Chapter 13

'Build-your-own' – MDDL equivalent schema

One option that a user may consider if the size and complexity of the MDDL schema is an issue and if, for instance, the user wishes to undertake run-time validation or bind with software, is to create an abridged MDDL schema to meet the requirements of a specific business function – thus allowing the user to take advantage of the use of terms and their relationship, as well as minimizing latency times that may occur if the full schema is used. It also will provide the opportunity to build validation into the new schema.

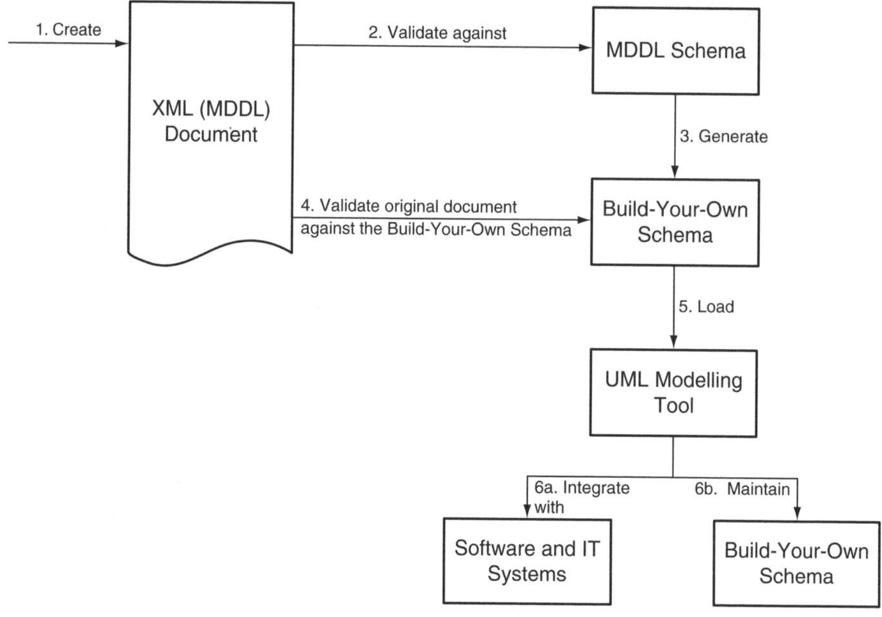

Figure 13.1 Steps required to build-your-own schema

Let us now examine an abridged schema that could be used to support the process of mark to market (MTM), which is a process used to regularly revalue holdings within a portfolio (Figure 13.1). Some organizations may wish to revalue only at the start of day based on the previous night's close, while others may wish to revalue at regular intervals. The example given does not include sender's information supplied in the header, nor date/time stamps.

To create a schema:

1. Create an instance of the MDDL document using one of the XML validation/editing tools such as XMLSpy. Always ensure that all the required definitions are populated – in the mark-to-market example, fill both the price fields – intraday day *<last>*, and *<close>* for close of business.
2. Validate the document against the schema. It's a real shame that business rules cannot be easily represented; this would make the role of the business systems analyst considerably easier! Perhaps this is something to look forward to in the near future.
3. The XML schema generation facility available in most XML Editor could be used to generate an abridged schema. The schema for representing the message requirements for a mark-to-market process would look like Figure 13.2; a visual

```
<xs:schema xmlns:xs="http://www.w3.org/2001/XMLSchema"
    elementFormDefault="qualified" attributeFormDefault="unqualified">
  <xs:element name="mddl" type="Mddl" />
  <xs:complexType name="Mddl">
    <xs:sequence>
      <xs:element name="snap" type="Snap" />
    </xs:sequence>
  </xs:complexType>
  <xs:complexType name="Snap">
    <xs:sequence maxOccurs="unbounded">
      <xs:element name="instrumentDomain" type="InstrumentDomain" />
    </xs:sequence>
  </xs:complexType>
  <xs:complexType name="InstrumentDomain">
    <xs:annotation>
      <xs:documentation>Representation of an instrument, of any
          type</xs:documentation>
    </xs:annotation>
    <xs:sequence>
      <xs:element name="instrumentIdentifier" type="InstrumentIdentifier" />
      <xs:element name="debtPricing">
        <xs:complexType>
          <xs:sequence>
            <xs:element name="mid" type="Mid" />
          </xs:sequence>
        </xs:complexType>
      </xs:element>
    </xs:sequence>
  </xs:complexType>
  <xs:complexType name="InstrumentIdentifier">
    <xs:sequence>
      <xs:element name="code" type="Code" />
      <xs:element name="name" type="xs:string" minOccurs="0" />
    </xs:sequence>
  </xs:complexType>
  <xs:complexType name="Code" mixed="true">
    <xs:sequence minOccurs="0">
      <xs:element name="mdString" type="xs:string" minOccurs="0" />
    </xs:sequence>
    <xs:attribute name="scheme" />
  </xs:complexType>
  <xs:complexType name="Mid">
    <xs:sequence minOccurs="0">
      <xs:element name="last" type="xs:decimal" />
      <xs:element name="close" type="xs:decimal" minOccurs="0" />
      <xs:element name="currency" type="xs:string" minOccurs="0" />
    </xs:sequence>
  </xs:complexType>
</xs:schema>
```

Figure 13.2 BYO schema to support mark to market (Continued/)

```
  <xs:complexType name="Mid">
    <xs:sequence minOccurs="0">
      <xs:element name="last" type="xs:decimal" />
      <xs:element name="close" type="xs:decimal" minOccurs="0" />
      <xs:element name="currency" type="xs:string" minOccurs="0" />
    </xs:sequence>
  </xs:complexType>
</xs:schema>
```

Figure 13.2 (/Continued)

representation is provided in Figure 13.3 (see page 199). However, it is cleaner to manually create the schema yourself as shown in the visual representation provided in Figure 13.3.

4. If an automated tool is used to create a schema it is also recommended that a manual sanity-check the schema is made to ensure it meets your expectations. For example, some generators may miss out the attribute that makes the *<close>* and *<currency>* definitions optional within the *mid* container. This can easily be rectified by added ' *minOccurs='0'* to each definition.
5. Assign the new schema to the instance document and revalidate.
6. Give the abridged schema to the development team to tweak so that it can be deployed. This may involve loading it into modelling tools such as C24 IO and Enterprise Architect. Once loaded into such tools, the schema can then be maintained centrally, simplifying the integration process with software applications.

Figure 13.4 (see page 200) shows the UML representation of the BYO schema to support mark to market.

Now let's examine a mark-to-market example that shows how to represent a couple of intraday Sovereign debt prices (Figure 13.5, see page 201).

The close of business pricing would be a similar document to the one above, but the *<last>* definition would be replaced by *<close>*.

It is worth appreciating that a good policy to adopt when more than one instrument is represented within an MDDL document, is to limit each domain to a single instrument. This will avoid potential confusion by the receiving applications. This situation is possible when a domain has subcategories of properties and these are grouped by class and/or subclasses.

Figures 13.6 (see page 201) and 13.7 (see page 202) both show valid MDDL, but only the latter is *good* MDDL.

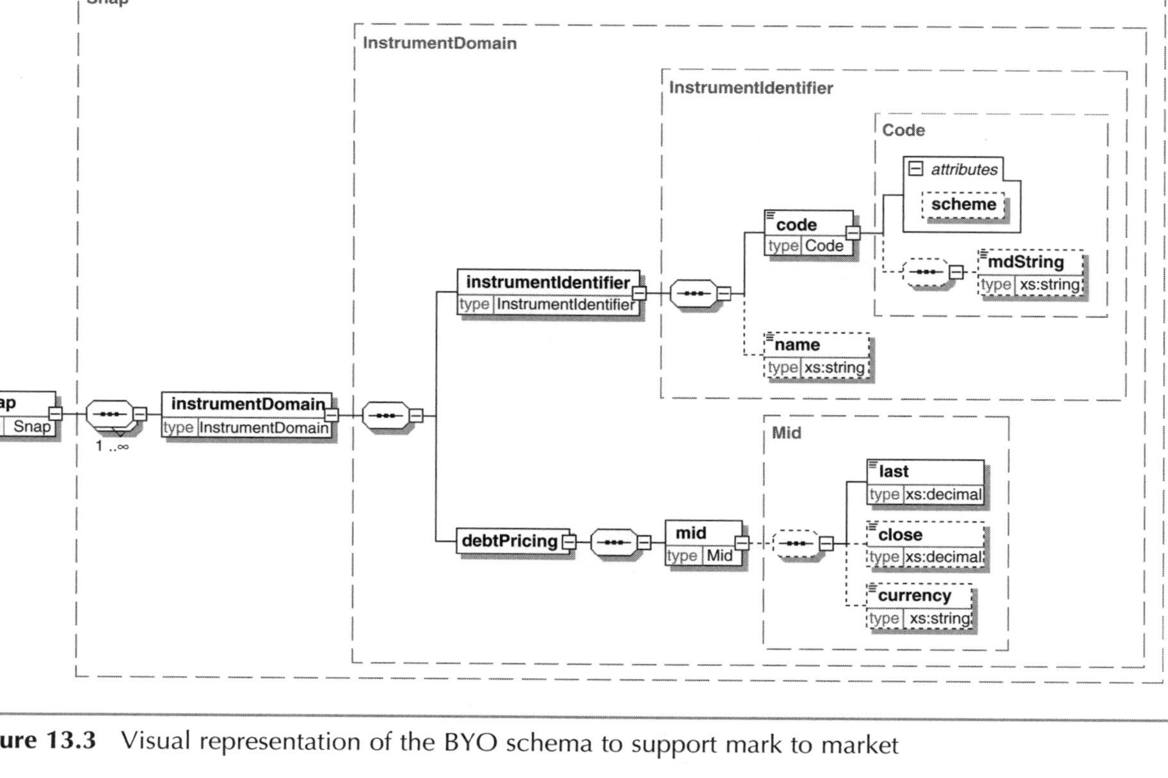

Figure 13.3 Visual representation of the BYO schema to support mark to market

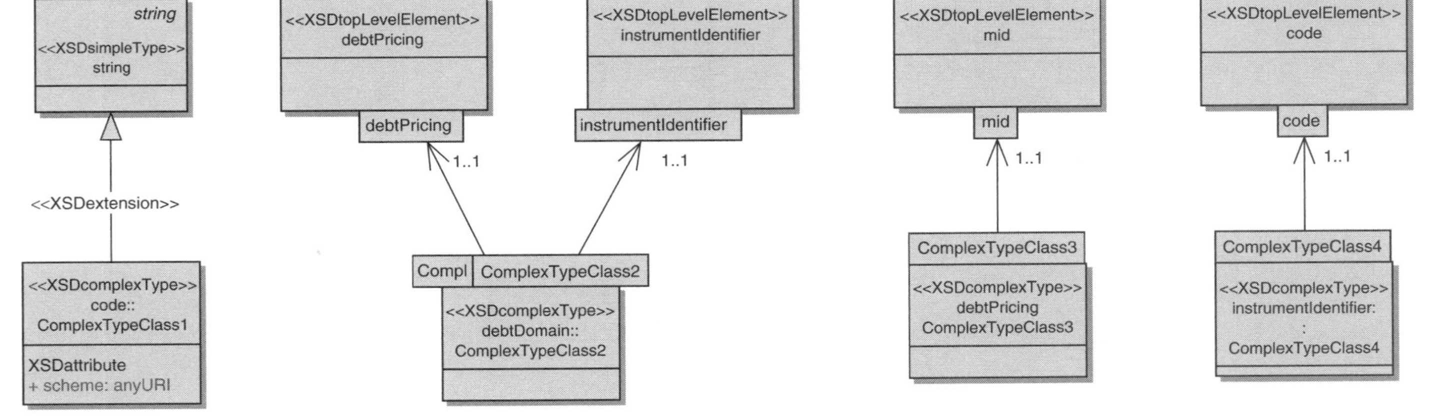

Figure 13.4 UML representation of the BYO schema to support mark to market

```
<snap>
  <instrumentDomain>
    <instrumentIdentifier>
      <name>US Treasury Bond 4.75% Mar
          2011</name>
      <code
          scheme="http://www.mddl.org/ext/scheme/SY
          MBOL?SRC=CUSIP"">912828FQ8</code>
    </instrumentIdentifier>
    <debtPricing>
      <mid>
        <last>98.50</last>
        <currency>USD</currency>
      </mid>
    </debtPricing>
  </debtDomain>
  <debtDomain>
    instrumentIdentifier>
      <name>UK Treasury 6.25% Nov 2010</name>
      <code
          scheme="http://www.mddl.org/ext/scheme/sy
          mbol?SRC=SEDOL"">0889016</ code>
    </instrumentIdentifier>
    <debtPricing>
      <mid>
        <last>195.59</last>
        <currency>GBX</currency>
      </mid>
    </debtPricing>
  </instrumentDomain>
</snap>
```

Figure 13.5 Mark-to-market intraday MDDL example

```
<snap>
  <entityDomain>
      <issuerClass>
        ... Content 1...
      </issuerClass>

      <businessClass>
        ...Content 2...
      </businessClass>
  </entityDomain>
</snap>
```

Figure 13.6 Valid MDDL, NOT good MDDL

```
<snap>
  <entityDomain>
        <issuerClass>
          ... Content 1...
        </issuerClass>
  </entityDomain>

  <entityDomain>
        <businessClass>
          ... Content 2...
        </businessClass>
  </entityDomain>
</snap>
```

Figure 13.7 Valid MDDL, good MDDL

Chapter 14

UML to XML schema generation

One of the recent developments in the financial industry is the transformation of UML (Unified Modeling Language) objects into XML. This is mainly as a result of the success of ISO 20022 (the UNIversal Financial Industry message scheme, or UNIFI), which is a standard that defines a process based on UML. It is a standard that models financial business processes, and the final output of this method is the creation of a suite of messages to support these functions.

The first time I came across this concept was when reading the book *Modeling XML Applications with UML*, by David Carlson; however, it wasn't until I read the

ISO standard and had the privilege of working with Anthony B. Coates and Michael Bennett that I was able to appreciate its significance. Thanks to Tony's efforts, MDDL is now maintained from a UML model.

Unlike using schema-generation facilities in products like Enterprise Architect, the MDDL and ISO 20022:2004 are based on using the XML Metadata Interchange (XMI) output. This is used as input into a process that finally results in the creation of message schemas. XMI was developed for exchanging models between modelling tools. In it's raw form XMI is a valid XML document; however, such output cannot be used for sourcing an XML schema without a little manipulation. Given its structure, the XMI output will require at least a couple of passes to obtain the desired result – an XML schema.

Creating schemas from UML models is not an exact science; however, ISO 20022 is a step in the right direction. Part 4: ISO 20022 XML Design Rules defines the mechanism for achieving this goal of transforming a model into XML schemas, thus allowing the user to take advantage of inherence, cardinality and hierarchical relationships, to define enumerated lists, constraints and validation, and transform UML attributes into XML element and or XML attributes. I am aware that this sounds like a cop-out, but the transformation process is a book in its own right. It is important to be aware of its potential significance and the benefits it may bring to any organization which wants to have better data management – especially given the ever-increasing burden of regulatory controls.

Chapter 15

Undertaking a mapping exercise?

The task of mapping data dictionaries, repositories and feeds onto any standard is, on the whole, considered to be a rather complex task. Given that MDDL was not designed around an existing feed that has developed over a number of years, like ISO 15022 or FIX, the impression is that it is a rather onerous task. Quotations from users include 'According to my analysis, I believe there are about 80% of the terms are missing', and another confided that 'I spent a few days attempting to map a Fixed Income product onto MDDL and found it too complex'.

The limited documentation, lack of training seminars and supporting material has not made the task of mapping any easier for users. London Market Systems (LMS), on its website, has provided some 'real-life' examples of how to use MDDL, supported by covering documentation that explains the context of their use. An example of this can be found in the White Paper on UK Treasury (Gilts) Issuance Process. There are also a couple of MDDL visual models available to assist developers in its deployment – there is one on the MDDL website, as well as an alternative model, that can be found on the front page of the LMS website. Users may find these extremely useful, as they clearly show the relationship of terms both hierarchically and via an alphabetical list of terms. Users may also wish to use the 'Find' facility (entering <Ctrl>F) available on web browsers to locate the appropriate term (Figure 15.1).

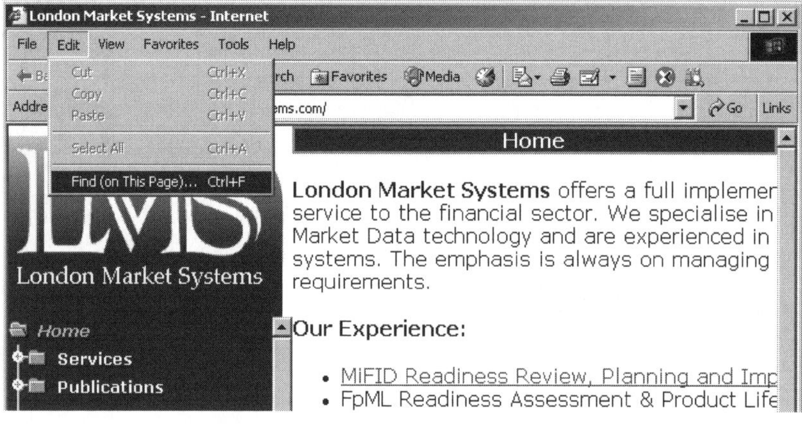

Figure 15.1 The Browser Find facility

London Market Systems has played an active role in supporting MDDL over the years, and was hired a few years ago by the FISD, owners of the standard, to undertake the requirements gathering exercise for the terms needed to support the Bond Market Association's (BMA) issuance portal. More recently, LMS was employed to define the framework of the MDDL Documentation Suite. It is hoped the Documentation Suite, alongside this manuscript, will meet the needs of the market and allow the standard to achieve the recognition it deserves.

When considering how to use MDDL, it is always important to remember the business context. In the early days, the lack of requirements, business process and activities models made the mapping exercise a little tricky, requiring users to undertake the exercise based on their own experience and not on the collective knowledge of others in the industry.

Based on personal experience, it appears that the number of unsupported terms tends to be far less than first assessed by customers. The example of 80 per cent missing terms identified earlier by a client was in fact nearer 2 per cent. If there is one piece of advice I would give to minimize effort, it is always to consider the business context and understand the business terms used prior to undertaking the task.

I am aware that a number of potential users, prior to the creation of the MDDL Documentation Suite in 2007, may be put off by simply undertaking a basic search and not finding an important term of interest. One example of this could be someone interested in representing fixed income products. A term to support the coupon (the annualized return on the principle amount) of an instrument would be of great significance to such a user. A search of MDDL terms for 'coupon' would return no items, and without adequate documentation to allow identification of the appropriate MDDL term (which is interestRate, by the way), a number of users might decide immediately that the standard does not support these products. It is easy to imagine a number of them going back to their manager and saying that MDDL doesn't meet the company's requirements – thus cutting short any gap analysis assignment planned.

There are many examples where the meaning of the terms can be confusing, and I have come across the occasional misunderstanding of such terms by organizations. I have read product terms sheets where *launch date* is, upon examination, in effect the *announcement date*. This in itself may not cause much grief; however, consider the situation where a maturity date in a prospectus meant the settlement date! The date actually referred to the date at which the investor was to receive the *redemption value* of the instrument purchased (the interest plus the principle). 'So what?', I hear you ask. Say that to a compliance officer and you are likely to hear the words 'You're fired!' Such a mistake could result in the company P&L and cash positions reports not reconciling between the trading desks and the general ledger. An audit would find that the organization did not have adequate control of its finance and had failed its regulatory obligations. The company would have lost its 'low risk' status and been fined too. I realize that I just put my Donald Trump hat on; however, it is worth remembering that inconsistent reference data can have costly implications for the business.

Data mapping process

To avoid some of the shortfalls in data mapping, the following process has been defined. In some situations, such as when employing an external consultant, it may be appropriate to go straight to step 5.

- *Step 1*: Define the business justification to ensure that there is a clear business case for the exercise.
- *Step 2*: Obtain the buy-in by the business. Do you have all stakeholders on board before undertaking the exercise, and are they aware of the benefits to the business? Without commitment from the management, business users and technicians, it will be difficult to undertake the analysis properly. Remember that one area of the business may use different terminology from another, and of course the experience of the people working in that area will be limited to a single business context, so it will be difficult for them to appreciate an alternative view. For example, the price an instrument was traded at will be seen differently by the Front Office desk and by the settlements department; the former may not consider it appropriate to add the cost of matching, clearing and settlement to a transaction, whilst the latter will.
- *Step 3*: Undertake the requirements gathering and business process analysis: Obtain a clear definition of the processes that is to be accessed and gather as much material as possible, such as sample messages and data formats – this is where it's important to use the stakeholder contacts, as a lot of the knowledge and understanding of the procedures will not be documented but stored away in individual's heads. Therefore, the use of workshops and personal interviews with key stakeholders should be considered. This will also apply to identifying the future requirements, although this will not be required at this stage. This should be documented, as is, or any existing documentation updated. This could take the form of an assessment report or time/resource permitting the creation of a UML model.
- *Step 4*: Model the requirements: document the communication requirements, identify the goals in the form of the business transactions and message sets, define the message flows between the various roles and the terminology used by business functions involved.
- *Step 5*: Armed with a clear definition of terminology (the models from previous steps), the inputs and outputs from the business functions (announcements, prospectus, reports, etc.) and sample data, it should be possible to initiate the mapping of terms onto MDDL.

Data mapping pointers

Here are some pointers to make the data mapping exercise go a little more smoothly.

1. If mapping an instrument onto MDDL, identify the appropriate domain, class and subclass. Remember that if a class or subclass exists, all properties should reside within the lowest of these containers. With version 3 of the standard, all

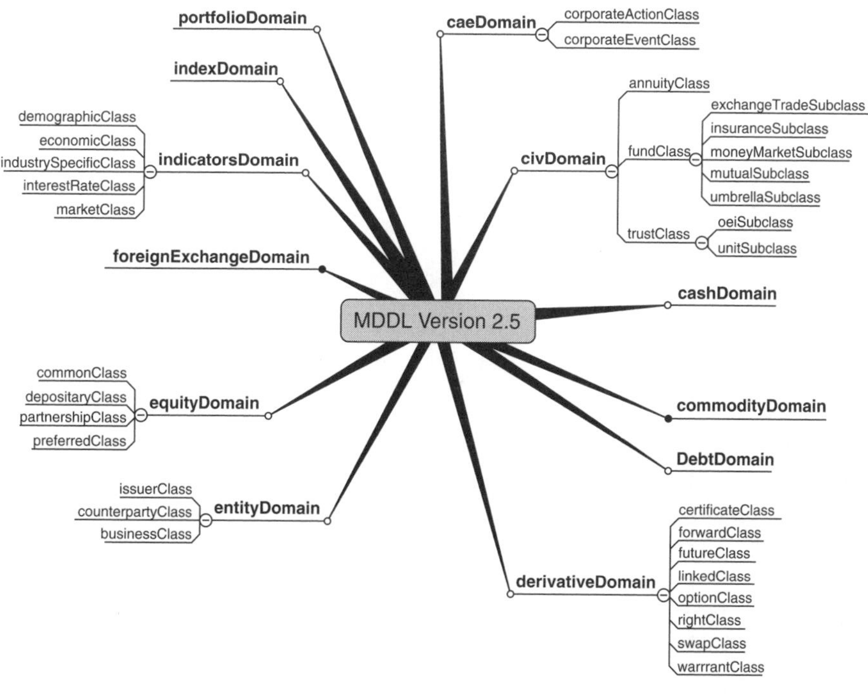

Figure 15.2 MDDL version 2.5 domain, class and subclass relationship

instrument terms are specified within the instrumentDomain and therefore this issue does not need to be considered. Figure 15.2 shows the top-level hierarchical relationship (domain/class and subclass) in the form of mind map; without such a diagram it may not be easy to identify the appropriate domain to use.

2. Where possible, use the capabilities of inheritance. Defining the elements such as currency at a high level within the document hierarchy reduces the need to repeat it every time it is associated with another property. Examine the opportunities to remove redundant containers where there is only a single 'child'. Similarly, it may be worth considering using the 'empty tag' technique; this is where the tag pair is replaced by a modified closing tag. In such a scenario, the forward slash within the closing tag itself becomes a suffix rather than a prefix when used as part of a tag pair. An example of this is *<trade/>*.

3. The next tip for undertaking a mapping exercise is to create a terms mapping matrix (see Table 15.1, overleaf). The minimum columns required are the data 'original' field, MDDL snippet, contents description, transformation considerations, plus a comments heading to add other information. It may also be useful to have a mapping reference to an MDDL sample to highlight the relationship of terms (see Table 15.2 on page 212).

Table 15.1 Terms mapping matrix

Mapping ref.	Field	MDDL snippet	Content	Comments
1.01	Instrument type	Domain and class (e.g.<equityDomain> <commonClass>) or domain alone (e.g.<debtDomain>)	The attributes associated with a common share are contained with the equity Domain/ common Class hierarchical structure	These are MDDL elements which must be generated, inside which the other elements sit; they will differ for different asset classes
1.02	Instrument name	<instrumentIdentifier> <name>x</name>	x = Instrument name contents	
1.03	Local market code	<code scheme="http://www.mddl.org/ext/scheme/?SRC=NYSE">x </code>	x = Local market code contents	
1.04	Open and time of first trade	<open> <mdDecimal>x </mdDecimal> <openType>firstTrade </openType> <dateTime>y </dateTime> </open>	x = Open y = Time	Transformation: prefix Time with 'T' and format output to hh:mm:ss

1.05	Close and time of last trade	<close> <mdDecimal>x </mdDecimal> <closeType> exchange </closeType> <dateTime>y </dateTime> </close>	x = Close x = Time	Transformation: prefix Time with 'T' and format output to hh:mm:ss
1.06	Low	<low> <mdDecimal>x </mdDecimal> </low>	x = Low	
1.07	High	<high> <mdDecimal>x </mdDecimal> </high>	x = High	
1.08	Change	<change> <mdDecimal>0.39 </mdDecimal> <valuationType> percentage </valuationType> </change>	x = Change	
1.09	Volume	<volume> <mdDecimal> 23799100 </mdDecimal> <volumeType>total </volumeType> </volume>	x = Volume	Transformation: removal of comma, spaces

Table 15.2 MDDL sample for cross-referencing into the terms mapping matrix

Mapping ref.	XML Document section
	<?xml version='1.0' ?> <mddl .... <header> <dateTime>2006-05-05</dateTime> <source> Martin Sexton (London Market Systems Limited) </source> </header> <snap>
1.01	<!- Equity Sample End of Day Snapshot for a single Instrument -> <equityDomain><commonClass>
1.02	<instrumentIdentifier> <name> Lucent Technologies Inc. </name>
1.03	<code scheme="http://www.mddl.org/ext/scheme/?SRC=NYSE"> LU.NYS </code> < /instrumentIdentifier>
1.04	<trade> <open> <mdDecimal>2.57</mdDecimal> <openType>firstTrade</openType> <dateTime>T09:01.00</dateTime> </open>
1.05	<close> <mdDecimal>2.58</mdDecimal> <closeType>exchange</closeType> <dateTime>T16:16:00</dateTime> </close>
1.06	<low> <mdDecimal>2.56</mdDecimal> </low>

Table 15.2

Mapping ref.	XML Document section
1.07	<high> <mdDecimal>2.61</mdDecimal> </high>
1.08	<change> <mdDecimal>0.39</mdDecimal> ....<valuationType>percentage</valuationType> </change>
1.09	<volume> <mdDecimal>23799100</mdDecimal> <volumeType>total</volumeType> </volume> </trade> </commonClass></equityDomain> </snap> </mddl>

Chapter 16

Compression

There is always a concern regarding the bandwidth usage of XML messages when compared with the binary or CSV (Comma Separated Values) equivalent formats. In high throughput scenarios, like streaming prices, 'static' data downloads or end-of-day valuations, compression may need to be considered necessity or even essential.

Firms may wish to develop their own schema-aware compression and stream-query interface based on zlib, XMill or gzip; the latter being supported over HTTP 1.1. A lot of interest has been shown in two compression specifications in particular. These are the xtcMessage (also known as the fisdMessage compaction library) and the FIX

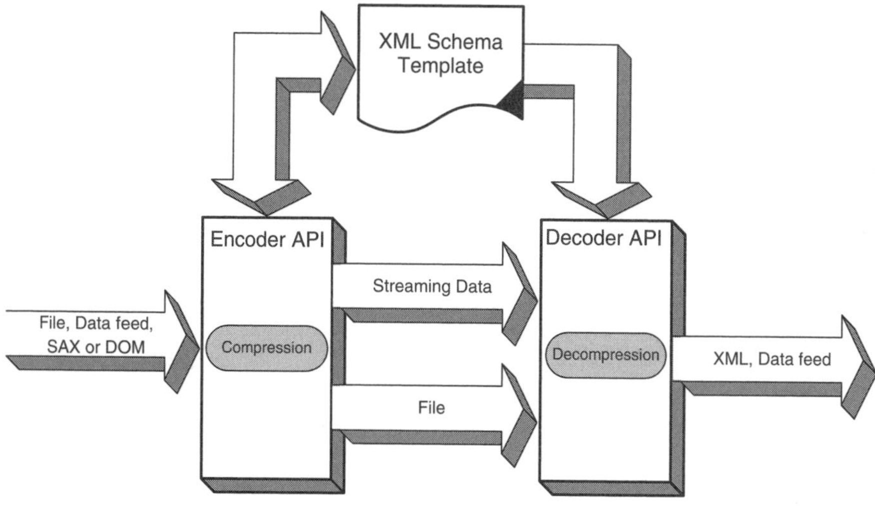

Figure 16.1 Template-based compression flow

Adapted for STreaming (FAST) Protocol℠ being developed by the FISD/SIIA and the FIX Protocol respectively. Both are what's known as template-based – that is, the template is either sent before transmission, or the template or structure is agreed between the parties (sender and receivers) prior to the transmission of the data (Figure 16.1). In addition to these two licence-free options there are many proprietary-based solutions available which, on the whole, provide better performance. One product that I have assessed is Expway's BinXML™, based on MPEG-7 (Moving Picture Experts Group-7) – a standard for describing the multi-media content data that supports streaming XML. Good latency times and results 180 times smaller than the original XML document, means that this is worth a mention.

xtcMessage (fisdMessage)

The xtcMessage specification (formerly known as fisdMessage), designed for the exchange of XML-structured content by James Hartley of MDDL fame, has not been developed with MDDL particularly in mind; however, the verbosity concerns regarding the standard was one driver behind its inception. It can be used to disseminate any XML specification, including FIXml, FpML, XBRL, to name just a few.

The protocol uses a template to define the content of the message, which is assumed to be a static structure. This means that a separate template will be required for each asset class – for example, an equity product will require different terms from a fixed income instrument. This forces the user to take a more structured approach to interface design and avoid having multiple asset classes within a single XML document. This is a particular consideration with bulk transfers such as end-of-day time and sales, valuations and reconciliations.

The default compression method for xtcMessage is zlib; however, the protocol has been designed to support others. Similarly, the user can also specify the encryption method.

For further information about xtcMessage, please refer to the MDDL website (http://www.mddl.org/fisdMessage/1.0-beta/).

FAST^{SM}

FIX Adapted for STreaming protocol^{SM} (FAST) has been developed by the FPL Market Data Optimization Working Group. Like xtcMessage, it uses templates to define the format of the message contents; however, it doesn't make use of existing compression methods (gzip, zlib and so on). It concentrates on converting string values into their binary equivalent, and with the appropriate template only sending information within a record that has changed (this is known as the delta) this has resulted in reduced latency times and has had positive feedback from the Chicago Mercantile Exchange (CME), International Securities Exchange (ISE) and the London Stock Exchange (LSE).

The FAST templates themselves are in XML (see Figure 16.2), based on the compact syntax of the RELAX NG schema language (RNC), but the specification has been designed primarily with FIX in mind and its tag-based massages rather than for XML message interchange.

There are a couple of points that should be highlighted. First, any XML message transport would require the schema validation to be undertaken outside of the API.

```
<templates xmlns="http://www.fixprotocol.org/ns/template-
definition"
    templateNs="http://www.fixprotocol.org/ns/templates/sample"
    ns="http://www.fixprotocol.org/ns/fix">
  <template name="MDRefreshSample">
   <typeRef name="MarketDataIncrementalRefresh"/>
   <string name="BeginString" id="8"> <constant
value="FIX4.4"/> </string>
   <string name="MessageType" id="35"> <constant
value="X"/> </string>
   <string name="SenderCompID" id="49"> <copy/> </string>
```

Figure 16.2 Fast template fragment (extract taken from FAST Specification Version 1.x.05 dated 11 July 2006) (Continued/)

```
    <uInt32 name="MsgSeqNum"
id="34"> <increment/> </uInt32>
    <sequence name="MDEntries">
      <length name="NoMDEntries" id="268"/>
      <uInt32 name="MDUpdateAction"
id="279"> <copy/> </uInt32>
      <string name="MDEntryType" id="269"> <copy/> </string>
      <string name="Symbol" id="55"> <copy/> </string>
      <string name="SecurityType" id="167"> <copy/> </string>
      <decimal name="MDEntryPx" id="270"> <delta/> </decimal>
      <decimal name="MDEntrySize"
id="271"> <delta/> </decimal>
      <uInt32 name="NumberOfOrders"
id="346"> <delta/> </uInt32>
      <string name="QuoteCondition" id="276"> <copy/> </string>
      <string name="TradeCondition" id="277"> <copy/> </string>
    </sequence>
  </template>
</templates>
```

Figure 16.2 (/Continued)

Moreover, there is the question of encryption, which may be important if the FIX session layer is not used or the participants are not part of a closed user group.

For further information about the FAST specification, refer to the FIX Protocol website (http://www.fixprotocol.org/working_groups/mdoptwg).

It is perfectly feasible to design the templates and develop the API to support MDDL or to manage the transformation to/from FIX and MDDL for market data messages.

Chapter 17

A final tribute to Jonathan Castaing

I thought it would be a nice touch to finish the book with an acknowledgement to Jonathan Castaing, and how better than taking the *The Course of the Exchange, and Other Things*, published in 1698, and examining how this would be represented in MDDL.

The example supplied in Figure 17.1 (overleaf) shows the equity stock 'Bank Stock', which is in the middle of the price list. Amazingly, bid and ask prices were being quoted on Saturday 1 January (would you get anyone working in London on New Year's Day today?). Similarly, two prices are quoted for Monday 3 January;

```
<header>
    <dateTime>2006-09-29</dateTime>
    <source>The Course of the Exchange, and other things by
        Jonathan Castaing, Broker, at his Office at Jonathans
        Coffee-house.</source>
</header>
<timeseries>
    <timeseriesType>eodHistory</timeseriesType>
    <event>
      <dateTime>1698-01-01</dateTime>
      <snap>
        <instrumentDomain>
            <instrumentIdentifier>
                <name>Bank Stock</name>
            </instrumentIdentifier>
            <bid>
                <close>85.5</close>
            </bid>
            <ask>
                <close>85.75</close>
            </ask>
        </instrumentDomain>
      </snap>
    </event>
    <event>
      <dateTime>1698-01-03</dateTime>
      <snap>
        <instrumentDomain>
            <instrumentIdentifier>
                <name>Bank Stock</name>
            </instrumentIdentifier>
            <bid>
                <close>85.5</close>
            </bid>
            <ask>
                <close>85.75</close>
            </ask>
        </instrumentDomain>
      </snap>
    </event>
    <event>
      <dateTime>1698-01-04</dateTime>
```


Figure 17.1 A snippet of Jonathan Castaing's *The Course of the Exchange, and Other Things* (published 1698), in MDDL

```
      <snap>
        <instrumentDomain>
            <instrumentIdentifier>
              <name>Bank Stock</name>
            </instrumentIdentifier>
            <bid>
              <close>85.75</close>
            </bid>
        </instrumentDomain>
      </snap>
    </event>
  </timeseries>
```


Figure 17.1 (Continued/)

however, on Tuesday 4 January there is only one price quoted. We can assume that this is the bid price.

So, if we are dealing with three days of closing prices, what would be the appropriate MDDL structure to use? If you answered '*timeseries*', give yourself an Amaretti biscuit.

It's a shame that Change Alley and, more importantly, Jonathan's Coffee House no longer exist, it would have been nice to be able to feel the ambience and smell the coffee dunk your biscuit. Oh, to be a Time Lord and travel back in time and read/feel the price list as it came hot off the press on that first day of publication!

I hope that I have shown that using MDDL and XML is not rocket science and that when the angle brackets are stripped away we are dealing with financial information in a human-readable form. In addition, it was my intention to convey my experience and knowledge of market data such as to inspire one to simplify the business operations of your organization.

Appendices

Appendix A: Glossary and acronyms

A large part of this glossary is reproduced, with kind permission, from *The Handbook of World Stock, Derivative and Commodity Exchanges*.

A la criée
See Auction market

Abandonment
Allowing an option to expire unexercised. Also, withdrawal from a cancellable forward contract to purchase securities.

Accrued interest
The amount of interest accumulated between the most recent payment and the sale of a fixed-interest security. For most bonds, accrued interest must be added to the purchase price, but that amount will be recovered by the purchaser in the next interest payment.

Action
French for share.

Action de jouissance
Share which grants the right to participate in the net profit of the company without conferring ownership rights. French/Belgian term.

Action ordinaire
French for ordinary share.

Action privilégiée
French for preference share.

Active fund
A fund in which the fund manager actively manages investments.

Active management
Fund managers who strive to outperform the market by identifying stocks that could produce better returns and beat the overall market (or target index).

Actuals
The physical or cash commodity, as distinguished from futures contracts.

After-hours dealing
On the London Stock Exchange, dealings done after the MQP. Such dealings are treated as dealings done on the following business day. In general, trading after the stock market has

closed. (For all major US stock markets, after-hours trading is 16:00–18:30 Eastern Standard Time). After-hours trading often takes place after the release of news after the close of trading that could make the price of a stock rise or fall sharply. Participation in the after-hours market is strictly voluntary, and may offer less liquidity and inferior prices.

After market
See Secondary market.

Agency cross
A trade in which a single broker acts as the agent for both the buyer and seller. This can occur when a member firm simultaneously receives a buy and a sell order from two different customers, but for the same number of shares in the same stock. When these orders reach the floor broker, he can easily cross them and complete the transaction, but only after going to the designated trading post for that stock and announcing the bid in case another broker is prepared to offer a better price.

Agency order
An order that a broker/dealer executes for the account of a customer with another professional or retail investor and for which a commission is typically charged.

Aktie
German for share.

Algorithmic trading
Trading in which buy or sell orders of a defined quantity are determined by a quantitative model that automatically generates the timing of orders and the size of orders based on goals specified by the parameters and constraints of the algorithm.

All or none (AON)
A condition that the full amount of an order to buy or sell is executed at an agreed price; a lesser amount is unacceptable.

Allotment letter
See Renouncable documents.

Alternative Trading System (ATS)
Non-traditional, computerized trading systems that compete with or supplement dealer markets and traditional exchanges. These private trading systems facilitate electronic trading in millions of shares of public issues every day, but do not provide a listing service. ECNs are alternative trading systems; however, not all ATSs are ECNs. (See Electronic communications network.)

American Depository Receipt (ADR)
A receipt or certificate issued by a US bank that represents a specific number of shares of foreign-based corporations held by a US banking institution in the country of origin on behalf of an investor in the US.

American option
An option which may be exercised at any time prior to expiration.

Amtlicher Handel
The official trade section of German stock exchanges.

Arbitrage
The simultaneous purchase on one exchange and sale on another of the same or equivalent financial instruments in order to benefit from price or currency differentials.

Arbitrageurs
Those looking for arbitrage opportunities.

Asian option
Asian options are based on an average price of a commodity over a period of time, rather than on a single price taken at the end of a period. Asian options are currently available only OTC.

Ask price
The price at which a seller has offered to sell a security or commodity.

Association Française des Sociétés de Bourse
A professional association which advises members of the French stock exchanges and represents them to outside bodies.

At best order
An order submitted to the order book with a specified size which may execute, either in part or in its entirety, against eligible orders at the price of those orders with any unexecuted portion being rejected from the book.

At-the-market
See Market order.

At-the-money
An option whose strike/exercise price is equal to or near the current price of the underlying instrument.

Attributes
An XML attribute is a parameter used within an XML element start tag that provides meaning to the contents of the XML element. XML attributes are not used widely within MDDL. One example is defining the scheme that applies to an instrument code (ISIN or ISO6166): <instrumentIdentifier><codescheme="http://www.mddl.org/ext/scheme/iso6166"> FR0000133308 </code></instrumentIdentifier>

Auction market
A system in which financial instruments are bought and sold through trading on an exchange floor by buyers and sellers competing via open-outcry with other buyers and sellers for the best price.

Authorized share capital
The maximum number of shares that a company can issue, as specified in the firm's articles of incorporation.

Automatic execution
An automatic trade executed by the trading system. Automatic trades are executed by matching buy and sell orders.

Avoir fiscal
A tax credit (on dividends) payable to French holders of French securities. In most cases, foreign holders are granted the *avoir fiscal* in accordance with tax agreements between France and their own country.

Azione
Italian for share.

Azione ordinaria
Ordinary share on Italian stock exchanges.

Azione privilegiata
Preference share on Italian stock exchanges.

Azione risparmio
Savings share on Italian stock exchanges normally issued in bearer form and enjoying privileged rights on the distribution of profits. Holders of these shares have no right to vote in shareholder meetings.

Backwardation
On futures markets, a market where a commodity is in shortage, causing near-contract months to sell at a premium and distant-contract months to sell at discount.

Balloon maturity
The last bonds of an issue maturing in a substantially larger amount than those of earlier maturities.

Bandhani
An Indian form of trading in which the contract price is not allowed to go beyond floor and ceiling prices, set on the first day, throughout the life of the contract, thus restricting excessive volatility.

Bank Interchange Code (BIC)
A unique code identifying a market participant.

Bargain
A transaction dealt through the London Stock Exchange which is a contract to buy or sell an agreed quantity of stock at an agreed price.

Basis
The difference between the cash price and the futures price.

Basis grade
The grade of a commodity used as the standard of the futures contract.

Basis point (bp)
1% of 1%.

Basis price
The price expressed in terms of yield to maturity or annual rate of return.

Basket
The purchase or sale of equity securities, which comprise a pre-defined group of securities.

Bear
An investor who believes that prices are going to fall.

Bear market
A prolonged period of generally falling prices.

Bearer security
A security whose owner is not registered on the books of the issuer.

Bed-and-breakfast deal
Selling shares one day and buying them back the next, done for tax purposes at the end of the financial year.

Benchmark
A standard used for comparison.

Beneficial owner
The true owner of a security. The registered holder of the shares may act as a nominee to the true shareholder.

Best ask
The lowest quoted offer of all competing market-makers to sell a particular stock at any given time.

Best bid
The highest quoted bid of all competing market-makers to buy a particular stock at any given time.

Best execution
The obligation of market-makers, broker/dealers and others to execute customer orders at the best price available at the time the trade is entered.

Beta
A measurement of the relationship between the risk of an individual stock or stock portfolio and the risk of the overall market. The beta is a measure of the sensitivity of an investment's return to market movements. A diversified portfolio of high beta stocks is more risky than a diversified portfolio of low beta stocks.

Bid price
The price at which a buyer has offered to purchase a security or commodity.

Bid/ask spread

The difference between the price at which a market-maker is willing to buy a security (bid), and the price at which the firm is willing to sell it (ask). The spread narrows or widens according to the supply and demand for the security being traded.

Bid/offer spread

The difference between the bid and offer prices of a security.

Big Board

A popular term for the New York Stock Exchange.

Big figure

A market expression for the part of the price which is the least significant in terms of quotation movement.

Black Box Trading

A proprietary computerized trading system whose formulas and calculations are not disclosed or readily accessible. Users enter information and the system utilizes pre-programmed logic to return output to the user, which may include trading signals and other data.

Black–Scholes model

An option pricing formula initially derived by Fisher Black and Myron Scholes for securities options, and later refined by Black for options on futures.

Block

A large amount of shares, normally 10 000 or more.

Block trade

The purchase or sale of stock in a large quantity, normally 10 000 shares or more.

Block volume

The aggregate volume of trades of 10 000 shares or more.

Blue chips

Shares with the highest status and quality as investments. Blue-chip stocks are normally relatively high-priced stocks with a long record of dividend payments.

Bonus issue

See Capitalization issue.

Book transfer

The transfer of title to a buyer without a physical movement of the product.

Book value

Common shareholder's equity on a per share basis. It is calculated by subtracting liabilities from assets and dividing the result by the number of outstanding shares of stock. The book value is not necessarily the same as the market value.

Borsa

Italian for stock exchange.

Bourse
French for stock exchange. The word *Bourse* is thought to originate from the town of Bruges in Belgium. In the early thirteenth century, merchants from the main commercial centres, particularly from Genoa and Venice, used to gather in front of the house of the Van der Buerse family in Bruges.

Briefkurs
The asked (offered price) on German and Swiss stock exchanges.

Broker
An agent, often a member of a stock exchange firm, who executes public orders to buy and sell securities and commodities. For this service a commission is usually charged. Brokers are agents working on commission, and not principals or agents acting on their own account.

Brokerage fee
A fee charged by a broker for executing a transaction.

Broker-dealer
See Dealer.

Bulge
A rapid price advance.

Bull
An investor who believes that prices are going to rise.

Bull market
A prolonged period of generally rising prices.

Bull spread
An option position composed of both long and short options of the same type, either calls or puts, designed to be profitable in a declining market. An option with a lower strike price is bought and one with a higher strike price is sold.

Bulldogs
Sterling bonds issued in the UK by foreign institutions.

Butterfly spread
(i) A futures butterfly spread is a spread trade in which multiple futures months are traded simultaneously at a differential. The trade basically consists of two futures spread transactions with either three or four different futures months at one differential. (ii) An options butterfly spread is a spread trade in which multiple options months and strike prices are traded simultaneously at a differential. The trade basically consists of two options-spread transactions with either three or four different options months and strikes at one differential.

Buyer/taker
The purchaser of an option, whether a call or put option. The buyer may also be referred to as the option holder. Option buyers receive the right, but not the obligation, to enter a futures/securities market position.

Buy-side trader
An individual, such as a pension or mutual fund portfolio manager, who effects trades for an institutional investor.

By-products
Products generated from the same raw materials.

Cabinet trade
A trade that allows options traders to liquidate deep out-of-the-money options by trading the option at a price equal to one-half tick.

Cable
A term used in the foreign-exchange market for the US dollar/British pound rate.

Calendar spread
Buying (selling) the calendar spread involves the simultaneous purchase (sale) of contract(s) in a near delivery month and the sale (purchase) of an equal number of contract(s) in a far delivery month of the same futures contract.

Call
A period of trading.

Call option
A call option confers the right but not the obligation to buy stock, shares or futures at a specified price within a predetermined time period. The buyer (taker) pays the seller (grantor) a premium for this.

Cap
An agreement with a counterparty that sets an upper limit to interest rates for the cap buyer for a stated time period.

Capital market
The market for medium- and long-term securities.

Capitalization
See Market capitalization.

Capitalization issue
The process whereby money from a company's reserves is converted into issued capital, which is then distributed to shareholders as new shares, in proportion to their original holdings. Also known as a bonus or scrip issue.

Carry
The interest cost of financing securities held.

Cash and carry
An arbitrage transaction involving the simultaneous purchase of a cash commodity with borrowed money and the sale of the appropriate futures contract.

Cash market
The market in the actual financial instrument on which a futures or options contract is based.

Cash settlement
Final disposition of open positions on the last trading day of a contract month. Occurs in markets where there is no actual delivery.

Central Securities Depository
A Central Securities Depository is a financial institution providing custodial and securities settlement services to one or several markets.

Certificate of deposit (CD)
A negotiable certificate issued by a commercial bank as evidence of a deposit with that bank which states the maturity value, maturity rate and interest rate payable. CDs vary in size, with maturities ranging from a few weeks to several years. CDs may normally be redeemed before maturity only by sale on the secondary market but may also be redeemed back to the issuing bank through payment of a penalty.

CFTC
The US Federal regulatory agency for futures traded on commodity markets.

Cheapest-to-deliver
The bond, deliverable against a futures contract, for which delivery is most attractive in terms of cost from the short position holder's point of view.

CIBOR
The rate at which the banks lend the Danish krone on an unsecured basis. The rate is calculated daily by the Danmarks Nationalbank (the Danish Central Bank), based on rules set out by the Danish Banker's Association.

Circuit breaker
A procedure that temporarily halts trading on all US stock markets for one hour when the Dow Jones Industrial Average falls 250 points or more within a trading day. The pause is designed to allow time for the markets to absorb the news that precipitated the decline. Should the average fall another 150 points within the same day, trading would again be halted, this time for two hours.

Class
In MDDL instruments are classified by the domain in which they reside, these are then subcategorized by class. For example an equity can be categorized by commonClass, depositaryClass, partnershipClass, preferredClass. Some instruments can be breakdown further by subclass.

Clean price
The price of a bond not including the accrued-interest element.

Clearing
The process of matching, registering and guaranteeing transactions.

Clearing house
An exchange-associated, usually independent organization through which all contracts are made, offset and delivered.

Clearing margin
Financial safeguards to ensure that clearing members (usually companies or corporations) perform on their customers' open futures and options contracts. Clearing margins are distinct from customer margins that individual buyers and sellers of futures and options contracts are required to deposit with brokers.

Clearing member
A member firm of a clearing house.

Close out
A transaction which leaves the trade with a zero net commitment to the market. A purchase if the initial transaction was a sale and *vice versa*.

Closed-end mutual funds
A mutual fund that issues a set number of shares, which then are only re-sold on the secondary market exchanges like regular stock shares.

Closing range
The high and low prices at which transactions took place at the end of the day's trading session.

Collar
A combination of a cap and a floor. A collar sets a band within which interest rates will apply (e.g. 10.5–13.75%), for a given period.

Collateralized Mortgage Obligations
CMOs package the mortgage payment stream from a portfolio of mortgages into several series of debt instruments which are prioritized in terms of their right to receive principal payments. In the most basic CMOs, each series must be repaid in full before any principal payments can be made to the holders of the next series.

Commission
The fee that a broker may charge clients for dealing on their behalf.

Commission des Opérations de Bourse (COB)
The French securities-market watchdog. The COB holds the status of an autonomous administrative body.

Committee of Wise Men on the Regulation of the European Securities Markets
See Lamfalussy Report.

Concentration rule
The rule in the current European Union Investment Services Directive allows European Union Member States to require that all retail investor transactions be executed on a regulated market. However, the European Union Commission considers that there must be convergence towards a single consensus view of marketplace regulation in order to create a single financial market in which supply and demand for a given financial instrument can interact across an integrated and efficient trading infrastructure.

Concert party
A group acting together in a takeover situation. Each member of the group (which acts in secret) buys a percentage of shares to avoid no longer being able to hide behind nominee status.

Confirmation
The process immediately following a transaction whereby the traders confirm the details of the trade.

Conseil des Bourses de Valeurs (CBV)
The French Stock Exchange Council which is the supervisory and regulatory authority of the French securities markets.

Consideration
On the London Stock Exchange the money value of a transaction (number of shares multiplied by the price).

Consolidated tape
The combined tapes of the New York and American stock exchanges. Network A covers New York Stock Exchange-listed securities, identifying the market where the trade takes place. Network B does the same for American Stock Exchange securities and securities listed on US regional exchanges.

Container
In MDDL, this is an element that contains other elements, an XML complex type, sometimes referred to as a component.

Contango
(i) On the London Stock Exchange a mechanism for detailing settlement of a bargain until the next account day. This mechanism is used when the selling party is unable to deliver the stock for the appropriate account day. The selling party pays an interest premium to the buyer to cover the extended settlement period. On futures markets, a market in which distant months sell at a premium over near months. (ii) In futures markets, a situation in which prices are progressively higher in the succeeding delivery months than in the nearest delivery month.

Contante price
Italian bond market cash price.

Contract
See futures contract.

Contract expiration date
The date on which a commodity must be delivered to fulfil the terms of the contract. For options, the last day on which the option holder can exercise his right to buy or sell the underlying security.

Contract month
The month in which a futures contract matures or becomes deliverable if not liquidated or traded out before the date specified.

Contract note

On the London Stock Exchange, on the day on which a bargain takes place a member firm must send to the client a contract note detailing the transaction, to include full title of the stock, price, consideration, commission and stamp duty (if applicable).

Contract size

For futures contracts, the quantity to be delivered.

Controlled vocabulary

A controlled vocabulary is a list of terms intended to constrain the values a particular property may contain. All properties that use controlled vocabularies are of base type String with classification Enumeration, and may take on any values listed in the controlled vocabulary. The controlled vocabularies are defined and modified external to the MDDL Schema or DTD and can be created as necessary by senders.

Conversion premium

The amount by which the price of a convertible bond exceeds the market price of the underlying stock.

Conversion price

The par value of a convertible security divided by the number of shares into which it may be exchanged.

Conversion ratio

The number of shares for which a convertible security may be exchanged.

Convertible bond

A bond which confers on the holder the right to exchange the bonds for other securities of the issuing company at a predetermined price and at, or during, determinable dates.

Convertible security

Bond or preferred stock that may be converted into another security at the holder's option.

Corporate bond

A long-term interest-bearing debt instrument that requires the issuer to pay the purchaser a specified sum of money, usually at specific intervals, and to repay the principal amount of the loan at maturity.

Correlation coefficient

A measure of the closeness of the relationship between two variables.

Côte Officielle

The market on Euronext Paris where securities of the largest French issuers (public or private) are traded.

Coupon

(i) On bearer stocks, the detachable part of the certificate exchangeable for dividends. (ii) Denotes the rate of interest on a fixed-interest security.

Coupon value

The annual rate of interest of a bond.

Cours
On Belgian and French exchanges, the market price of a share.

Covariance
A measure of the comovement between two variables.

Cover
The total net profit a company has available for distribution as dividend, divided by the amount actually paid gives the number of times that the dividend is covered.

Crack spread
A hedge used in the energy futures market to offset the risk of buying (or selling) crude oil with an opposite transaction in the refined products that may be derived from it.

Crore
A *Crore* equates to 10 million.

Cross rates
Rates between two currencies, neither of which is the US dollar.

Crossed market
The situation which exists when a broker's bid is higher than the lowest offer of another broker.

Cross-trade
A cross-trade transaction is a transaction where either the buy-broker and the sell-broker are the same, or the buy-broker and the sell-broker belong to the same firm.

Crush
The meal and oil products resulting from processing soya beans.

Crush margin
The ratio of oil and meal resulting from crushing a given volume of soya beans.

Crush spread
The spread between soya beans and soya bean products created by buying soya bean futures and selling soya bean oil and soya bean meal futures.

Cum
Latin for 'with' (used in the abbreviations cum cap, cum div, cum rights, etc.), to indicate that the buyer of a security is entitled to participate in the forthcoming capitalization issue, dividend or rights issue. See also Ex.

Cum all
A stock trading with the right to all supplementary advantages attached to the share.

Cum capitalization
The purchaser of stock which is cum capitalization is entitled to receive an issue of new shares made fully paid by the capitalization of reserves and given free of charge in proportion to his or her existing holdings.

Cum dividend

The purchaser of a stock which is cum dividend is entitled to receive the declared dividend.

Cum period

A period during which a buyer of securities is entitled to the dividend regardless of whether or not he is on the register at the record date.

Cum rights

The purchaser of a stock trading cum rights is entitled to buy shares of a new issue of stock in direct proportion to his or her existing holdings.

Current delivery month

The most current calendar month in which a futures contract comes to maturity and becomes deliverable. Also known as the spot month.

CUSIP code

The CUSIP numbering system is the standard method for identifying securities throughout the US financial industry. The CUSIP number is a nine-digit alphanumeric number which is permanently allocated to each issue and identifying that single issue and no other issue. CUSIP numbers are also assigned to most Canadian securities. (Exceptions being issues of purely domestic interest such as municipal debt securities. Such securities are issued CUSIP compatible codes by the Canadian Depository for Securities Ltd.)

Customer margin

Within the futures industry, financial guarantees required of both buyers and sellers of futures contracts and sellers of options contracts to ensure fulfilling of contract obligations. FCMs are responsible for overseeing customer margin accounts. Margins are determined on the basis of market risk and contract value. Also referred to as performance-bond margin.

Daily official list

The London Stock Exchange's daily official list is the list of listed securities and the prices of transactions published each day.

dateTime

The MDDL dateTime property is ISO 8601 compliant, the International Standard for the representation of dates and times, where: YYYY = four-digit year; MM = two-digit month (01 = January, etc.); DD = two-digit day of month (01 through 31); hh = two digits of hour (00 through 23) (am/pm NOT allowed); mm = two digits of minute (00 through 59); ss = two digits of second (00 through 59); s = one or more digits representing a decimal fraction of a second; TZD = time zone designator (Z or +hh:mm or −hh:mm).

Day order

An order placed for execution, if possible, during only one trading session. If the order cannot be executed that day, it is automatically cancelled.

Day trader

Speculators who take positions in commodities which are then liquidated prior to the close of the same trading day.

Dealer

An individual or firm acting as a principal, rather than as an agent, in the purchase and/or sale of securities. Dealers trade for their own account and risk.

Debenture

A non-secured loan raised by a company, paying a fixed-rate of interest.

Decimalization

The process that converted stock prices from fractional pricing to pricing in decimals; that is, in increments from eighths or sixteenths of dollars to nickels (USD0.05) or pennies (USD0.01). Decimalization and the reduction of tick sizes are not the same and are not necessarily dependent on each other.

Declaration date

The latest day or time by which the buyer of an option must indicate to the seller his intention to exercise the option.

Default

The non-performance of a stated obligation.

Deferred shares

Stocks whose dividends are not paid until the expiration of a stated date, or until a specified event, such as the company's profitability reaching a certain level, has taken place.

Delivery

The settlement of a futures contract by receipt or tender of a financial instrument.

Delivery month

The calendar month in which a futures contract comes to maturity and becomes deliverable.

Delivery points

Those locations designated by futures exchanges at which stocks of a commodity represented by a futures contract may be delivered in fulfilment of the contract.

Delivery versus Payment

A delivery instruction where the delivery of securities and the payment of the cash consideration are linked.

Delta

The change in the value of the option premium relative to the instantaneous change in the value of the underlying instrument, expressed as a coefficient.

Déport

A discount on carrying over a position on a French equity from one settlement period to next.

Depository trust company

In the US, a central securities repository, owned by banks and brokerage houses, where stock and bond certificates are exchanged.

Depreciation

The reduction in the book or market value of an asset.

Depth of market
A measure of how much a price has to move in order to execute larger than normal transactions. The smaller the price movement and the larger the transaction, the deeper the market.

Derivatives
Financial instruments or arrangements that derive their value from some underlying stock, bond, commodity or other asset. Futures, swaps, some forwards, options and warrants, and certain mortgage-backed securities are the most common derivative forms.

Dilution
The diminution in the proportion of income to which each share is entitled.

Dirty prices
Bond prices which include the accrued interest.

Discount
When the market price of a newly issued security is lower than the issue price.

Discount factor
The present value of one unit of currency received at a stated future date.

Discount rate
The rate used to calculate the present value of future cash flows.

Discounted bond
Zero coupon bonds are corporate or municipal debt securities that trade at a deep discount from the face value, as the bond pays no interest to the bondholders during its lifetime.

Discounted cash flow
Future cash flows multiplied by discount factors to obtain the present value.

Distribution date
See Payment date.

Dividend
The distribution of (post-tax) earnings to shareholders declared by the board of directors of a corporation to be paid per share to the shareholders. Dividends are usually paid in cash, but can be paid in stock or by means of stock and cash.

Domain
In MDDL in domain is the highest categorization of data. These are principally instrument groups such as equity, debt, derivative and foreign exchange, which can then be subcategorized by class and, in some cases, subclass. These are domains to identify a corporate action or an indicator such as an interest rate etc.

Down tick
The sale of a security at a price lower than the previous one.

Dual-currency bond
A bond with the interest paid in one currency and the principal paid in another.

Durante price
Fluctuation price established during trading sessions other than the official opening and closing dealings on Italian exchanges.

Duration
A measurement of the change in the value of an instrument in response to a change in interest rates. It is the primary basis for comparing the effect of interest rate changes on prices of fixed-income instruments.

Earnings per share
The total net profit of a company per share.

EDGAR
Electronic Data Gathering, Analysis and Retrieval System – the Securities and Exchange commission's system for the electronic submission by direct transmission, magnetic tape or diskette, of most filings and related correspondence.

Efficient market
A market in which security prices reflect information instantaneously.

Electronic communication network (ECN)
Any electronic system that widely disseminates to third parties orders entered by an exchange market-maker or OTC market-maker, and permits such orders to be executed against in whole or in part.

Element
Is the main XML document building, each element has a name and content. The content is delimited by special mark-ups known as start and end tags. In MDDL an element is referred to as a property.

Equity
The ordinary shares of companies. The ownership interest in a company of holders of its common and preferred stock.

Equity warrant bonds
See Subscription warrant.

ETFs
See Exchange Traded Funds (ETFs).

Eurobonds
A long-term loan issued in a currency other than that of the country or market in which it is issued. There is no withholding tax applied to interest payment. Eurobonds are internationally underwritten and available in bearer form. They are cleared through Cedel and Euroclear, and are traded crossborder.

Eurodollar strips
Strips of Eurodollars are the coordinated purchase or sale of a series of futures contracts with successive expiration dates. The object is to lock in a yield for a period or term equal to the length of the strip.

Eurodollars
US dollars deposited in a bank (US or non US) located outside the USA.

European option
An option that can be exercised only on its expiration date rather than before that date.

Ex
The opposite of cum, and used to indicate that the buyer is not entitled to participate in whatever forthcoming event is specified (ex cap, ex dividend, ex rights, etc).

Ex all
The sale of a security without dividends, rights, warrants or other supplementary privileges associated with that security.

Ex capitalization
A stock or share sold without the right to the capitalization issue which has been announced.

Ex date
The date, for a benefit event (e.g. a dividend) used to determine whether the buyer or seller of the security is entitled to the benefit. The ex date divides the cum period from the ex period. Bargains dealt prior to the ex date (during the cum period) are dealt with the benefit attached, unless stated to the contrary as a bargain condition. Bargains dealt after ex date (during the ex period) are dealt without the benefit attached, unless stated to the contrary by a bargain condition.

Ex dividend
A stock or share sold without the right to the recently declared dividend. A stock quoted ex dividend has the amount of the dividend which is about to be paid deducted from the price.

Ex rights
Stock sold without the right to participate in an offer of securities to existing shareholders by a company in proportion to their existing holdings.

Ex warrants
Stock sold with the buyer no longer entitled to the warrants formerly attached to the stock.

Exchange of futures for cash
A transaction in which the buyer of a cash commodity transfers to the seller a corresponding amount of long futures contracts, or receives from the seller a corresponding amount of short futures, at a price difference mutually agreed upon. In this way, the opposite hedges in futures of both parties are closed out simultaneously.

Exchange of futures for physicals
A futures contract provision involving an agreement for delivery of a physical product that does not necessarily conform to contract specifications in all terms from one market participant to another, and a concomitant assumption of equal and opposite futures positions by the same participants at the time of the agreement.

Exchange Traded Funds (ETFs)
Exchange traded funds are collective investment vehicles which track indices – they can allow low-cost exposure to the performance of an index as quickly and efficiently as the most liquid stocks.

Ex-dividend date
The date on which a stock goes ex dividend. After this date the right to receive a current dividend will not automatically transfer from the seller of the stock to the buyer.

Exercise
The use of the right to purchase the underlying instrument by the holder of a call, or to sell the underlying instrument by the holder of a put. Upon exercise of an option on a futures contract, an option seller will be assigned (at the exercise price) a futures position opposite to the position acquired by the option buyer. Upon exercise of an option on equity shares, an option seller will be required to deliver shares at the exercise price (in the case of a call option) or purchase shares at the exercise price (in the case of a put option). Exercise of an option on an equity-index contract, either a call or a put, results in a cash settlement based on the difference between the exercise price and the index at the time of exercise.

Exercise notice
The formal notification that the holder of a call (or put) option wishes to buy (or sell) the underlying security at the exercise price.

Exercise price
See Strike price.

Exercise value
For a call option, this is the amount by which the strike price is below the underlying investment; for a put option, it is the amount by which the strike price is above the underlying investment.

Exotic option
Any of a wide variety of options with unusual underlying, strike price calculations, strike price determinations, payoff mechanisms or expiration conditions.

Expiration date
(i) Options – the last date after which the option can no longer be exercised. (ii) Bonds – the date on which a bond matures.

Expiration month
The month in which an option expires.

extraMark
The London Stock Exchange market for innovative investment companies and products, is dedicated to providing investors with special investment opportunities.

Extrinsic value
See Time value.

Face value
See Par value.

Fair value
An option value derived from a mathematical option valuation model.

Fannie Mae
Securities issued by the Federal National Mortgage Association (FNMA) of the US.

Fast market
Rapid movement in a market caused by strong interest by buyers and/or sellers. In such circumstances, price levels may be omitted and bid and offer quotations may occur too rapidly to be fully reported.

Fill or kill order
An order submitted to the order book with a specified size and at the option of the member firm, a specified limit price which either executes in its entirety against eligible orders at the price of those orders or is rejected in full from the order book.

Final dividend
The dividend paid by a company at the end of its financial year, recommended by the directors, but authorized by the shareholders at the company's Annual General Meeting.

Financial future
A futures contract based on a financial instrument.

Financial Services Action Plan (FSAP)
The FSAP is the European Commission's response towards improving the single market in financial services. Adopted in 1999, the FSAP contains a list of 42 measures to be implemented, grouped around 4 strategic objectives (retail markets; wholesale; prudential rules and supervision; and wider conditions for an optimal single financial market). The Markets in Financial Instruments Directive forms a major part of the implementation of the FSAP.

Firm quote
A market-maker's quote which is a price at which he/she is committed to deal.

First notice day
The first day on which notices of intention to deliver actual commodities against futures market positions can be received.

FISD
Financial Information Services Division of the Software and Information Industry Association.

fisdMessage
see xtcMessage.

Fixed-interest security
A security or bond which offers an annual guaranteed interest payment. There is usually a fixed date at which the bond is redeemed.

Flexible exchange (FLEX) option
A semi-customized, exchange-traded put or call option issued by a clearing house. Customization is limited to expiration date, strike and exercise style (European or American).

Floor
An agreement with a counterparty that sets a lower limit to interest rates for the floor buyer for a stated time period.

Flotation
The occasion on which a company's shares are offered on the market for the first time.

Forward rate agreement (FRA)
An agreement to borrow or lend at a specified future date at an interest rate that is fixed today. The borrowing and lending is purely notional as the contract allows the purchaser to fix interest costs for a specific future period.

Fourth market
The direct trading of securities between institutional investors without the use of brokers or dealers.

Free float
The number of shares not held by corporate insiders that are freely tradable in the public market or markets on which a company's securities are listed.

Freimakler
Independent dealers admitted to trade on German stock exchanges by the board of governors of the individual exchange. *Freimakler* participate in stock exchange dealings as intermediaries. They do not conclude business directly with buyers or sellers of securities. *Freimakler*, unlike *Kursmakler*, are not subject to any legal restriction with regard to the execution of business on their own account. The main area of trading of *Freimakler* is trading in the securities on other markets than the official trade. They may, however, also deal in officially listed securities.

Freiverkehr
The free market section of German stock exchanges.

Front month
The nearest active contract month of a futures contract. See also Spot month.

Front running
A situation where the employees of a brokerage firm or a bank trade in equity shares using price-sensitive information that is privately available to the firm.

Fully paid
Applied to new issues, when the total amount payable in relation to the new shares has been paid to the company.

Fungibles
Instruments that are equivalent, substitutable and interchangeable in law.

Furthest month
The month that is furthest away from settlement of a futures or options contract.

Futures contract
A contract traded on a futures exchange which requires the delivery of a specified quality and quantity of a commodity, currency or financial instrument in a specified future month, if not liquidated before the contract matures.

Gamma
The rate at which a delta changes over time.

Gearing
A company's debts expressed as a percentage of its equity capital.

Geldkurs
The bid price on German and Swiss exchanges.

Genussscheine
Dividend right certificate (German and Swiss stock exchanges). Security incorporating the right to participate in the net profit and the liquidation proceeds of a company as well as the right to subscribe to new shares in the case of a rights issue. However, the holder has no membership rights; in particular, he cannot attend shareholder meetings. The dividend-right certificate may be in bearer or registered form.

Geregelter Markt
The regulated market section of the German stock exchanges.

Gilt edged
(i) In the UK, loans issued on behalf of the government to fund its spending. Longs are gilts with a redemption date greater than 15 years; mediums are those with a redemption date between 5 and 15 years; shorts are those with a redemption date within 5 years. (ii) In the US, top-quality stocks issued by corporations with a known record for profit and of paying dividends over the years. In the US, the term also refers to high-quality bonds.

Ginnie Mae
Securities issued by the Government National Mortgage Association (GNMA) of the US.

Giovannini Group
The Giovannini Group was formed in 1996 to advise the European Commission on issues relating to EU financial integration and the efficiency of euro-denominated financial markets. The Group consists of financial-market participants and meets under the chairmanship of Dr Alberto Giovannini. The Commission's Directorate-General for Economic and Financial Affairs provides the secretariat, with officials from the Directorate-General for the Internal Market and from the European Central Bank (ECB) also supporting the Group's work.

Global Depositary Receipt (GDR)
Certificate, denominated in US dollars, which represents ownership of a given number of a company's shares and which can be listed and traded independently from the underlying shares.

Going long
The purchase of a stock or commodity for investment or speculation.

Going short
The selling of a stock or commodity not owned by the seller.

Green shoe
A provision in an underwriting agreement that if there is an exceptional public demand, an issuer will authorize additional shares for distribution by the syndicate.

Greenmail
The situation by which a large block of stock is held by an unfriendly company, which forces the target company to repurchase the stock at a substantial premium to prevent a takeover.

Grey market
The market in a new issue prior to formal offering.

Gross
Before deduction of tax.

Grossing-up
Calculating a gross or pretax rate of interest or dividend by adding a notional amount of tax to the net, or post-tax amount received.

H share
A share of a mainland Chinese company listed on HKEx (the Hong Kong stock and derivatives exchange).

Hedge
The purchase or sale of options or futures contracts as a temporary substitute for a transaction to be made at a later date. Usually it involves opposite positions in the cash or futures or options market.

Hedge ratio
For futures, the number of contracts required to hedge one contract's value of the underlying asset. For options, see Delta.

Historical volatility
The annualized standard deviation of percentage changes in futures prices over a specific period. It is an indication of past volatility in the marketplace.

Horizontal spread
A calendar or time spread.

Hors-côte
The market on the Paris Stock Exchange where issues not traded on the official list or second market are traded.

Implied volatility
A measurement of the market's expected price range of the underlying commodity futures based on the market-traded option premiums.

Index
A number that measures changes in financial markets. Some indexes are used as benchmarks that financial performance is measured against.

Indexed bond
A bond whose payments are linked by an index (such as a consumer-price index).

Index-linked gilt
A gilt, the interest and capital of which change in line with the Retail Price Index.

Indicative quote
A market-maker's price which is not firm.

Inhaberaktien
Swiss or German bearer shares.

Initial margin
The margin required to secure a new futures or options position.

Initial public offering (IPO)
A company's first sale of stock to the public. Companies making an IPO are seeking outside equity capital and a public market for their stock.

Inside information
Inside information is information of a precise nature which has not been made public, relating, directly or indirectly, to one or more issuers of financial instruments or to one or more financial instruments and which, if it were made public, would be likely to have a significant effect on the prices of those financial instruments or on the price of related derivative financial instruments.

Inside spread (Inside quote)
The difference between the best bid and best ask being quoted among all of the market-makers competing in a security. Since the inside spread is the aggregate of individual market-maker spreads, it is narrower than an individual dealer spread or quote (see Market-maker).

Insider dealing
The purchase or sale of shares by someone who possesses 'inside' information about the company – i.e. information on the company's performance and prospects which has not yet been made available to the market as a whole and which, if available, might affect the share price.

Institutional investor
A bank, mutual fund, pension fund or other corporate entity that trades securities in large volumes.

Instrument groups
In MDDL, instruments are categorized by domain, class and subclass.

Interbank rates
The bid and offer rates at which international banks place deposits with each other.

Intercommodity spread
The purchase of a given delivery month on one futures market and the simultaneous sale of the same delivery month on a different futures market.

Interdealer broker
A specialist broker who acts as an intermediary between market-makers who wish to buy or sell securities, to improve their book positions, without revealing their identities to other market-makers.

Interdelivery spread
The purchase of one delivery month of a given commodity futures contract and the simultaneous sale of another delivery month of the same commodity futures contract on the same exchange.

Interim dividend
A dividend declared part of the way through a company's financial year, authorized solely by the directors.

Intermarket spread
See Intercommodity spread.

Intermarket Trading System (ITS)
A computer system that interconnects competing US exchange markets for the purpose of choosing the best market. ITS is operated by the Securities Industry Automation Corporation (SIAC).

Intermediary
An institution acting between two or more other entities by assuming certain rights and obligations.

Internal rate of return
The discount rate at which an investment has a zero net present value.

Intersettle
A sister company of the Swiss Securities Clearing Corporation (SEGA), which has been set up for international settlement purposes.

In-the-money
A call option is in-the-money if the price of the underlying instrument is higher than the exercise/strike price. A put option is in-the-money if the price of the underlying instrument is below the exercise/strike price. See also Out-of-the-money.

Intramarket spread
See Interdelivery spread.

Intrinsic value
The amount by which an option is in-the-money. The intrinsic value is the difference between the exercise/strike price and the price of the underlying security.

Inverse floater
A bond with a coupon rate structured to move in the opposite direction of interest rates.

Investment Services Directive
The European Union Investment Services Directive, adopted in 1993, sought to establish the conditions in which authorized investment firms and banks could provide specified services in other European Union Member States on the basis of home country authorization and supervision. It has subsequently been extended by the Markets in Financial Instruments Directive.

Investment trust
A company whose sole business consists of buying, selling and holding shares.

ISD
See Investment Services Directive.

ISD 2
See Markets In Financial Instruments Directive (MiFID).

ISIN code
The structure of the ISIN code is: two-digit alphacountry code (ISO 3166) or XS for securities numbered by CEDEL or Euroclear; nine-digit alphanumeric code based on the national securities code or the common CEDEL/Euroclear code; a check digit computed according to the modulus 10 'double-add double'.

Issue price
The gross price placed on a new bond issue, expressed as a percentage of the principal amount.

Issuer
A corporation or governmental agency which borrows money through the sale of securities.

Issuing house
An organization, normally a merchant bank, that arranges the details of an issue of stocks or shares, and the necessary compliance with the London Stock Exchange regulations in connection with the listing of that issue.

Itayose
A method of trading employed on Japanese exchanges. Under the *itayose* method, which is used in the case of opening trades and the like, all orders reaching the floor before the opening are treated as simultaneous orders, and, in accordance with the principle of priority, each buy order is compared with sell orders till its quantity and price are matched by a sell order and the price is treated as a single price for the consummation of the transaction.

Kassakurs
On German stock exchanges, the official cash settlement price established once per day, for orders of the amount of less than 50 shares.

Kassenverein
German securities clearing and deposit bank.

Kerb trading
Trading that takes place after the market has closed.

Kursmakler
The function of the *Kursmakler* is to act as an intermediary between persons admitted to deal on German stock exchanges and to fix official prices of those securities to which he/she is entrusted. The *Kursmakler* are subject to certain legal restrictions in the conclusion of business on their own account.

Kursmaklerkammer
A public body representing the *Kursmakler* of the German stock exchanges. The *Kursmaklerkammer* is responsible for the allocation of securities among the *Kursmakler*, for the control of the settlement of prices and for the editing of the Official List.

Lakh
A *Lakh* is a unit that equates to a hundred thousand.

Lamfalussy Report
The Committee of Wise Men on the Regulation of European Securities Markets under the chairmanship of Alexandre Lamfalussy was established by ECOFIN with a mandate to assess the current conditions for the implementation of the regulation of securities markets in the European Union. It was asked to assess how the mechanism for regulating those markets can best respond to developments, and, in order to eliminate barriers, to propose scenarios for adapting current practices to ensure greater convergence and cooperation in day-to-day implementation.

Lapsed rights
Rights for which call payments have not been made by the acceptance date.

Last notice day
The final day on which notices of intent to deliver on futures contracts may be issued.

Last trading day
The day on which trading ceases for an expiring contract.

Latency
Latency is the technical term for the delays in computer systems caused by both distance and processing. Distance creates latency because of simple physics. Messages travel at the speed of light, and over long distances the delays are measurable. Processing creates latency by delaying messages at every instance where a process occurs.

Less liquid stocks
The London Stock Exchange has classified those of its listed and USM company shares that have a normal market size of 1000 or less as liquid stocks.

Letter of renunciation
On the London Stock Exchange, this applies to a rights issue and is the form attached to an allotment letter which is completed should the original holder wish to pass his entitlement to someone else, or to renounce his rights absolutely.

Leverage
The ability to control large amounts of a financial asset with a comparatively small amount of capital.

LIBID
The rate charged by one bank to another for a deposit.

LIBOR
The rate charged by one bank to another for lending money.

Life of contract
The period between the beginning of trading in a particular future and the expiration of trading.

LIMEAN
The average of the LIBOR and LIBID rates.

Limit
The maximum price fluctuation permitted by an exchange from the previous session's settlement price for a given contract.

Limit down
The maximum price decline from the previous trading day's settlement price permitted in one trading session.

Limit move
A price that has advanced or declined the limit permitted during one trading session.

Limit order
An order to buy or sell a specified amount of a security at a specified price or better.

Limit up
The maximum price advance from the previous trading day's settlement price permitted in one trading session.

Liquid
A characteristic of a security or commodity market with enough units outstanding to allow large transactions without a substantial change in price. Institutional investors are inclined to seek out liquid investments so that their trading activity will not influence the market price.

Liquid stocks
The London Stock Exchange has classified its listed shares and USM-company shares that have a normal market size greater than 1000 as liquid stocks.

Liquidity
The level of trading volume in a market.

Listed security
The securities of a private company or public body which is traded on a securities exchange and has signed a listing agreement with the stock exchange.

LMIL
London Market Information Link, The London Stock Exchange's broadcast market data feed.

Loan stock
Stock bearing a fixed rate of interest. Unlike a debenture, loan stock may be unsecured.

Local
A futures trader who normally trades on an exchange on his/her own account.

Local Market Identifier
Normally referred to as a Tiches Symbol.

Locked market
For equities a market is locked when the bid price equals the asked price. In futures markets a locked market is one where trading is halted because prices have reached their daily limit move.

Long
Owning a security.

Maintenance margin
The minimum margin which an investor must keep on deposit in a margin account at all times.

Make-a-market
A dealer is said to make-a-market when he or she quotes bid and offer prices at which he or she stands ready to buy and sell.

Mandatory quote period (MQP)
On the London Stock Exchange, the period during which all registered market-makers are obliged to display prices.

Marché au comptant
The French cash market. All securities on the official list not traded on the monthly settlement market are traded on this market. Cash transactions comprise the least active shares and the great majority of bonds; any quantity may be negotiated for immediate settlement and delivery.

Marché officiel
Official list of French stock exchanges.

Margin
(i) In equity markets, the amount paid by the customer when he/she uses his broker's credit to buy a security. (ii) For options, the sum required as collateral from the writer of an option. (iii) For futures, a deposit made to the clearing house on establishing a futures position.

Margin call
A demand for additional funds to be deposited in a margin account to meet margin requirements because of adverse future price movements.

Market abuse
Conduct that adversely affects a financial market and falls below the standards expected by the regular user of that market. The Financial Services Authority (FSA) can enforce disciplinary action against those who commit such abuses.

Market capitalization
The current total market value of a company's issued shares, obtained by multiplying the current market price by the current number of shares in issue.

Market operator
A market operator is a person or persons who effectively direct the business of a regulated market.

Market order
An order to buy or sell a financial instrument immediately at the best possible price.

Market value
The number of shares in issue multiplied by their current market price.

Market-maker
A market-maker is a person or firm authorized to create and maintain a market in a security. Market-makers commit themselves to always being ready to deal in the range of stocks for which they are registered.

Markets in Financial Instruments Directive (MiFID)
European Union legislation covering investment intermediaries and financial markets which replaces the previous Investment Services Directive (ISD). MiFID, part of the EU's Financial Services Action Plan, extends the coverage of the ISD regime and introduces new and more extensive requirements for firms, in particular in relation to their conduct of business and internal organization.

Mark-to-market
The daily adjustment of an account to reflect accrued profits and losses.

Material news
News released by a public company that might reasonably be expected to affect the value of a company's securities or influence investors' decisions. Material news includes information regarding corporate events of an unusual and non-recurring nature, news of tender offers, unusually good or bad earnings reports, and a stock split or stock dividend (see Trading halt).

Maturity date
Date on which a bond matures, at which time the face value will be returned to the purchaser. Sometimes the maturity date is not one specified date but a range of dates during which the bond may be repaid.

Maximum on-line publication level
On the London Stock Exchange, the maximum size of bargain in each SEAQ security which will be published on-line on SEAQ, immediately following trade reporting.

Member firm
A trading firm on the London Stock Exchange which may act as an agency broker on behalf of clients or a principal.

Mercato ristretto
Italian regulated market for unlisted securities.

Mid-price
The price half-way between the two prices shown on the London Stock Exchange's daily official list under quotation, or the average of both buying and selling prices offered by the market-makers.

MiFID
The European Commission's proposals in the Markets in Financial Instruments Directive can be summarized broadly as seeking to clarify and expand the list of financial instruments that may be traded on regulated markets and between investment firms; to broaden the range of investment services for which authorization is required under the Directive, notably to include the provision of investment advice and clarification of ancillary services investment firms can provide; to reinforce the requirement that investment firms execute orders in a way that provides best results for the client (often referred to as 'best execution obligations'); to set in place new rules for handling clients orders; to set requirements for managing conflicts of interest; to clarify standards for regulated markets and MTFs; and to enhance the principles for cooperation between competent authorities.

Minimum price fluctuation
The smallest increment of market price movement possible in a given futures contract.

Minimum quote size
On the London Stock Exchange, the minimum number of shares in which market-makers are obliged to display prices on SEAQ for securities in which they are registered.

Modaraba
Modaraba is an Arabic word which means a business (project) in which capital is provided by one party (a company or individual) while effort and skill are contributed by the other party (beneficiary, entrepreneur or borrower). During the lifetime of the project, the lender is the sole owner of the project and the borrower is the manager. In a *Modaraba* arrangement, financial losses have to be borne exclusively by the lender. In Pakistan, the sponsor of a *Modaraba* has to be a company which must be registered under the Modaraba Companies and Modaraba (Flotation and Control Ordinance 1980).

Money market
The market for short-term investments. 'Short term' is usually defined as less than a year.

Money-market fund
An open-ended mutual fund that invests in very short-term instruments such as US Treasury bills, corporate commercial paper and certificates of deposit of US and foreign banks.

MTF
See Multilateral Trading Facility.

Multilateral Trading Facility
Multilateral trading facility (MTF) is a multilateral system which brings together multiple third-party buying and selling interests in financial instruments – in the system and in accordance with non-discretionary rules – in a way that results in a contract.

Multiply-listed option
Any option contract that is listed and traded on more than one national options exchange.

Mutual fund

An open-end investment company. Equivalent to unit trust.

Nakadachi

Regular members of the Osaka Stock Exchange buy and sell securities on the trading floor through the medium of *nakadachi* members, who serve as intermediate agents in transactions between members. *Nakadachi* members are prohibited from trading on their own account.

Namenaktien

On German and Swiss exchanges, shares made out in the name of the owner who is entered in the register of shareholders of the company concerned.

Nasdaq

The Nasdaq stock market is the second largest equity market in the US. It is screen-based, with multiple competing market-makers. The Nasdaq system is the market's electronic communications facility.

Nearby contracts

The closest active futures contracts, i.e. those that expire the soonest.

Net-asset value

The market value of all assets owned by an investment trust minus liabilities and divided by the number of shares outstanding. In mutual funds, the market value of a fund share.

Netback

An industry term referring to the net FOB cost of product offered on a delivered or CIF basis. It is derived by subtracting all costs of shipment from the landed price.

New issue

A company coming to the market for the 1st time or issuing additional new shares.

New shares

Shares recently issued by a company; these shares can usually be transferred on renouncable documents.

New time

On the London Stock Exchange, new time dealings may be transacted by special arrangement in the last 2 days of an account, and settled as if they had been done during the following account.

Nil paid

A new issue of shares, usually as the result of a rights issue, on which no payment has yet been made.

No brainer

A transaction guaranteed to make a profit.

Nominal quotation

(i) Securities. An approximation of a security's market value, given for the purpose of valuation.

(ii) Futures. An estimated price for a future month or date for which there is no bid, ask or trade price.

Nominee name
Name in which a security is registered and held in trust on behalf of the beneficial owner.

Normal market size (NMS)
A value expressed as a number of shares used to calculate the minimum quotation size for UK domestic equities and ADRs traded on the London Stock Exchange. The NMS values, which range from 500 shares to 200 000 shares, are based on each individual stock's average market turnover value in the previous 12 values.

Notice day
Any day on which notices of intent to deliver on futures contracts may be issued.

Odd lot
A block of securities bid or offered which is smaller than the standard lot size for that particular security.

Offer for sale
A method of bringing a company to the market. The public can apply for shares directly at a fixed price. A prospectus containing details of the sale must be printed in a national newspaper.

Offer price
The price at which a seller is willing to sell. The best offer is the lowest such price available.

Official list
The list of securities which have obtained a formal listing on the main market of an exchange.

Offset
The closing-out or liquidation of a futures position.

Open interest
The total number of outstanding option or futures contracts that have not been closed out by offset or fulfilled by delivery.

Open order
An order to buy or sell a security which remains in place until it is either executed or cancelled.

Open range
Price (or price range) recorded during the opening period of the market.

Open-end fund
A mutual fund with no limit to the number of shares that can be issued.

Open-outcry
A public auction method of trading conducted by calling out bids and offers across a trading ring or pit and having them accepted.

Option

A contract conferring the right but not the obligation to buy (call) or to sell (put) a specified amount of an instrument at a specified price within a predetermined time period.

Option class

All options of the same type – calls or puts – listed on the same underlying instrument.

Option series

All options of the same class having the same exercise/strike price and expiration date.

Optionspreis

German for premium. The price a put or call buyer must pay to a put or call seller for an option contract.

Optionsscheine

German for warrant.

Order book

Compiled list of orders received that are away from the current best price in the market.

Order ticket

The document on which the details of the order are manually recorded, as soon as the order is received.

Ordinary share

The most common form of share or stock. A certificate that represents share ownership in a corporation.

Out trade

A trade that cannot be reconciled in the clearing process.

Out-of-the-money

A call option is out-of-the-money if the price of the underlying instrument is lower than the exercise/strike price. A put option is out-of-the-money if the price of the underlying instrument is above the exercise/strike price. See also In-the-money.

Over-the-counter (OTC)

In the US, a market where small capitalization stocks (and some large capitalization stocks as well), shell companies, inactively traded and unregistered stocks trade. The pink sheets and the OTC Bulletin Board (OTCBB) are the only places left in the US where unregistered stocks trade. See also Pink sheets.

Par

(i) Price of 100%. (ii) The principal amount at which the issuer of a debt security contracts to redeem at maturity. (iii) The nominal value of a security.

Par value

The amount, exclusive of interest or premium, due to a security holder at maturity. The face value (par value) of a security is shown on the face of the security's certificate.

Partizipationsscheine
On Swiss exchanges, a bearer security incorporating the same rights as the dividend-right certificate and thus similar to that. It is issued for the purpose of raising capital, and its nominal value is part of the equity of the company.

Passive managers
Fund managers who do not attempt to beat the market. Instead, they try to mirror the performance of a selected market index.

Payment date
The date on which a dividend or bond interest payment is scheduled to be paid.

Penny stocks
Low-priced stocks selling at less than USD1 a share, often highly speculative.

Perpetual
A security without a time limit for redemption.

Pink sheets
A list of securities which are traded by OTC market-makers, published by the National Quotations Bureau; the price quotations for equity securities are published on pink sheets, those of debt securities on yellow sheets.

Pip
1/100 of 1% of the nominal value of a security.

Pit
See Ring.

Point
The smallest increment of price movement possible in trading a given futures contract.

Portfolio
A collection of securities held by an investor.

Position limit
The maximum position, either net long or net short, in one commodity future or in all futures of one commodity combined which may be held or controlled by one person.

Preferential form
The London Stock Exchange allows companies offering shares to the public to set aside up to 10% of the issue for applications from employees and, where a parent company is floating off a subsidiary, from shareholders of the parent company.

Preferred ordinary shares
See Preferred stock.

Preferred stock
Shares that pay dividends at a specified or sometimes adjustable rate and have preference over ordinary shares (common stock) in the payment of dividends and liquidation of assets.

Premium
(i) Options, the price a put or call buyer must pay to a put or call seller for an option contract.
(ii) The amount by which the market price of a bond exceeds its par value.

Present value
The discounted value of future cash flows.

Price-earnings ratio
Current price of a stock divided by its trailing 12-months earnings.

Primary market
The market relating to the original issue or first sale of new securities.

Principal
A dealer who buys or sells stock for his/her own account.

Principal orders
Activity by a broker/dealer when buying or selling for its own account and risk. Also called principal trades.

Principal trades
See Principal orders.

Private placement
An issue that is offered to a single or a few investors, as opposed to being publicly offered.

Privatization
The conversion of a state run company to PLC status, often accompanied by a sale of its shares to the public.

Probate price
In the UK, the price used to assess the value of shares for inheritance tax purposes. The probate price is calculated by dividing the difference between the bid and offer prices by four and adding the result to the lower of the two prices.

Program trade
Program trading is defined as a wide range of portfolio trading strategies involving the purchase or sale of 15 or more stocks having a total market value of US$1 million or more.

Property
AN XML element upon which the rules of the MDDL schema applies. A property may be a container for other properties.

Property type
Each MDDL property has a base type defined. The base type specifies the kind of value the property can contain in much the same way a type constrains a variable in most programming languages. Base types include Boolean, DateTime, Decimal, Duration, String and URI.

Prospectus
A document, giving the details that a company is required to make public, to support a new issue of shares.

Proxy
A form which, when completed by the shareholder, grants another person the authorization or power to vote on his/her behalf at company meetings.

Public Limited Company (PLC)
In the UK, a public company limited by shares and having a share capital, and which may offer shares for purchase by the general public. Only PLCs may qualify for listing or trading on the London Stock Exchange.

Put option
A put option confers the right but not the obligation to sell stock, shares or futures at the option exercise price within a predetermined time period.

Quotation
The price quoted by a market-maker at which he/she will trade.

Quotation size
The maximum number of shares per order of a particular security that a market-maker is willing to buy or sell at his or her current price.

Quote-driven system
A service that does not allow automatic execution. Trading of quote-driven securities is conducted via telephone dealing.

Range
The difference between the highest and lowest price of a future recorded during a given trading session.

Rating
A grade – usually denoted by a letter or series of letters – signifying a security's investment quality.

Real Estate Investment Trust (REIT)
An organization similar to an investment company in some respects but concentrating its holdings in real estate investments.

Recognized Clearing House (RCH)
In the UK, the Financial Services Authority has recognized and supervises a number of Recognized Clearing Houses (RCHs) under the Financial Services and Markets Act 2000. Recognition confers an exemption from the need to be authorized to carry on regulated activities in the United Kingdom. In order to be recognized, RCHs must comply with the recognition requirements laid down in the Financial Services and Markets Act 2000 (Recognition Requirements for Investment Exchanges and Clearing Houses) Regulations 2001.

Recognized Investment Exchange (RIE)
In the UK, the Financial Services Authority has recognized and supervises a number of Recognized Investment Exchanges (RIEs) under the Financial Services and Markets Act 2000. Recognition confers an exemption from the need to be authorized to carry on regulated

activities in the United Kingdom. In order to be recognized, RIEs must comply with the recognition requirements laid down in the Financial Services and Markets Act 2000 (Recognition Requirements for Investment Exchanges and Clearing Houses) Regulations 2001.

Recognized Overseas Clearing Houses (ROCH)
In the UK, the Financial Services Authority has recognized and supervises a number of Recognized Overseas Investment Exchanges (ROIEs), and has the power to recognize and supervise Recognized Overseas Clearing Houses (ROCHs) under the Financial Services and Markets Act 2000 (FSMA). In order to be recognized, ROCHs must satisfy the requirements of S.292(3) of FSMA.

Recognized Overseas Investment Exchange (ROIE)
In the UK, the Financial Services Authority has recognized and supervises a number of Recognized Overseas Investment Exchanges (ROIEs), and has the power to recognize and supervise Recognized Overseas Clearing Houses (ROCHs) under the Financial Services and Markets Act 2000 (FSMA). In order to be recognized, ROIEs must satisfy the requirements of S.292(3) of FSMA.

Record date
The date on which a shareholder must be registered as the owner of shares in order to be entitled to a dividend.

Redemption
The extinguishing of a debt through cash payment.

Redemption date
The date on which a security (usually a fixed-interest stock) is due to be repaid by the issuer at its full face value. The year is included in the title of the security; the actual redemption date being that on which the last interest is due to be paid.

Reduced size market-maker
On the London Stock Exchange, a market-maker concerned primarily with retail business who has permission to display prices in reduced sizes on SEAQ.

Registered representative
The employee of a member firm who gives advice on which securities to buy and sell, and who collects a percentage of the commission income he or she generates.

Registrar
The registrar is responsible for keeping track of the owners of bonds and the issuance of stocks. Working with the transfer agent, the registrar keeps current files of the owners of a bond issue and the stockholders in a corporation. The registrar ensures that no more than the authorized amount of stock is in circulation. If the registrar and transfer agent are the same company, then there must be a Chinese Wall separating the functions.

REG-NMS
Regulation Nation Market System, the new regulation relating to best execution and market transparency laid down in the United States by the Securities and Exchange Commission. There is an overlap between the EU Directive, MiFID and REG-NMS.

Regulated market
A market, normally taking the form of an exchange with strict regulations relating to Official Trading – examples being the New York Stock Exchange and the London Stock Exchange.

Remisier
A self-employed stockbroker who gets commission for buying and selling for his own clients.

Renouncable documents
On the London Stock Exchange, temporary evidence of ownership, of which there are four main types. When a company offers shares to the public, it sends an allotment letter to the successful applicants; if it makes a rights issue, it sends a provisional allotment letter to its shareholders or, in the case of a capitalization issue, a renounceable certificate. All of these are in effect bearer securities, and are valuable. Each includes full instructions on what the holder should do if he/she wishes to have the newly issued shares registered in his/her name, or wishes to renounce them in favour of somebody else.

Report
A premium on carrying over a position on a French equity from one settlement period to the next.

Reverse split
The reduction in a corporation's outstanding common stock. This is accomplished by replacing outstanding common stock by fewer shares and increasing the stated or par value per share. The total number of shares will have the same market value immediately after the reverse split as before.

Reverse-crush spread
The spread between soya beans and soya-bean products created by buying soya-bean oil and soya-bean-meal futures, and selling soya-bean futures.

Rights issue
An offer of securities to existing shareholders by a company in proportion to their existing holdings.

Ring
An area on a trading floor where futures or equities are traded.

Risk factor
The risk factor (delta) indicates the risk of an option position relative to that of the related futures contract.

Risk premium
The expected additional return for making a risky investment rather than a safe one.

Road show
A series of meetings with potential investors in key cities, designed and performed by a company and its investment banker as the company prepares to go public.

Rolling over
The substitution of a far option for a near option of the same underlying stock at the same strike/exercise price.

Round lot

(i) For stocks, a unit of trading – usually 100 shares. (ii) For futures, an amount of a commodity equal in size to the futures contract for that commodity.

Round trip

Buying and selling of a futures or options contract.

Saitori

Saitori members of the Tokyo Stock Exchange function as middlemen in transactions between regular members. *Saitori* members cannot trade for their own account, nor can they accept orders from members of the public.

SAPIB

Sociedad Anónima Promotora de Inversión Bursátil (Stock Investment Promoting Corporation) – a type of Mexican company which, once registered, has a 3-year transition period before it is required to comply with the full regulatory regime governing public companies. The shares of a SAPIB may only be bought and traded by certain institutional and qualified investors.

Sarbanes–Oxley Act

The Sarbanes–Oxley Act of 2002, was signed into law by US President George W. Bush and became effective on 30 July 2002. The Act contains sweeping reforms for issuers of publicly traded securities, auditors, corporate board members, and lawyers. It adopts tough new provisions intended to deter and punish corporate and accounting fraud and corruption, threatening severe penalties for wrongdoers, and protecting the interests of workers and shareholders.

Scheme

The scheme attribute is used to provide a semantic description of what is inside the associated property.

Scrip issue

See Capitalization issue.

SEAQ

An electronic system for displaying market-makers' quotations in UK quotations admitted to the London Stock Exchange. SEAQ forms the interface between the market-makers and their customers, allowing the entry and display of bid and ask prices on the SEAQ system.

SEAQ International

The London Stock Exchange's electronic price quotations system for non-UK equities, similar to SEAQ.

SEATS

A London Stock Exchange service which supports the trading of listed UK equities in which turnover is insufficient for the market-making system.

SEC

The Securities and Exchange Commission, established by Congress to protect investors in securities transactions.

Second Marché

Second Market of Euronext Paris. This market is chiefly intended for medium-sized firms.

Secondary market

Trading in a new issue, either OTC or on an exchange, immediately following its original issuance.

Secondary offering

A registered offering of a large block of a security that has been previously issued to the public. The blocks being offered may have been held by large investors or institutions, and proceeds of the sale go to those holders, not the issuing company. Also called secondary distribution.

Securities analyst

An individual who does investment research and makes recommendations to buy, sell or hold. Most analysts specialize in a single industry or business sector.

Securitized derivative

Instruments that derive their value from another security (the underlying security), such as a share, share price index, currency or bond.

Security

Generic name for a stock or share. Stocks are fixed-interest securities and shares are the rest.

SEDOL code

The stock code used to identify all securities issued in the UK or Eire. The SEDOL code, which is the basis of the ISIN code for UK securities, consists of a seven-digit number allocated by the master file service of the London Stock Exchange.

Self-regulatory organization (SRO)

In the UK, a recognized controlling body which regulates a specified class of investment business.

Seller/grantor

Also known as the option writer. The seller of an option is subject to a potential obligation if the buyer chooses to exercise the option.

SEQUAL

The London Stock Exchange trade confirmation service.

Serial expiration

Options on the same underlying futures contract which expire in more than 1 month.

Series

All options of the same class which share a common strike price.

Settlement date

The date by which an executed order must be settled by the transference of securities and funds between buyer and seller.

Settlement price

The official closing price for a future set by the clearing house at the end of each trading day.

Share Price Index
An index measuring movements in the prices of shares but not their dividends; as opposed to a Total Return Index, which measures both price movements and dividend income.

Shares
See Security.

Shares outstanding
The number of shares that have been issued that are actually in the hands of investors.

Short interest
The total number of shares of a security sold short.

Short sale
The sale of a security or commodities futures not owned by the seller at the time of the trade. Short sales are usually made in anticipation of a decline in the price.

SICOVAM code
A five-digit code allocated to French securities.

SIIA
Software and Information Industry Association.

Single stock futures
Futures contracts on individual stocks.

Sinking fund
The repayment of debt by an issuer at stated regular intervals through purchases in the open market or drawings by lot.

Size
(i) The number of shares or bonds which are available for sale. (ii) A term used when there are a large number of shares for sale.

Sociétés de Bourse
Member firms on the French Bourses. *Sociétés de Bourse*, previously known as *Agents de Change*, are empowered to conduct trade in securities and financial instruments, manage private and institutional portfolios, and set up and manage investment funds. Member firms are also entitled to deal as principals.

***Société des Bourses Françaises* (SBF)**
This body applies regulations drawn up by the *Conseil des Bourses de Valeurs* to market operations of the French stock exchanges. Its activities include registering trades and listings, and keeping investors informed of transactions.

Specialist
A member of a US stock exchange who holds an exclusive franchise to trade in one or more securities on the exchange floor. The specialist in return is obliged to maintain a fair and orderly market in the stocks in which he or she is registered.

Split
The division of the outstanding shares of a corporation usually into a larger number of shares.

Spot commodity
The actual physical commodity, as opposed to the futures contract.

Spot month
The contract month closest to delivery or expiry.

Spot price
The price at which the spot or cash commodity is currently trading in the spot market.

Spread
(i) The difference between the bid and ask price of a security. (ii) The difference between the price of two related futures contracts. (iii) For options, transactions involving two or more option series on the same underlying security.

Stag
One who applies for a new issue in the hope of being able to sell the shares alloted to him/her at a profit as soon as dealing starts.

Stammaktie
German for ordinary share.

Stamp duty
In the UK, a tax levied on the purchase of shares.

Stillhalter option
Swiss form of covered warrant.

Straddle
The simultaneous purchase/sale of both call and put options for the same share, exercise/strike price and expiry date.

Strike price
Also called exercise price. The price at which an options holder can buy or sell the underlying instrument.

Strip
For futures, buying (selling) the strip involves the simultaneous purchase (sale) of contracts of four or six consecutive delivery months in the same futures contract. For options, a stock option contract made up of two puts and one call.

subClass
In MDDL this refers to the lowest level of instrument classification, with instruments being grouped by domain and class. An example is <civDomain> <fundClass> <exchangeTradedSubclass>

Subscription warrant
A type of security that entitles the holder to purchase a specified number of shares at a fixed price within a fixed- or perpetual-time period. The conversion price per share at which the warrants are exercised is adjusted in the event of a rights issue or a stock split.

SuperMontage
The next-generation electronic trading system in both order display and execution for Nasdaq securities, launched by The Nasdaq Stock Market in 2002.

Swap
A forward type of contractual agreement to exchange one type of cash flow or asset for another, according to predetermined rules.

Swiss certificate (schweizer zertifikat)
Original share certificate of a foreign company, mainly originating in the US, the UK or Canada, which is quoted on a Swiss Stock Exchange and is registered in the nominee name of a specified Swiss nominee endorsed in blank. For dividend payments or participation in corporate actions it must be stamped by the nominee company.

Swiss Index
The Swiss index family with 2 major components: the Swiss Market Index (SMI) which comprises 23 blue chips and the Swiss Performance Index (SPI) which comprises all listed and major OTC stocks.

Tap stocks
UK Government stocks which the government broker will supply at a given price. The price chosen provides a means of influencing interest rates in general.

Tender offer
In an offer by tender, buyers of shares specify the price at which they are willing to purchase.

Termine price
Italian bond market forward price.

Theta
The measure of the change in an option's premium given a change in the option's time until expiration. Equal to the change in the option's premium divided by the change in time to expiration.

Third market
In the US, the trading of exchange-listed securities on the OTC market by non-exchange member broker-dealers and institutional investors.

Tick
A minimum change in price, up or down.

Tick size
This is the minimum price movement for a futures contract.

Ticker symbol
Characters that identify a financial instrument on an exchange ticker.

Time value
That part of an option premium which reflects the length of time remaining in the option prior to expiration – the longer the time remaining until expiration, the higher the time value.

Top level contents wrappers (or MDDL constructs)
Top level content wrappers (or constructs, as they are referred to in earlier versions of the documentation) are the collections and groupings of properties necessary to convey a particular reason for providing the market data. For example, the construct snap denotes that the included data is a snapshot of a quote – perhaps at end of day.

Total Return Index
An index that calculates the performance of a group of stocks, assuming that dividends are reinvested into the index constituents. For the purposes of the index calculation, the value of the dividends is reinvested in the index on the ex-dividend date.

Touch
The best buying and selling prices available from a market-maker on SEAQ and SEAQ International in a given security at any one time.

Tracker
See Exchange Traded Funds (ETFs).

Trade date
The date on which a trade occurs.

Traded options
Transferable options with the right to buy and sell a standardized amount of a security at a fixed price within a specified period.

Trading halt
The suspension of trading in a security while material news from the issuer is being disseminated. A trading halt generally lasts 30 minutes, and gives all investors equal opportunity to evaluate news and make buy, sell or hold decisions on that basis.

Trading range
The range of prices that have been traded over a particular period.

Traditional options
Traditional options cannot be traded, and are offered by three market-makers acting as principals.

Transaction
The buying or selling of securities resulting from the execution of an order.

Transfer
On the London Stock Exchange, the form signed by the seller of a security authorizing the company to remove his or her name from the register and substitute that of the buyer.

Transparent market
The degree to which trade and quotation information is available to the public on a current basis.

Treasury bills
Short-term obligations of a government issued for periods of 1 year or less. Treasury bills do not carry a rate of interest and are issued at a discount on the par value. Treasury bills are repaid at par on the due date.

Treasury bonds
Government obligations with maturities of 10 years or more.

Treasury notes
Government obligations with maturities greater than 1 year but less than 10 years.

Treasury stock
Previously issued stock that has been repurchased by, donated to, or otherwise reacquired by the issuing firm. Treasury stocks pay no dividends and have no voting privileges.

Triple-witching
The simultaneous expiry of index futures, index options and individual stock options.

Turnover
The total money value of securities traded, as calculated by multiplying price by the number of securities traded.

Underlying security
The instrument upon which traded options are listed.

Underwriting
An arrangement under which a company is guaranteed that an issue of shares will raise a given amount of cash, because the underwriters, for a commission, undertake to subscribe for any of the issue not taken up by the public.

Unit
More than one class of securities trading together as one (e.g. a stock and a warrant).

Unit trust
A fund which raises money from investors and invests it in a range of securities.

Unlisted securities
Securities that are not listed on an exchange.

Unlisted trading privileges
The trading of securities not listed on a US exchange but traded on that exchange at the request of a member of that exchange, and not at the request of the issuing corporation.

Unregulated markets
A market not so strictly bound to regulations, normally known as a Multilateral Trading Facility (MTF), is a multilateral system which brings together multiple third-party buying and selling interests in financial instruments – in the system and in accordance with non-discretionary rules – in a way that results in a contract. Nasdaq is classified as an MTF.

Up tick
A transaction executed at a price greater than the previous transaction.

Valorennummer

The Telekurs securities identification number, consisting of up to six digits.

Value date

The date up to and including which accrued interest is calculated.

Variation margin

Profits or losses on open positions in futures and options contracts which are paid or collected daily.

Vega

The measure of the change in an option's premium for a 1% change in the volatility of the underlying futures contract. Equal to the change in premium divided by 1% change in volatility.

Volatility

Usually defined as the standard deviation of returns of an asset. Volatility generally refers to the magnitude of price movements in a specific asset. Large price movements are said to be more volatile, and *vice versa*. Volatility has a major direct influence on option premium levels. When volatility is high, premiums increase (all other assumptions remaining the same). When volatility is low, premiums decline.

Volume

Amount of trading activity, expressed in shares or dollars, experienced by a single security or the entire market within a specified period, usually daily, monthly or annually.

Vorzugsaktie

German for preferred share.

VWAP

VWAP – 'volume-weighted average price' – represents the total value of shares traded in a particular stock on a given day, divided by the total volume of shares traded in that stock on that day. Calculation techniques vary: some will use data from all markets or just the primary market, and may or may not adjust for resubmits and other error corrections. VWAP is a method of pricing transactions and also a benchmark to measure the efficiency of institutional trading or the performance of traders themselves.

Warrant

A certificate giving the holder the long-term and at times perpetual privilege, but not the obligation, of purchasing securities at a specified price.

Wash trade

A matched deal which produces neither a gain nor a loss.

Wertpapierkennummer

Security code number on German stock exchanges. The German securities identification number is a six-digit numeric code. Codes up to 499 999 are allocated to fixed-interest securities, codes from 500 000 are allocated to shares, warrants and unit trusts.

When issued
A transaction made conditionally in a security authorized but not yet issued.

White knight
A company which rescues another that is in financial difficulty, especially one which saves a company from an unwelcome takeover bid.

xtcMessage
The xtc stands for XML transmission compaction. This is an industry-standard compaction protocol for broadcasting XML content (not just MDDL) with encryption capabilities.

Yield
The percentage rate of return computed by dividing a security's annual dividend by its current market price.

Zaraba
A method of trading employed on Japanese exchanges. Under the *zaraba* method, transactions are consummated by auction based on (i) price priority, in that the selling (buying) order with the lowest (highest) price takes precedence over other orders; and (ii) time priority, in that an earlier order takes precedence over other orders at the same price.

Zero coupon bonds
Zero coupon bonds are corporate or municipal debt securities that trade at a deep discount from the face value, as the bond pays no interest to the bondholders during its lifetime.

Appendix B: MiFID terms

The terms identified in the CESR publication *Expert Group Cooperation and Enforcement – Technical Task Force on Transaction Reporting – Draft to the Final Report* Ref. CESR/05-398 concentrates on the reporting of trades to a Competent Authority (CA). These have been supplemented by others that were required to support the trade workflow and order/quote reporting processes.

The grey fields denote proposed terms, identified by CESR, and in addition described in Annex B of the Technical Advice; other additional terms are highlighted in ***bold italic***.

Technical data fields	Data field name	MiFID article	Data field values	Data type	Description
Authority Key	AuthorityKey		ISO 3166 Country Code	Code	The competent authority is identified based on its country code. If more than one Authority Key is needed on a country level a sequential number will be added for each of the competent authorities.
Reporting Party Name and Identification	Reporting PartyName	25(5-6) – Entity identification – source of the report		Text identifier	Full name of the reporting party in uppercase.
	ReportingParty Identification Code		'BIC' = ISO 9362 – SWIFT/Bank Identifier Code (BIC) 'BEI' = ISO XXXX – Business Entity Identifier 'EXC' = External acronym/code on the Trading Platform 'INT' = Internal acronym /code used by the Reporting Party	Code	The ReportingPartyIdentificationCode provides information on the Reporting Party Identification Scheme.

Technical data fields	Data field name	MiFID article	Data field values	Data type	Description
	ReportingParty Identification		ISO 9362 – SWIFT/Bank Identifier Code (BIC) (if ReportingPartyIdentification-Code = 'BIC') if ReportingPartyIdentification-Code = 'BEI' if ReportingPartyIdentification-Code = 'EXC' if ReportingPartyIdentification-Code = 'INT'	Identifier	
Trading day ***(Would the term Event Date be more appropriate as not all transactions are trade reports?)***	TradingDay		ISO 8601 Date Format	Datetime	

Trading Time ***(Would the term Event Time be more appropriate as not all transactions are trade reports?)***	TradingTime		ISO 8601 Time Format	Datetime	
Time identifier	TimeIdentifier		ISO 8601	Datetime	
Order quote expiry date	***OrderQuoteExpiry Date***		ISO 8601	Datetime	Date at which an Order or Quote Expires.
Order quote expiry time	***OrderQuoteExpiry Time***		ISO 8601 Time Format; HHMMSSNN	Datetime	Time at which an Order or Quote Expires.
Buy/sell indicator	BuySellIndicator		'B' = Buy 'S' = Sell	Code	
Trading capacity	TradingCapacity		'O' = Own account 'C' = Customer/client account	Code	

Technical data fields	Data field name	MiFID article	Data field values	Data type	Description
Transaction type	TransactionType		'MC' = Minimal content 'SL' = Securities loans 'EO' = Exercising options 'CC' = Conversion of convertibles 'ES' = Exercising subscr. rights 'RP' = Repos and reverse repos 'PR' = Primary market transactions (excluding Derivatives) 'OT' = Others	Code	Resulting from the exercise of subscription rights.
Transaction type	TransactionType Description			Text	
Instrument identifica-tion	***ISIN***	25(5-6) Content and standards	ISO 6166 – International Securities Identification Number (ISIN)	Identifier	
	ProprietaryCode Identification	25(5-6) Content and standards		Identifier	

Instrument security code type	***InstrumentSecurity CodeType***	25(5-6) Content and standards	A set of enumeration of identify the propriety code source: SEDOL, BLOOMBERG, RIC, QUIK, VALOREN, CommonCode, etc…	Code	
Place of trade	***PlaceOfTrade***				
	InstrumentName	25(5-6) Content and standards		Text identifier	Instrument name in uppercase.
Underlying instrument identifica-tion	UnderlyingInstrument Identification	25(5-6) Content and standards	ISO 6166 – International Securities Identification Number (ISIN) (if InstrumentSecurity CodeType = 'IS') if InstrumentSecurity CodeType = 'OT'	Identifier	
	UnderlyingInstrument Name	25(5-6) Content and standards		Text-Identifier	Instrument name in uppercase.

Technical data fields	Data field name	MiFID article	Data field values	Data type	Description
Underlying instrument security code type	UnderlyingInstrumentSecurityCode Type	25(5-6) Content and standards	'IS' = ISO 6166 – International Securities Identification Number (ISIN) 'OT' = Proprietary code	Code	The InstrumentSecurityCode Type information on the Instrument Identification Scheme.
Instrument type	InstrumentType		'E' = Equity 'B' = Bond 'Q' = Equity derivative 'O' = Bond derivative 'C' = Commodity derivative 'I' = 'Index rate derivative 'X' = Index derivative 'N' = Others	Code	
CFI instrument type	CFIInstrumentType	25(5-6) Content and standards	ISO 10962 – Classification of Financial Instruments (CFI)	Code	
Maturity date	MaturityDate		ISO 8601 Date Format; YYYYMMDD	DateTime	

Derivative type	DerivativeType	'O' = Option 'F' = Future 'W' = Warrant 'O' = Other	Code		
Put/call	PutCallIndica tor	'P' = Put 'C' = Call	Code		
Strike price	StrikePrice		Amount		
Price multiplier	PriceMultiplier		Quantity		Default value is 1.
Price	Price		Amount or rate		
Price notation	PriceNotation		ISO 4217 Currency Code 'PCT' = Percentage	Code	The PriceNotation provides information on the Price field type which is an amount in case of a currency code and a rate in case of 'PCT'.
Quantity	Quantity			Quantity	
Quantity notation	QuantityNotation		'F' = quantity expressed in number of pieces of financial instruments 'B' = quantity stands for the nominal value of bonds 'D' = quantity stands for the number of derivative contracts	Code	The QuantityNotation provides information on the Quantity field type.

Technical data fields	Data field name	MiFID article	Data field values	Data type	Description
Order type	***OrderType***		B – At Best, L – Limit …	Code	Hit (At Best) Limit etc. Term can affect the "realistic price" that can be achieved. Thus required for reporting.
Order quote expiry date	***OrderQuoteExpiryDate***		ISO 8601 Date Format; YYYYMMDD	Datetime	Date at which an Order or Quote expires.
Order quote expiry time	***OrderQuoteExpiryTime***		ISO 8601 Time Format; HHMMSSNN	Datetime	Time at which an Order or Quote expires.
Fill indicator	***FillIndicator***		S – Single fill, P – Partial fill	Code	
Fast market	***FastMarket***		Y – Fast market		
Aggregated price	***AggregatedPrice***	22(2) Publication of client limit orders		Amount or rate	
Aggregated price notation	***AggregatedPriceNotation***	22(2) Publication of client limit orders	ISO 4217 Currency Code 'PCT' = Percentage	Code	The PriceNotation provides information on the Price field type which is an amount in case of a currency code and a rate in case of 'PCT'.

Aggregated quantity	***AggregatedQuantity***	22(2) Publication of client limit orders		Quantity	
Aggregated quantity notation	***AggregatedQuantityNotation***	22(2) Publication of client limit orders	'F' = quantity expressed in number of pieces of financial instruments 'B' = quantity stands for the nominal value of bonds 'D' = quantity stands for the number of derivative contracts	Code	The QuantityNotation provides information on the Quantity field type.
Nondisclosure reason	***NonDisclosure Reason***	24 Transactions executed with an eligible counter parties. 24(2) on a trade by trade basis. Article 22 – Client order handling.	M – Market practice exempt (Delayed reporting) E – Eligible counterparty…	Code	Non disclose due to transaction undertaken by, or on behalf of an eligible counterparty

Technical data fields	Data field name	MiFID article	Data field values	Data type	Description
Counterparty name and code	CounterParty Name	25(5-6) - Entity identification – source of the counterparty initiating the transaction		Text-identifier	(Full) name of the counter party in upper case.
	CounterPartyCode Type		'BIC' = ISO 9362 – SWIFT/Bank Identifier Code (BIC) 'BEI' = ISO XXXX – Business Entity Identifier 'EXC' = Internal acronym/code on the Trading Platform 'INT' = Internal acronym/code used by the Reporting Firm 'CUC' = Customer/client	Code	The CounterPartyCode Type provides information on the Counter Party Code Scheme. If the CounterPartyCode Type = 'CUC' there is no Counter Party Code.
	CounterPartyCode	ISO 9362 – SWIFT/Bank Identifier Code (BIC)	Identifier		

	(if CounterPar-tyCode Type = 'BIC') if CounterPar-tyCode Type = 'BEI' if CounterPar-tyCode Type = 'EXC' if CounterPar-tyCode Type = 'INT'				
Customer/ client identification	CustomerClient Identification		Text-identifier		
Trading venue	TradingVenueId entificationType	25(5-6) – Entity identification of where the transaction was reported	'MIC' = ISO 10383 Market Identifier Code (MIC) 'BIC' = ISO 9362 – WIFT/Bank Identifier Code (BIC) 'BEI' = ISO XXXX – Business Entity Identifier 'OTH' = Proprietary/ Domestic Code 'OFF' = Off-exchange	Code	The TradingVenueIdentifi cationType provides information on the Trading Venue Identification Scheme. If the TradingVenueIdentifi cationType = 'OFF' there is no Trading Venue Identification.

Technical data fields	Data field name	MiFID article	Data field values	Data type	Description
	TradingVenueIde ntification		ISO 10383 Market Identifier Code (MIC) (If TradingVenue IdentificationType = 'MIC') ISO 9362 – SWIFT/Bank Identifier Code (BIC) If Trading Venue Identification Type = 'BIC' If Counter Party Code Type = 'BEI' if Trading Venue Identification Type If Counter Party Code Type = 'BEI' If Trading Venue Identification Type	Identifier	
Receiving time stamp by CA	ReceivingTimes tampByCA		ISO 8601 Date Time Format	Datetime	Receiving Timestamp of the report by sending CA (YYYY = year, MM = month, DD = day; HH = hour (00 though 23), MM = minute, SS = second, DD = fraction (decimals); expressed in local time; 4 digits offset from UTC; HH = hour, MM = minutes).

Transaction reference number	Transaction ReferenceNumber	27(6) Ability to limit multiple orders from the same client (Monitoring, validation, correction etc.)		Identifier	(Unique) Transaction Reference Number attributed or managed by the CA for TR.
Transaction reference number code	Transaction ReferenceNumber Code		'C' = Transaction Reference Number attributed by CA 'M' = Transaction Reference Number 'R' = Transaction Reference Number attributed by Reporting Party Code		The TransactionRefere nceNumberCode provides information on the Transaction Reference Number Identification Scheme.
Cancellation/ amendment indicator	CancellationAme ndmentIndi cator		'N' = Normal 'C' = Cancellation 'A' = Amendment (1-step modification) 'R' = Amendment with new TR (2-step modification)	Code	

Technical data fields	Data field name	MiFID article	Data field values	Data type	Description
Modified transaction sequence number	ModifiedTransactionSequence Number			Code	Default value = 1. This field is an incremental field to order multiple TR modifications.
Previous transaction reference number	PreviousTransactionReference Number			Identifier	The Previous Transaction Reference Number field could be used in case CAs attribute a new transaction reference number each time a transaction is modified.

References and further reading

Al-Khalili, J. (2004). *Quantum: A Guide for the Perplexed* Weidenfeld & Nicolson.

Bond Markets Association (2002). *Securities Master Database – Request for Proposals*. Bond Markets Association.

Coates, A. B. (2001). *How and Where XML is Changing the Markets*. Paper published as part of an xml-europe Conference, 21–25 May, Berlin, Germany (http://about.reuters.com/researchandstandards/events/2001/05/xml-europe/how-and-where-xml-is-changing-the-markets-paper.htm).

Daly, W. K. (1989). *Doctor Who – The Ultimate Evil*, the Missing episodes series. W. H. Allen.

Grinbaum, M., Malabre, F., Maynard, G., Shriver, R. and Simpson, M. (2006). *FIX Book Management Recommended Practices V 1.0*. FIX Protocol Ltd.

Harold, E. R. (2004). *XML Bible*, 3rd edn. Hungry Minds Inc.

Hartley, J. (2001). *MDDL Market Data Definition Language* (available at www.idealliance.org).

Hennessy, E. (2001). *Coffee House to Cyber Market*. Elbury Press.

ISITC Europe (2003). In Search of Unique Instrument Identifier. Discussion Paper, ISITC Europe.

ISO (2004). ISO/TS 20022-4:2004 Financial Services – UNIversal Financial Industry Message Scheme. ISO.

Kay, M. (2004). *CSLT 2.0, 3rd Edition Programmer's Reference*. Wiley Publications Inc.

Lee, R. (1998). *What's an Exchange?* Oxford University Press.

London Stock Exchange (2003). *Data Formats – Trading and Information Services*. LSE.

London Stock Exchange (2005). *EDOL Masterfile™ – Technical Specifications Version 5.7*. LSE.

Mahony, S. (1997). *A–Z of International Finance*. Pitman Publishing.

Pollock, J. T. and Hodgson, R. (2004). *Adaptive Information*. John Wiley & Sons, Inc.

Ray, E. T. (2003). *Learning XML Guide to creating Self-Describing Data*. O'Reilly & Associates.

Reference Data User Group (RDUG) and Reference Data Coalition (REDAC) (2005). *The Implications for Reference Data under the Markets in Financial Instrument Directive (MiFID – Directive 2004/39/EC)*, Discussion Paper Version 1.9, 7 December. ISITC Europe.

Rosenborg, D. and Furuhed, A. (2006). *FAST Specification Version 1.x.05*. FIX Protocol, Ltd.

Si Alhir, S. (1998). *UML in a Nutshell*. O'Reilly Associates.

The Handbook of World Stock, Derivative and Commodity Exchanges. Mondovisione.

Unknown authors (2006). *Expert Group Cooperation and Enforcement – Technical Task Force on Transaction Reporting – Draft to the Final Report*. CESR.

van der Eijk, P., Nickull, D., Dubray, J. J. *et al.* (2001). *Professional ebXML Foundations*. Wrox Press Limited.

van der Vlist, E. (2002). *XML Schema*. O'Reilly & Associates.

Index